More praise for
The Moral Compass of the American Lawyer

P9-CER-528

"Zitrin and Langford have managed to present in their lively and highly readable study, *The Moral Compass of the American Lawyer*, many of the most difficult dilemmas, moral and practical, faced today by the profession and its clients. They have also proposed some modest and sensible solutions. Their book is challenging and eminently readable."

—LOUIS BEGLEY
Lawyer and author of *Mistler's Exit*

"Lawyers, law students, and everyone who has to live or work with them will gain fresh insights into their behavior from *The Moral Compass*."

—GERALD F. UELMEN
Professor of Law at Santa Clara University

"Cogent, incisive, and unsparingly honest . . . *The Moral Compass of the American Lawyer* deals with a hard truth—the ethical and moral confusion which pervades our legal system—and how it might be fixed."

—RICHARD NORTH PATTERSON
Bestselling author of *Degree of Guilt*
and *Dark Lady*

"Zitrin and Langford raise key questions about the behavior of many in their profession. . . . This book will interest and inform adult readers."

—*Library Journal*

"A worthy read for lawyers and nonlawyers alike."

—*Booklist*

"*The Moral Compass of the American Lawyer* is a well-crafted indictment of the state of the legal profession. Easy to read, it can serve as a classroom text, a basis for in-house discussion of the issues or merely an engaging book for the curious."

—*The Professional Lawyer*

THE
MORAL COMPASS
OF THE
AMERICAN
LAWYER

TRUTH, JUSTICE, POWER, AND GREED

Richard Zitrin
Carol M. Langford

BALLANTINE BOOKS · NEW YORK

A Ballantine Book
Published by The Ballantine Publishing Group

Copyright © 1999 by Richard A. Zitrin and Carol M. Langford

All rights reserved under International and Pan-American Copyright Conventions. Published in the United States by The Ballantine Publishing Group, a division of Random House, Inc., New York, and simultaneously in Canada by Random House of Canada Limited, Toronto.

Ballantine and colophon are registered trademarks of Random House, Inc.

We would like to thank the following for permitting us to use excerpts of their work:

Mark F. Bernstein, *J.D.* cartoon published in *The* [San Francisco] *Recorder*, June 1997, © 1997, Mark F. Bernstein.

Monroe Freedman, *Lawyers' Ethics in an Adversary System*, Bobbs Merrill, 1975, © 1975 Monroe H. Freedman. Professor Freedman has updated and expanded his analysis in *Understanding Lawyers' Ethics* (Matthew Bender, 1990).

Stephen Gillers, Counsel Connect on-line comments of January 26, 1997. Used with permission.

David Luban, *Lawyers and Justice: An Ethical Study*, © 1989 Princeton University Press. Reprinted by permission of Princeton University Press.

Arthur Miller, *All My Sons*, 1947, renewed 1975, © Arthur Miller, All Rights Reserved. Courtesy of Viking Penguin, a division of Penguin Putnam Inc.

John B. Mitchell, "Reasonable Doubts Are Where You Find Them: A Response to Professon Subin's Position on the Criminal Lawyer's 'Different Mission,' " 1 *Georgetown Journal of Legal Ethics* 343 (1987). Reprinted with the permission of the publisher, Georgetown University, and the *Georgetown Journal of Legal Ethics*, © 1987.

Columbia Pictures, *Anatomy of a Murder*, 1959, renewed 1987, © Otto Preminger Films, Ltd., All Right Reserved, Courtesy of Columbia Pictures.

Harry I. Subin, "The Criminal Defense Lawyer's 'Different Mission': Reflections on the 'Right' to Present a False Case," 1 *Georgetown Journal of Legal Ethics* 125 (1987). Reprinted with the permission of the publisher, Georgetown University, and the *Georgetown Journal of Legal Ethics*, © 1987.

Gerald B. Wetlaufer, "The Ethics of Lying in Negotiations," published in 75 *Iowa L. Rev.* 1219 (1990), reprinted with pemission.

www.randomhouse.com/BB/

Library of Congress Catalog Card Number: 00-105863

ISBN: 0-449-00671-9

Manufactured in the United States of America

First Hardcover Edition: May 1999
First Trade Paperback Edition: September 2000

10 9 8 7 6 5 4 3 2 1

To Richard's parents, Charlotte and Arthur Zitrin,
who have always taught by both word and deed;
and to Laurie Jean Robertson, May 18, 1956–November 7, 1997,
still with us in inspiration

CONTENTS

ACKNOWLEDGMENTS

No book like this could ever be written without a great deal of help from others and inspiration from many more. It is telling that despite this book's criticisms of the legal profession, most of those to whom we owe thanks are themselves lawyers, including many who frankly and candidly shared their thoughts with us. Some, including Barry Baskin, Leslie Bruekner, Elizabeth Cabraser, Clarence Ditlow, Monroe Freedman, Bill Gwire, Michael Josephson, and Bill Ross, are quoted in these pages. Others, among them our San Francisco colleagues Bill Bernstein, Bob Calhoun, and Mark Chavez, are not, though they too gave us important insights.

We are indebted to many we never met, including Frank Armani, who has so candidly and publicly told the story of his most difficult case; Hon. Lloyd Doggett, a passionate believer in openness of court records; and Leslie Scanlon, whose Louisville *Courier-Journal* articles doggedly pursued a story about an important case that got little publicity elsewhere.

Back home, Stephanie Dolan provided much of the research for an entire chapter, and Laura Goldsmith added other sources. Len Mastromonaco gave us long-term unequivocal support. Meredith LeVene, early on, and Rolie Vera and Clint Mitchell, later, added their valuable two cents. Bob Hill provided both his labor and faith in us. Maggie Vera's labor, loyalty, and abiding belief in our project were invaluable. Bob D'Arcy, more than a copy editor, read every word and provided consistent editorial advice. The University of California's Hastings Law campus gave us new teaching opportunities. And, as it has for years, the law school at the University of San Francisco continued to be a home base where we could test our ideas in an ongoing dialogue with our fellow teachers and our enthusiastic and outspoken students.

We have been fortunate to know a great many lawyers who have inspired and taught us. Significant among them are these: Glenn Becker, Angela Bradstreet, Tom Bruyneel, Hon. Walter Calcagno, Martin Checov, Hon. Maxine Mackler Chesney, Peter Cling, Paul Cummins, Morris Dees, Randy Difuntorum, Willy Fletcher, Larry Fox, Monroe Freedman, Jack Friedman, Nate Harrington, Mike Hennessey, Steven Hobbs, Michael Josephson, Peter Keane, Phil Martin, David Ross Mayer, Hon. E. Warren McGuire, Roger Meredith, Gaile O'Connor, Eva Jefferson Patterson, Paul Persons, Hon. Beverly Savitt, Bart Sheela, Jacob Smith, Wally Smith, William Reece Smith, Marvin Stender, Harry Subin, Bob Taylor, Mark Tuft, Lish Whitson, David Wilkins, and Mary Williams. We thank them all.

Six lawyers whom we interviewed extensively have proven by their lives in the law that they represent the best our profession has to offer: Robert Doggett of Dallas; Horace Green of San Francisco; Howard Moore of Oakland and Atlanta; Ronald Pohl of New York; Arlene Popkin of White Plains, New York; and Pat Wagner of Seattle. If all lawyers were like these six, the moral compass of the American lawyer would never waver from its true course.

We are deeply grateful to Jules Tygiel, Charlotte and Arthur Zitrin, and Elizabeth Zitrin, who read our manuscript draft from start to finish, giving us plain, unvarnished critiques along with their unwavering support. Simply put, they made this a better book. So too did Doris Ober, who read every line with her unique combination of passion and a keen editor's eye, and who pulled no punches in her comments along the way. Faith Hamlin, our agent, was a constant source of wisdom, and had confidence in us from the first moment. And Leona Nevler, our editor at Ballantine, gave us supportive and invariably helpful feedback and advice.

Most especially, we thank Lexis Law Publishing, the Michie Company, and Lee Freudberg of Lexis, for permitting us free rein to use ideas developed in our first book on legal ethics; and the indispensable Claude Piller, attorney, friend, and research assistant extraordinaire, without whom this book simply never could have been written.

Richard Zitrin and Carol M. Langford
San Francisco, California
September 1998

Introduction

Courage is the most important attribute of a lawyer. It is more important
than competence or vision. . . . It can never be delimited, dated, or
outworn, and it should pervade the heart, the halls of justice, and the
chambers of the mind.   —Robert F. Kennedy at the University of
                                    San Francisco School of Law, 1962

When her kids reached school age, Sabrina Jones went back to
work as a nurse's aide at a health care facility run by Just
Like Home, Inc. She soon became concerned by what she saw. She
had worked at other nursing homes where cleanliness was a pri-
ority. But at Just Like Home, when she was assigned to clean the
common areas and medical examination rooms, she was given ordinary household cleansers instead of the industrial-strength products that she knew were necessary to meet strict state standards.
And she sometimes saw medical instruments that appeared un-
sterilized lying about the exam rooms.

Sabrina was just an hourly worker and reluctant to say anything.
But after she felt she had developed a good relationship with her
boss, she went to him with her concerns. Three days later she was
fired, allowed back into the facility only to clean out her locker in the
company of a security guard. Jones was shocked and upset. She hired
a lawyer, who sued Just Like Home for wrongful discharge.

Across town, Laura Bernardi, a senior associate at a large urban law firm, has been working seventy hours a week trying to impress her partners so she can make partner herself. Just Like Home is one of Laura's biggest clients, and she is assigned to defend the company in the Jones case. Laura knows that the Jones suit could mean big trouble for her client: Just Like Home has a pattern of cutting corners on more than just cleaning products. And Laura has seen an internal memo stating that Jones was fired because of what she suspected about the company's sloppy attitude about cleanliness.

But Laura has been taught that her primary ethical duty is to represent her client zealously. And she knows that she and Just Like Home have the upper hand. Sabrina's lawyer has taken a job in another state, leaving her without counsel. Still unemployed, Sabrina has little money to prosecute the lawsuit herself, and almost no knowledge about how to do it.

Knowing that Sabrina has moved in with her sister eighty miles south of the city, Laura sets the Jones deposition at a branch of her law firm that will require Sabrina to travel by train to the city center, then by bus out of the city, and then change buses. It's a time-consuming and costly trip for an unemployed mother of two. When Sabrina calls to plead with Laura to set the deposition at the firm's main city office, Laura politely but firmly refuses.

Knowing Sabrina is not likely to show up at the deposition, Laura has a certified shorthand reporter ready and waiting. When Sabrina is not there on time, Laura waits ten more minutes, notes it on the reporter's official transcribed record, and heads back to her office to sign an already-prepared motion to dismiss the case based on Sabrina's failure to appear. Overwhelmed and daunted by the legal system, Sabrina again calls Laura, pleading for more time to reply to the motion and to find a new lawyer. Again Laura refuses. Her motion is heard and granted by the court, and Sabrina has lost her case almost before it's begun.

The story of Sabrina Jones and Laura Bernardi is true, though the names have been changed. Lawyers may have mixed feelings about what Laura did, but most would say she acted properly—doing it by the book, using legal procedure to gain an advantage for her client. Few, if any, would call it unethical. Yet most nonlawyers would say that something wrong has taken place—that justice has been not served but denied.

•

Americans have long regarded lawyers with suspicion and criticism. A hundred and fifty years ago Abraham Lincoln cited a "vague popular belief that lawyers are necessarily dishonest." But never in our country's history have lawyers—and how they think, speak, and act—been as controversial as they are today. People ask why lawyers so rarely seem to owe allegiance to the truth or basic concepts of justice. Many consider the typical American lawyer to be either immoral or amoral, while many others believe that our justice system no longer protects the interests of the average person. Polls show that public confidence in lawyers has never been lower.

Many of the rules of legal ethics originated in the moral precepts that govern the conduct of human affairs. But today, almost 150 years after Judge George Sharswood first set down rules "on the Aims and Duties of the Profession of Law," many people question whether the ethical behavior of lawyers is sufficiently tied to those ordinary moral precepts. There is a palpable tension between the rules of legal ethics and other important principles of our society: telling the truth, being fair and compassionate, seeking justice, being courageous, acting as a moral human being. While the public looks to the legal system for the truth, lawyers often look to spin the truth from their clients' perspectives. While the public looks to the legal system for justice, lawyers ask, "Justice for whom?" and point to their duty to protect their clients' version of justice above all others.

In these pages we'll examine whether lawyers should ever be allowed to ignore the real "Truth" while purveying their clients' "truths" to both judge and jury. And we'll reexamine what we call the "adversary theorem," an idea endorsed by legal thinkers from Dr. Samuel Johnson to Alan Dershowitz, that when lawyers do their utmost to represent their clients "zealously," Justice somehow triumphs.

Every day, American lawyers in a wide variety of practices face competing ethical principles—among the most important, the choice between representing a client's interests diligently and being truthful in one's words and deeds. But there are larger issues than those raised by the "black-letter" ethical rules themselves. Just as the rules of ethics are based substantially on moral standards, each lawyer must ultimately decide how to balance ethics with the moral principles of our society: whether being "ethical" should be defined by what a lawyer can "get away with"; whether a lawyer must remain loyal to a client who insists on acting illegally; whether a lawyer is willing to pay the practical and economic consequences of "doing the right thing," even if it means losing a job; and whether, and to what extent, a personal sense of morality should play a part in a lawyer's behavior.

As ethics teachers and consultants, we have taught thousands of law students and lawyers and consulted with several hundred more. We have seen lawyers do things that were not only unethical but immoral and, to us, indefensible. We have known others who honestly believed that they were acting with the highest ethical standards, but who had never stopped to think about how their behavior actually affected their clients or society. We've also seen other lawyers who conduct their professional lives in a way that makes them worthy of the highest praise. There are tens of thousands of these ethical and moral men and women, some of whom you'll meet in these pages. More often, though, we focus on those who, for reasons ranging from greed to simple lack of understanding, serve the profession less well.

But we cannot examine the behavior of lawyers, or reach hard conclusions about what conduct can no longer be tolerated under our legal system, without also examining the system itself: how it succeeds—or fails. We'll look at the public's expectations as well as our own. And we'll determine where our justice system still works, and where it has gone so far wrong that major change is needed.

We begin each chapter with an illustrative story like that of Sabrina Jones and Laura Bernardi. Each story is based on events that actually took place, familiar to us through our own experiences consulting with and advising lawyers and their clients over the years. Except for Chapter One, the stories are composites, the names changed to protect the innocent—and the guilty. Each story sets the table for a discussion of actual cases and hard facts. And—as is typical of facts, especially when it comes to lawyers—truth is indeed stranger than fiction.

PART ONE

TRUTH, JUSTICE, AND THE AMERICAN LAWYER

Buried Bodies:
Robert Garrow and His Lawyers

The most difficult ethical dilemmas result from the frequent conflicts between the obligation to one's client and those to the legal system and to society.   —Professor (later U.S. District Court judge)
Jack B. Weinstein

On the evening of August 9, 1973, just as Frank Armani was sitting down to dinner with his family, he received a phone call that not only would change his life, but would set him on a course of conduct that years later he couldn't fully justify, even to himself. The caller was the wife of Robert Garrow, convicted rapist, accused child molester, and suspected serial killer. Police had captured Garrow that morning after the largest manhunt in New York State history, wounding him seriously in the process. Now Garrow lay in his hospital bed in critical condition, refusing to talk to anyone except his wife and his lawyer, Frank Armani.

Armani lived and worked in Syracuse, New York. Due north of Syracuse are the Adirondacks, one of our nation's most beautiful natural treasures. These five million acres of protected parkland, tree-covered mountains, and idyllic lakes are where people go to escape the heat, crowds, and violence of the Northeast's urban sprawl—where they go to get away from it all.

That's just what eighteen-year-old Philip Domblewski and his three friends, Nick Fiorello, David Freeman, and Carol Ann Malinowski, had in mind in late July 1973. They had pitched their tents for the night in a clearing on the edge of the woods just off State Route 8. They woke up to see Robert Garrow, a rifle at his side.

Grabbing a coil of rope, Garrow herded the four friends into the thick woods. He forced Nick to tie David to a tree trunk, then moved deeper into the forest, where Phil was forced to tie up Nick. Finally, after Carol Ann had tied up Phil Domblewski, Garrow took her to another tree and tied her up as well. Garrow then returned to Phil. Carol Ann couldn't be sure what was happening, but she could hear Phil's screams. Desperately she managed to work her way out of her bonds and ran off to hide in the woods.

Nick too had broken free. He made it back to the campsite and drove off in search of help. He returned a short time later with a small posse of armed men. They searched until they found David running in the forest in fear of his life and Carol Ann sitting by the body of Phil Domblewski. Phil had been slashed and stabbed repeatedly in the chest and finally killed with a knife wound through the heart. Garrow was nowhere to be found.

Phil Domblewski's friends soon gave police a positive identification of Robert Garrow. Garrow was a man whose mug shot was well known to the cops. The New York Bureau of Criminal Investigation and the state police quickly organized a massive manhunt. There were good reasons for their urgency. The police knew that Garrow, an experienced backwoodsman who grew up in the area and could live off the land, needed only to cross one state highway to escape into the vast expanse of the Adirondack wilderness. But most important, they feared for the safety of Susan Petz.

Nine days before the Domblewski killing and just fifty miles up the road, police had found the body of Daniel Porter, a twenty-one-year-old Boston College student, tied up and stabbed to death. The pattern of the stab wounds was similar to the stabbing torture inflicted on Domblewski. Porter's companion, Susan Petz, a Boston College student from Skokie, Illinois, had disappeared. Robert Garrow now became the police's star suspect in the Porter/Petz case. If Garrow had abducted Susan Petz, she might still be alive—if they could find her in time.

·

Hoping that he would be willing to help in their search, the police called Frank Armani, a former deputy DA who now ran his own small law firm. He handled some criminal law work, but concentrated mostly on personal injury cases. He had met Robert Garrow a year earlier, when Garrow asked for advice about a minor automobile injury case. Nothing had ever come of the case, but a few months later, in November 1972, Garrow called Armani from the local jail. Garrow was accused of the false imprisonment of a young Syracuse University couple and possession of marijuana found in his car.

Armani knew that Garrow was on parole for rape, but he also knew that officials considered Garrow an exemplary parolee. He had found good work as a master mechanic at a Syracuse bakery and had worked hard to put his family back together. The New York State Crime Commission had even used Garrow as one of their "poster boys," an example of the parole system at its best. Garrow swore to Armani that he had done nothing wrong, and when the college couple admitted that the marijuana belonged to them, the case against Garrow was dismissed.

Six months later, though, Robert Garrow was back in trouble. Police claimed that Garrow had driven two young girls, ages ten and eleven, to a secluded area outside Syracuse, where he forced them to masturbate him and perform oral sex. Garrow called Frank Armani. When Armani read the girls' statements, he was struck by how well organized, detailed, and precise they were. He was convinced that no eleven-year-old could remember so much so precisely, and that the police had coached the girls. At the least, the police were guilty of overzealousness. At the most, his client might just be telling the truth. Armani agreed to represent Garrow. He had started to doubt his client, but he doubted the police work, too.

Armani succeeded in getting Garrow out on bail, and Garrow returned to his job at the bakery. But when the case was called for trial on July 26, Garrow failed to appear in court and the judge issued a bench warrant for his arrest. Three days later Phil Domblewski was killed.

When the police called Armani about the Domblewski killing, they also told him about their suspicions in the Porter/Petz case. Armani offered to help the police bring Garrow in. He even went on

TV. "Running away will do you no good, Robert," Armani said on the air. "I'm willing to help. Come on in, and you won't get hurt."

For the next ten days, despite numerous reported sightings, the police had almost no idea where Robert Garrow was. Hope for finding Susan Petz alive faded with each passing day. Finally, on August 7, Garrow made a mistake. He stole a late-model Pontiac from the parking lot of a resort lodge. He headed north but found his way barred by a police roadblock. Garrow accelerated down the highway's double yellow line and broke through the barricade. He had gotten away again, but this time police thought they knew his destination.

Two days later, in the northeastern corner of the state, troopers flushed Garrow out of the woods behind his sister's home. As he dashed for another stand of trees, a sharpshooter with a high-powered rifle dropped him with shots in the leg, back, and arm. Garrow was taken to a Plattsburgh hospital in critical condition. There he instructed his wife to call Frank Armani.

Armani had never before handled a murder defense, but he had already represented Garrow in the molestation case. Garrow, who didn't have enough money for a lawyer on the murder charge, asked the court to appoint Armani. The local trial judge was ready to oblige. By now Armani had strong and serious reservations about Garrow, but this case, already one of the most notorious in upstate New York history, was headline news, a chance to be in the spotlight. With mixed feelings he accepted the appointment.

By the end of August Armani had been joined on the Garrow defense team by Francis Belge, a criminal defense specialist who had handled some of the region's most difficult cases. Given the overwhelming evidence and the bizarre history and behavior of their client, both lawyers believed that their only chance to save Garrow was an insanity plea, preferably one that included Garrow's confession to every crime he had committed, not just the Domblewski case. The lawyers figured that the more aberrant and abhorrent Garrow's behavior was, the easier it would be to prove his insanity.

But three weeks after his capture, Garrow continued to maintain that he could not recall the specific events of the Domblewski killing or the Porter/Petz case, in which the police strongly suspected his involvement. Years later Frank Armani would describe how he finally used party-trick hypnosis to suggest to Garrow that when Belge visited later that day, Garrow would remember everything. It worked; the floodgates opened. Not only did Garrow remember killing Phil Domblewski, he recalled details of the rape and murder of Alicia Hauck, a sixteen-year-old Syracuse girl who had been missing since late July. The more Belge prodded, the more Garrow revealed, in graphic and gruesome detail.

Garrow told how he picked up Alicia Hauck as she was hitchhiking, drove her to a hill near Syracuse University, and raped her. He forced her to walk with him into a cemetery near the campus, and when she tried to run, he "hit her" with his knife over and over, killing her. Garrow described burying the young girl's body in thick underbrush near a maintenance shack in the cemetery.

Under Belge's prodding, Garrow began to recall bits and pieces of the murder of Daniel Porter and the kidnapping of Susan Petz. At first all Garrow could remember was fighting with Porter and having a terrible headache. He didn't recall tying Porter to a tree, but eventually remembered "hitting him" with his knife again and again. Then he had forced Susan Petz into his car and headed north to his parents' home, four hours away. There he pitched a tent in the woods, tied up his victim, and periodically raped her. When he went off to see his parents or to spend the night at his aunt's home, he tied Petz with rope and hose, leaving food and water at her feet. After a few days he took Petz to a swimming hole, where she grabbed for his knife and tried to escape. When he described this to Belge, Garrow seemed genuinely puzzled as to why the young woman tried to escape. "We talked, we had great conversations," Garrow explained. But when Susan Petz went for his knife, Garrow killed her and shoved her body down the air shaft of an abandoned mine.

The lawyers may have gotten more than they had bargained for by the time Garrow was done with his confessions. If hearing this horrific tale were not enough, Armani and Belge now had to decide what to do with their newfound knowledge. They represented Garrow only on the Domblewski case. But now they had confirmation of what the DA had long suspected about Garrow's involvement in the Porter/Petz case, as well as information on several new crimes, including the truth about the disappearance of Alicia Hauck, still listed as a possible runaway.

This new knowledge presented the lawyers with a terrible and serious dilemma. Should they reveal the information to the police or the district attorney? Could they at least tell the judge? Or must they maintain their silence, even though it meant concealing evidence of multiple murder? As they analyzed it, the lawyers both felt that the principle of lawyer-client confidentiality—that everything a client tells them must be "held inviolate" and never revealed—required them to say nothing to anyone. Instead the lawyers asked Robert Garrow to tell them exactly where the bodies of Alicia Hauck and Susan Petz were buried, and set out to find the evidence—evidence they felt would support the insanity defense they intended to build for their client.

First Armani and Belge drove to Mineville, the remote upper New York State town where Garrow's parents lived. Equipped with a flashlight and camera, they climbed Barton Hill and searched for the abandoned mine that Garrow had described. They walked past the mine opening several times before feeling the cool breeze from the air shaft. Then one lawyer lowered the other down into the shaft to locate and take pictures of Susan Petz's corpse. Interestingly, when the two lawyers described the same grisly scene after the fact, each claimed that he had taken the photographs. Belge told the *New York Times* that Armani had held him by his feet as he snapped pictures. But Armani told a biographer that he and Belge had looped their two belts together as Belge lowered Armani into the shaft, camera in hand.

Finding Alicia Hauck's body was far more difficult. Even though Oakwood Cemetery was located right in the center of Syracuse, the underbrush was so thick that the lawyers' first forays into the brambles resulted only in cuts and scrapes all over their arms and legs. Finally, after several failed attempts, Belge found Alicia Hauck's headless and badly decomposed remains. Her skull lay about ten feet from her body. To get a picture of both, Belge moved the skull and placed it near the shoulders of the body before snapping his photos.

By this time, of course, Armani and Belge knew that Garrow's stories were true and that he was a vicious, crazed killer. This made their dilemma about their confidential information all the more difficult. To make matters worse, they now knew, literally, where the bodies were buried, and they also knew that both the Petz and Hauck families were searching for their children.

Still, Armani and Belge chose silence. Even when Susan Petz's father flew east from Chicago in search of his daughter and met with each lawyer to plead for information, their resolve to keep their client's secrets "inviolate" did not break; the two attorneys told him nothing. Later Alicia Hauck's father tried several times to see Armani, but the lawyer refused to talk to him.

But the lawyers did discuss the two girls' bodies with the prosecution, at least indirectly. Armani and Belge hoped that they could convince the prosecutors that their client was insane, and that it was in the state's best interests to accept a plea bargain. They pushed for this alternative mostly because they felt it was their client's best option. A plea of not guilty by reason of insanity would mean that instead of being sent to prison, Garrow would be housed in the much friendlier confines of a state hospital, where medical treatment would be available. Also, since Garrow would technically be found not guilty due to his mental condition, there would be at least the possibility of a future release if hospital psychiatrists ever deemed him "cured." The possibility of release might be slight, but it was far better than any chance he had of ever being paroled from prison.

Belge and Armani had three arguments to support their position. First, only a crazy man would do what Garrow had done. Second, a guilty plea would save the taxpayers of tiny Hamilton County, the most rural county in the state, hundreds of thousands of dollars in trial costs. Third, the lawyers told the DA that as part of the plea bargain, they and their client would clear up several unsolved disappearances and disclose where the remains of missing victims had been buried.

This was a daring but dangerous strategy. The lawyers insisted that they were bound by the cloak of confidentiality, refusing to be more specific about what crimes could be resolved. Saying too much too soon could breach confidentiality and give the police the evidence they needed to charge Garrow with the other crimes. So while the prosecutors undoubtedly surmised that Belge and Armani were talking about the Petz and Hauck cases, they could do no more than speculate.

Perhaps more significant, however, was how far the attorneys felt they should go in fulfilling their duty as lawyers to "zealously represent" their client. Armani and Belge surely knew that using the girls' bodies as bait for their deal was walking a very thin line. Implying Garrow's involvement in other terrible crimes might help them convince the prosecutors that their client was insane, but they would be using those other crimes—and the victims' bodies—as bargaining chips.

The lawyers' tactic infuriated the DAs of both Hamilton County and Onondaga County, where Syracuse is located. To the prosecutors, it was one thing for the lawyers to decline to reveal a client's confidential confession, but something else entirely to use their knowledge of the deaths of two girls—knowledge so desperately sought by the girls' families—to cut a deal for their client. The prosecutors refused to negotiate.

During the fall and winter of 1973 Armani and Belge spent a considerable amount of time in the small town of Lake Pleasant attending pretrial hearings, conducting their investigation, and otherwise preparing for trial. Since the town was a good two-hour drive from Syracuse, they looked for a place to rent rooms and set up a satellite office. This proved unexpectedly difficult, since they had become the most unpopular people in town. When they finally set up shop at a local inn, the innkeepers themselves were shunned by many of their friends.

Things weren't much better for the lawyers back in Syracuse that winter. They were both drinking more than they should, and Armani suffered increasingly from insomnia. Armani's office was broken into on several occasions, while at home, his wife and daughters received numerous obscene and threatening phone calls. These disruptions caused Armani to hide and finally destroy the photographs of the two girls' bodies, as well as some tapes he had made of Garrow's admissions. He was afraid that these confidential items could be stolen and then revealed.

Then in December a Syracuse University student found a decomposed body in a remote part of Oakwood Cemetery. Dental records identified the body as Alicia Hauck. An autopsy revealed that she had been strangled to death and then repeatedly stabbed. Less than two weeks later some schoolchildren playing near the abandoned mines in Mineville saw what they thought was a human foot. They called their teacher, who soon discovered the body of Susan Petz. The autopsy showed she had been stabbed in the chest repeatedly and hit over the head with a blunt object. Police announced that Robert Garrow was the prime suspect in both killings.

The case of Robert Garrow went to trial in May 1974 in the highly charged atmosphere of the Lake Pleasant courthouse. It began with a lengthy jury selection process. Hamilton County had less than five thousand inhabitants; over half were screened for service on the Garrow jury. There were three common reasons that prospective jurors gave to explain why they could not serve on the case. One excuse came from those whose jobs depended on the seasonal tourist trade, which started in May. The two other excuses were from jurors who were personally acquainted with the judge or DA and those who were already convinced that Robert Garrow was guilty.

In contrast to the five weeks it took to select a jury, the trial itself lasted only two weeks. The prosecutors needed just four days to put on their case. The pathologist testified about the stab wounds and the evidence that Phil Domblewski had been tortured before being killed. Domblewski's three friends told about their ordeal, and how cool and calculating Robert Garrow had been throughout.

Then it was the defense's turn at last to present its insanity defense. To prove insanity, Armani and Belge would have to show not just that Garrow was mentally ill, but that because of that illness he lacked "the capacity to know or appreciate the nature and consequences of [his] conduct or that such conduct was wrong." Belge began by calling Robert Garrow. Still wounded, his left leg and left arm permanently damaged by the police sharpshooter's bullets, Garrow testified from his wheelchair alongside the witness box. The story he told was more horrific than anyone could possibly have suspected.

First Garrow recounted his tormented childhood on the farm owned by his parents. He talked about his short-tempered, alcoholic father and his cruel and violent mother; about his father whipping him with a belt and making him stand in a corner for hours at a time. Perhaps worse, he described how his mother beat him at almost every opportunity, once hitting him over the head with a piece of firewood when he was five, knocking him unconscious. He also detailed how she made him wear his sister's bloomers when he misbehaved. When he spoke of his siblings, he referred to each of them as "it" rather than "he" or "she."

Garrow testified that at age seven or eight he was sent to live at a neighbor's farm as an indentured servant. Then, to the shock of everyone in the courtroom, Garrow described how at age eleven or twelve, alone on the neighbor's farm with no friends or other children, he had started having sex with the animals—dogs, cows, and sheep.

He stayed at the neighbor's farm until he was fifteen, when his parents sent him to an industrial school for incorrigible children. He joined the air force at seventeen but spent most of his two years' service in the stockade for stealing a camera and selling pornographic pictures. After his discharge he got in trouble again when he started a fight and quit his job. The lawyer who got him out of jail used him as a sex toy, forcing Garrow to masturbate him, and whipping Garrow while he took pictures. At some point Garrow had gotten married, but soon after, he was convicted of rape. He swore he didn't remember whether he had committed the rape or not, but he was sent to prison and served eight years.

Then Robert Garrow described what little he could remember of several rapes he had committed after his release from prison. What he remembered most clearly were the terrible headaches, the pounding and pressure in his head that preceded each incident. Finally Garrow described what he recalled of the homicides: the Porter/Petz case, the Hauck rape and homicide, and the Domblewski killing. As he talked about the two men he had killed, he referred to them as "it" rather than "he." By the time his testimony was finished, Garrow had admitted to four homicides and seven rapes or sexual assaults.

Garrow's testimony was shocking beyond belief. But it was no more shocking to some than the revelation his lawyers made the next day. Garrow's testimony had freed them from their vows of silence. They held a press conference announcing that they had known since the previous summer of Garrow's involvement in the Porter, Petz, and Hauck homicides and the locations of the two girls' bodies. The lawyers were under no compulsion to reveal this; why they chose to do so remains a mystery.

The Garrow case took only a few more days to complete. Belge and Armani did their best to present the strongest possible insanity defense. They called several psychiatrists who explained Garrow's psychosis by citing several incidents in his early childhood. The doctors explained that Garrow saw himself as he would see a cow, horse, or sheep—an impersonal, unfeeling animal—and that he depersonified others in much the same way. One psychiatrist described asking Garrow to imagine that the doctor was Garrow's father. The psychiatrist described what followed as the most frightening thing he had ever seen. Garrow's face got red and his pupils became enlarged, and he complained of a loud rushing sound in his ears. "I've got to kill it, Dad," said Garrow, staring hard at the doctor, before the petrified doctor calmed him down.

Armani and Belge had laid it all on the line in their defense of Robert Garrow, but on June 26, 1974, after less than two hours of deliberations, the jury rejected the insanity defense and found Garrow guilty of first-degree murder.

Now public outrage shifted from Garrow to his lawyers. The local grand jury investigated both men, ultimately indicting Belge on two felonies: failing to report a dead body, as required by the health code, and failing to provide a body with a decent burial. Central to the charges—and perhaps to the grand jury's decision not to indict Armani—was the fact that Belge had moved Alicia Hauck's body in order to get a better picture.

But the trial court threw out the indictment, saying enigmatically that "a trial is in part a search for truth, but it is only partly a search for truth." The court said Garrow's lawyers had to "maintain . . . a sacred trust of confidentiality," and even applauded Francis Belge for "conducting himself as an officer of the Court, with all the zeal at his command to protect the constitutional rights of his client."

When the prosecutors appealed the court's dismissal of the

Belge indictment, the appeals court upheld it, but the opinion was hardly a ringing endorsement of Belge or Armani. Emphasizing their "serious concern" about the lawyers' reliance on absolute confidentiality and insisting that lawyers "also must observe basic human standards of decency," the appeals judges were far more critical than the trial court had been. So were Alicia Hauck's parents, who filed an ethics complaint with the state bar disciplinary authorities.

But the ethics charges were also dismissed. The ethics committee concluded that "[p]roper representation of a client calls for full disclosure by the client to his lawyer of all possibly relevant facts, even though such facts may be the client's commission of prior crimes. To encourage full disclosure, the client must be assured of confidentiality." Alicia Hauck's father saw it another way. "When you get lawyers against lawyers," he summed up in an interview many years later, "it's kind of a closed fraternity."

Francis Belge and Frank Armani walked away from the Garrow incident unscathed by any official penalty. But they fared less well in the court of public opinion. To many, these two attorneys typified the image of the unfeeling, unscrupulous modern-day American lawyer. But years later, in an interview for a PBS television special, Frank Armani described the internal conflict he and Belge felt. "Your mind's screaming one way, 'Relieve these parents' . . . and the other is your sworn duty." When asked about "common decency," Armani replied that he tried to find "the higher moral good at the moment . . . the question of the Constitution, of even a bastard like him having a proper defense . . . against the fact that I have a dead girl, the fact her body's there [and] the breaking heart of a parent." Clearly distressed, Armani told journalist Fred Graham that "it's a terrible thing to play God."

Both Belge and Armani were particularly tormented by having to keep silent in the face of inquiries from the girls' families. Belge told the *New York Times* that "I spent, many, many sleepless nights" about the decision to remain silent, especially after Mr. Petz visited from Chicago. Armani explained that he had refused to see Alicia Hauck's father because he had been so upset by Petz's visit. He feared he would tell the bereaved father what he felt sworn not to reveal: "I just couldn't trust myself to meet him face to face." In fact,

Armani acknowledged some years later that his own brother had been lost on an air force reconnaissance mission in 1962, and the body had never been recovered. This made it even more difficult for Armani to keep his terrible secret.

Throughout, the two lawyers and their supporters pointed to important constitutional principles to explain why the attorneys had done the right thing, in spite of how unfeeling it might have seemed. What principles could be so important as to justify the lawyers' actions to the citizens of New York State? The court that dismissed the Belge indictment put it this way:

> A hue and cry went up from the press and other news media suggesting that the attorneys should be found guilty of such crimes as obstruction of justice or becoming an accomplice after the fact. From a layman's standpoint, this certainly was a logical conclusion. However, the Constitution of the United States of America attempts to preserve the dignity of the individual and to do that guarantees him the services of an attorney who will bring to the bar and to the bench every conceivable protection from the inroads of the state against such rights as are vested in the Constitution for one accused of crime.

When Fred Graham asked Armani what the point was in applying such important principles to "a piece of scum like Garrow," Armani replied that if a principle "doesn't belong to the worst of us, then it can't belong to the best. Where do you make the exception?" Armani was echoing the words of another New York lawyer, Judge Learned Hand. Hand, a legendary figure who served for over fifty years as a federal judge, is considered by many the greatest judge in the history of the state. His speeches and monographs emphasized that a society of laws must be measured by how it treats its worst examples, not its best.

But when Alicia Hauck's sister Cindy wrote Frank Armani to ask why he had remained silent in the face of the family's grief, the lawyer was never able to answer, though he started to many times. On the verge of breaking down, he explained it this way in his PBS interview: "I caused them pain, I prolonged their pain. . . . There's nothing I can say to justify that in their minds. You couldn't justify it to me."

•

Rarely will ethics rules and society's morals conflict more graphically and directly than in the choices that faced Francis Belge and Frank Armani. On one side was the obligation to protect their client's interests, their "sworn duty" never to reveal a client's confidences and secrets, their ethical mandate to provide their client with "zealous representation." On the other was "common decency" and the fundamental notions of justice, fairness, and compassion. There was also the moral imperative that so distressed both lawyers—to ease two families' pain rather than prolong it.

Belge and Armani made the decisions they did—to maintain their silence, to protect a "piece of scum" like Robert Garrow at all costs—in part because of the concept of "fiduciary duty."

A lawyer who agrees to take a client's case takes on a "fiduciary duty" to that client. That term includes loyalty to the client, zealous advocacy on the client's behalf, and a duty to protect the client's confidences and secrets. But the concept of fiduciary duty is even greater than the sum of these parts. It has often been defined as the duty a lawyer owes to each client by virtue of the lawyer's special position of trust over the client's affairs. Fiduciary duty requires the lawyer to place the client's cause above the lawyer's own individual interests, and to always act on the client's behalf in the utmost good faith.

If we accept their version of events, Belge and Armani indeed placed their client's cause above their own individual interests. By protecting Robert Garrow's horrible secrets, they suffered great personal costs—economically, emotionally, and to their own reputations. But what about the other side of the equation—telling the truth, seeing justice is done, "doing the right thing"? Does their fiduciary duty exempt lawyers from following these principles? Where do individual rights stop and the interests of society begin?

When asked, many, perhaps most, lawyers will candidly admit that seeking truth—discovering what really happened—is rarely their job. They might argue that the real truth is often hard to know, and that their role—their fiduciary duty—is to explain the truth as their clients perceive it. Some may admit that they present the truth as their clients would *like* it to be perceived. Most agree, though, that at best it's someone else's responsibility, the judge's or perhaps the jury's, to divine the real truth—Truth with a capital *T*.

The traditional view, espoused by lawyers from the old school, is that the adversary process, with one side arguing its version of truth and the other side arguing another version, somehow results in the emergence of absolute Truth. To many others, though, this is nonsense. One side may have much more money or a vast array of legal talent at its disposal, while the other side struggles simply to stay afloat. In the minds of some, the "little guy," America's favorite hero, has little chance against fat-cat corporations with large war chests and flashy law firms. Proving the truth, these people would argue, has far less to do with the facts of a case than money and power.

If lawyers don't see themselves as purveyors of Truth, they are much more comfortable with the idea that they are seekers of Justice. They point to a common concept of our legal system, the "legal fiction," which by its very nature chooses justice over truth. Here is an example of a legal fiction based on our Constitution, in this case the rights protected under the Fifth Amendment.

A suspect in a criminal case confesses, but only after he is put in isolation for twenty-four hours, threatened with beatings, and denied water to drink and the use of a bathroom. A judge later determines that the confession is unlawful because it was "coerced" by these unfair tactics. The judge notes that even an innocent person might have confessed under these circumstances. But the circumstances and the judge's opinion will never be presented to the jury. The jury will never hear anything about the confession at all. If the subject comes up, even police witnesses will testify in a way that makes it appear that the defendant never confessed.

The theory behind the legal fiction is this: Letting the jury hear the confession at all would be unfair, because it might influence the jury despite the circumstances. Some jurors, for example, might believe that no one would falsely confess to a crime after only a single day's deprivation, while for others the effect of the confession might be more subtle, such as tending to lend credibility to circumstantial evidence that would otherwise be weak. Instead of taking this chance, the theory is that the justice system owes it to the defendant to take matters into its own hands. So the judge strikes the confession from the record. The guilt or innocence of the defendant will then be tested only by the *admissible* evidence, leaving out all those things that the judge has determined would be unfair to one side or the other.

But while the concept of legal fiction makes a lot of sense to most lawyers, it raises some important questions for the rest of us. For instance, some people wonder why the judge doesn't simply allow the jury to hear about the confession and the surrounding circumstances, leaving the issue of the confession's fairness to the jury's common sense. Some people want to know the other facts of the case. For example, why did the police treat the accused so brutally? Was it because of the horrible nature of the crime and the overwhelming physical evidence of the defendant's guilt? If this is the case, then why are we so worried about the confession, no matter how it was obtained?

In other words, while lawyers and the legal system are seeking justice for the defendant, the American public is asking, "What about justice for society?" There is an increasing public perception that Justice is routinely done a disservice by lawyers who serve the needs of their clients by buying it at any price, even when they are clearly in the wrong.

While Francis Belge and Frank Armani saw themselves as seekers of justice, most of the public saw hired guns who shoved truth and justice under the rug, along with fundamental notions of compassion and decency. The lawyers claimed not only that they had acted properly under the rules of ethics, but that their actions served the greater good—"the higher moral good at the moment," as Armani put it. They pointed to their client's horrific childhood and what they considered to be his legitimate claim of insanity. They argued that only by protecting Garrow's confidence could they fulfill their fiduciary duty, not to mention upholding our Constitution. But this argument fell largely on deaf ears.

To the public, the best one could say about Belge and Armani is that they failed to see the forest for the trees. In their single-minded efforts to protect a rapist and murderer, they had lost touch with the larger needs of society: to see justice done, to put a killer behind bars, to alleviate the suffering of the victims' families.

But if it were that simple, why would any lawyer ever do what these two did? They became pariahs in their own city. Their families were shunned by former friends and harassed by obscene phone calls. Armani's marriage almost ended as a result of the case. On one occasion a Molotov cocktail was left at Armani's home. On another he got a death threat on his breakfast napkin: "We can take you out at any time. That kid killer better not get off."

Their law practices fared even worse. Frank Armani went from heading a four-attorney office with five secretaries to a one-man office with a secretary who came in three afternoons a week. His total compensation from the state for representing Garrow on murder charges was less than $10,000. Despite being deserted by many of his old clients, Armani managed to put the pieces of his life back together and rebuild a small practice, though he suffered two serious heart attacks. Francis Belge eventually gave up the practice of law completely.

If asked, Belge and Armani would undoubtedly say that it was the public and not the two attorneys who missed the forest for the trees. For the lawyers, the trees were the horrible facts of the Garrow case, while the forest was the American system of justice and the principle that unless every person's rights are protected—even someone as despicable as Robert Garrow—then ultimately no one's are. In this instance, protecting the "forest" came at great personal cost—to the families of the victims, to all the citizens of the little town of Lake Pleasant, New York, and ultimately to the lawyers themselves.

This point of view echoes a traditional theme of the American legal system—that protecting the rights of individuals is the best way to protect society. The theory is that this time the system protected a "piece of scum" like Robert Garrow, but the next time it might be you or me.

To illustrate this point, let's return to the confession scenario. We've said that many people think society shouldn't worry too much about how the confession was obtained when the accused is clearly guilty. But is that really true? Are we comfortable letting our police decide how far they can go in coercing a confession based on how guilty *they* think the suspect is? Do we want them to feel free to deny a suspect—*any* suspect—food and water for twenty-four hours, refuse to let him use the bathroom, and threaten him with beatings? That doesn't justify such conduct even if the accused turns out to be guilty.

Let's assume the accused in question is Robert Garrow on the day after his capture. He's wounded and hurting; the evidence seems strong. Once he's out of immediate medical danger, the police refuse to feed him, deny him medical treatment and pain pills, and force him to confess. If Garrow's rights are not protected here, what happens with the next Robert Garrow, where the evidence is a little less clear? Or the one after that? As Frank Armani put it, "Where do we make the exception?"

In this fictional scenario, when Frank Armani and Francis Belge move to strike Garrow's confession, they are doing it to protect Garrow's rights. But in another sense, they are protecting the rights of all individuals in our society to be free from the kinds of abuses that their client suffered, abuses that we usually associate with societies less free, less democratic, than ours.

Judge Learned Hand said that it was "better 100 guilty men go free than one innocent man go to jail." But he spoke these words over a half century ago, when there was less crime in the streets, a simpler, less cumbersome legal system, and a less jaded American public. Today the average American is much less willing to accept Learned Hand's aphorism than the words of the distraught father of another victim, Ronald Goldman. When Fred Goldman declared at a press conference in the middle of the O.J. Simpson trial that "this is not justice," he struck a chord with the American people. Mr. Goldman, and much of the public, was frustrated by endless months of testimony, an endless stream of witnesses, and a trial that seemed to become less about the accused, and still less about the victims, as time went on.

Many lawyers, perhaps Francis Belge and Frank Armani among them, might well be sympathetic to Goldman's plea. But they would also argue that this point of view sends us down a slippery slope, where we may lose far more than we think. Do we really want to let the American public decide who is guilty and who is not, which trials are too long, and which present defenses so implausible they should not be allowed? If the American public gets to decide, will we find ourselves voting on the guilt or innocence in the next celebrated case by *USA Today* poll or by pushing a button on interactive TV?

Epilogue:
The End of the Saga of Robert Garrow

Robert Garrow began his life sentence in the high-security surroundings of Dannemora State Prison, where he had served out his prior rape sentence. But he complained continually to prison authorities that his wounds, which had left him in a wheelchair, meant he should be moved to Fishkill, a medium-security institution housing the elderly and infirm. He backed up his complaints with a lawsuit against the state prison system. In 1978 Garrow got his wish—a transfer to Fishkill.

On September 8, 1978, well after lights-out, Robert Garrow got out of bed, placed a dummy stuffed with rags in his cot, grabbed a radio and the gun his son had smuggled in to him, jumped the fourteen-foot fence that separated him from freedom, and disappeared into the densely wooded terrain that surrounded the prison. It was his kind of terrain. His left leg and arm were not nearly what they once were, but neither was he the wheelchair-bound invalid he led the prison system to believe he was. Robert Garrow, serial killer and rapist, experienced woodsman, was once again at large.

Again, as in 1973, one of the first people the police contacted was Frank Armani. They asked him for anything that could help them apprehend his former client. This time, according to what he told his biographer years later, Armani did not remain silent, despite the cloak of confidentiality that is never lifted even when a lawyer's representation ends. Armani thought back to the secrets Garrow had told him from his hospital bed in Plattsburgh about how best to avoid a police dragnet, and reported what he recalled to the police: Garrow would stay near the prison and let the manhunt pass him by rather than try to outrun it; he'd have a radio to monitor reports of police activity and blockades; he would hide in the deepest part of the underbrush and wait it out until the police felt they had exhausted their search of the area.

The police followed Armani's advice and continued to search the area surrounding the prison. On the third day, as dusk approached, a search team discovered Garrow in the underbrush. Garrow shot first, wounding the team's point man, and was immediately gunned down in a hail of police bullets. Thanks in part to confidential information revealed to the police by his former lawyer, Robert Garrow was dead.

Another Day Spent
Representing the Guilty

He who defends the guilty, knowing him to be so, forgets alike honour and honesty, and is false to God and man!
> —Letter to the London *Times* in 1840,
> about barrister Charles Phillips's zealous defense
> of a man he knew to be a murderer

Maintaining the system is not maintaining justice. Representing someone you know is guilty is not justice, it's rhetoric.
> —University of California law student in 1995,
> commenting on the case of *People v. O.J. Simpson*

They are the two questions perhaps most frequently asked of lawyers: "How can you justify representing someone you're convinced is guilty? Even worse, how can you actually try to get that person off?" Richie Richewski has heard the questions hundreds of times, at his friends' cocktail parties, his kids' soccer games—wherever he goes in his life away from the courthouse. To Richie, the answers are clear, but many lawyers are themselves uncomfortable with these questions, and would never do what Richie Richewski does for a living.

Simeon "Richie" Richewski is one of the most respected criminal defense lawyers in River City. Although he is a private lawyer, not a public defender, he accepts more than his share of "assigned cases" where he's appointed by the court. These cases don't pay very well, but Richie likes the work more than defending wealthy clients accused of drunk driving, or white-collar embezzlement cases. Richie often says that assigned cases are "what doing criminal defense work is all about."

Not all of Richie's cases are a walk in the park, however, and Kirk Hopman is a case in point. Richie has been appointed by the court to represent Hopman on three counts of child abuse with great bodily injury. The indictment charges that on several occasions Hopman struck his girlfriend Rowena Soo's three-year-old child, and once threw the child against the walls of their apartment, causing brain damage. Soo is also accused and faces the same charges, though the deputy DA assigned to the case has made it clear that she considers Hopman the perpetrator and Soo only an aider and abettor.

Richie first meets Hopman in a jail conference room, where Hopman denies he did anything wrong, but tells a story that includes several factual inconsistencies. Richie is almost certain that Hopman is guilty, but he can't be absolutely sure. He finds the crimes charged repugnant, and though he likes many of his clients, he finds Hopman manipulative, whiny, and demanding. Still, Richie knows that there are "winning chances" if the case goes to trial. The witnesses against his client—especially the one who claims to have seen Hopman actually "tossing that kid around"—are "flaky," the type of witnesses whose credibility Richie knows he can successfully attack at trial.

At a settlement conference before the trial, the DA tells Richie that if Hopman pleads guilty to one count of child abuse carrying a seven-year prison term, she'll drop the other two counts. Hopman insists to Richie that he wants to go to trial. The DA, convinced Hopman committed the actual assaults, offers Soo a much better deal: a long term of closely supervised probation if she cooperates in testifying against Hopman. But even though Soo steadfastly denies that she hit her child, the policy of the district attorney's office is that Soo must plead guilty to one of the counts in the indictment as charged—that she committed an assault and personally inflicted great bodily injury on the child.

Privately Richie agrees with the DA's assessment that Hopman committed the assaults, while Soo, easily the weaker of the two, found herself unable to stop him. But Richie realizes that if Soo testifies against Hopman, her guilty plea could help create a reasonable doubt defense that Soo, by her own admission, was the one who committed the injuries, not Hopman.

This line of attack may afford Kirk Hopman a possible defense, but it doesn't offer Richie much comfort. He faces several difficult ethical issues: How hard should he fight at trial for a client he's convinced is guilty? Does the terrible nature of this crime make a difference? How far should Richie go in cross-examining Rowena Soo? Should he come out with both guns blazing, even though he believes Soo's version of events? How vigorously should he argue to the jury that his client is not guilty?

As Richie and his client go over strategy the night before trial, Hopman suddenly admits his guilt: In a rage he threw Soo's child against the wall, and he "hit the kid pretty hard" on a few other occasions. The next morning, as he heads to the courthouse, Richie evaluates his situation. Hopman's admission of guilt is upsetting, even alarming, but can Richie allow it to affect his defense? After all, Kirk may be a very bad man, but Richie has promised him the best he can give.

.

We've often made heroes of criminal defense lawyers, but usually because they were saving the world from injustice. Perry Mason, perhaps our most famous fictional lawyer, used all the tricks of the trade, but only for his seemingly limitless stable of innocent clients. Would Perry represent a man like Hopman? Perhaps not, but the fictionalized criminal defense lawyer who rides to the defense of justice and rights wrongs done to innocent victims never really existed. Far more accurate is the world-weary, calculating Teddy Hoffman, who in the very first episode of the controversial television drama *Murder One* readily admits that he represents guilty clients all the time.

It shouldn't be a great surprise to learn that some of our real-life heroes also represented the scourge of society. Clarence Darrow represented guilty criminal clients as often as not, and he was more than once accused of unethical conduct in defense of their causes. His most famous defense was undertaken on behalf of two guilty killers, Leopold and Loeb.

Even our most sacrosanct hero is not immune. Abraham Lincoln's most celebrated case was the defense of "Duff" Armstrong, in which Lincoln used an almanac to prove that the key eyewitness could not have seen by the light of the moon because the moon had already set when the crime took place. But what is often omitted in the telling of this tale is that "Duff" Armstrong was almost certainly guilty.

The reality is that at trial, the job of the criminal defense lawyer is to make every effort to convince the jury to acquit a guilty client. The public may be asking, "How can you work to get that guilty person off?" But to most experienced criminal defense lawyers, that question is old news. The answer comes with the territory; it's a fact of life from the very first day on the job.

Lawyers who zealously defend the guilty are of considerable current interest, but this controversy is hardly new. In 1840 the story of Charles Phillips, one of England's leading barristers, captivated the British public and press. Phillips had defended an accused murderer to the utmost, though he knew the man was guilty. Phillips gained little but disapprobation, including from the bishop of London, who called his defense "a late most melancholy and remarkable occasion" and presented a petition from "the inhabitants of London" on the floor of the House of Lords that said "God's word" could not be reconciled with what Phillips had done.

We grapple with the same issues today. The traditional justification often advanced is that this is the way our adversary system works. While most of the world's legal systems use some form of adversarial model, with different lawyers for each side, the Anglo-American system has operated under a strong "adversary theorem" in which the lawyer does not adopt the views of the client, but merely defends them. Since all people, even the most unpopular, have the right to representation, separating the lawyer's personal values from those of the client allows the lawyer to be loyal to the client without being responsible for the client's actions. This is a cornerstone of the American adversary theorem, making the job of the advocate not to present the truth, but to explain the client's story. The theory is that truth emerges when both sides have lawyers who play by these rules.

Learning the adversary theorem has long been a major part of the typical law school education. Teaching young men and women how to "think like a lawyer" includes showing them how to argue both sides of a legal point with equal vigor and conviction. Almost every school holds a moot court competition in which students argue one side of a hypothetical case on one day and the other side on the next. The winner is the person who does the best job for *both* sides, regardless of personal convictions.

Not everyone in the profession accepts this old-school view. Some years ago a law professor named Gerald Postema pleaded with lawyers to "apply moral principles" to their conduct and to recognize the "moral costs" of their actions. He criticized lawyers who simply distance themselves from their clients' views, and argued that lawyers should accept personal moral responsibility for their behavior.

Is it possible to be moral and represent guilty clients with all the vigor and zeal the law requires? Many say no, while others remind us that all who stand accused are innocent until a guilty verdict is returned in court. Some point to another traditional tenet of the American legal system: taking the side of the underdog. A California statute reads: "It is the duty of an attorney . . . [n]ever to reject, for any consideration personal to himself or herself, the cause of the defenseless or the oppressed."

Law professor and advocate supreme Michael Tigar raised this banner when agreeing to represent John Demjanjuk, accused of being Treblinka's Ivan the Terrible, who helped oversee the murder of 850,000 Jews. Though an Israeli court acquitted Demjanjuk of being Ivan, it became clear that he had worked in the death camps and had lied rather than admit it.

Interestingly, according to Tigar's old friend and debate opponent, Monroe Freedman, of Hofstra (New York) Law School, it was Tigar who had once convincingly argued that lawyers should ask two questions in each case: "Is this really the kind of client to which I want to dedicate my training, my knowledge, my skills?" and "Did I go to law school to help a client that harms other human beings?"

Professor Freedman dubbed this the "burden of public justification." But Tigar replied to Freedman by renouncing this burden, calling it "pernicious," and arguing that he should never have to explain why he represents a client. Acting consistently with this principle, Tigar later agreed to represent Oklahoma City bombing suspect Terry Nichols.

A similar principle motivated Anthony Griffin, who in 1993 agreed to represent the grand dragon of the Texas Knights of the Ku Klux Klan against the efforts of the State of Texas to obtain the Klan's membership list. Griffin is African-American, and was at that time chief counsel to the Texas branch of the NAACP. He made it clear that he found his new client personally repugnant. But, he told the *New York Times* in 1993, Texas's arguments were the same as those "always used against every organization 'We' do not like. It was used against the N.A.A.C.P. [and] the Black Panther Party." Indeed, Griffin based his defense of the Klan on the U.S. Supreme Court case that first established an organization's right to keep its information private, *N.A.A.C.P. v. Alabama*, in which the civil rights group successfully resisted the state's attempts to get its membership lists.

Most of Griffin's NAACP colleagues believed that he should not represent both the Klansman and the NAACP. Griffin was discharged from his NAACP post, and as the Klan litigation went forward, the NAACP filed a "friend of the court" brief supporting the State of Texas and opposing the applicability of *N.A.A.C.P. v. Alabama*, the case it had filed itself and won thirty-five years before.

Eventually, however, Griffin prevailed both in and out of court. In June 1994 the Texas Supreme Court sided with Griffin's client on First Amendment grounds. As for Griffin, he received the first annual William Brennan Award, named in honor of the former Supreme Court justice, long a champion of free speech. Perhaps more important, Griffin regained his reputation in the black community, and was invited to work with the NAACP's sister organization, the NAACP Legal Defense Fund.

From the beginning, Griffin had maintained that he was doing the right thing. "In our role as lawyers, we're not God," he told the *New York Times*. "If lawyers backed off because someone is unpopular or hated, then our whole system of justice would just fall apart."

In his remark that lawyers aren't God, Griffin echoed the sentiment of many legal scholars, who caution that the last thing a good advocate should do is judge a client. Proponents of this view have been around since Dr. Samuel Johnson:

BOSWELL: But what do you think of supporting a cause which you know to be bad?

JOHNSON: Sir, you do not know it to be good or bad till the judge determines it. . . . An argument which does not convince yourself may convince the judge to whom you urge it; and if it does convince him, why then, sir, you are wrong and he is right. It is his business to judge; and you are not to be confident in your opinion that a cause is bad, but to say all you can for your client, and then hear the judge's opinion.

In today's world, more people question the justification for Dr. Johnson's perspective than ever before. But most criminal defense lawyers would find it impossible to perform their jobs if they sit in judgment of their clients as well as defend them. Representing the criminally accused is a serious and difficult responsibility. Often the lawyer is the only person on the defendant's side. Besides, clients frequently deny their involvement in the crimes they are accused of. While the lawyer may assume or even strongly suspect that the client is guilty, in many cases it is difficult to *know* for sure which clients "did it" and which may just possibly be telling the truth. Most criminal defense lawyers have asked themselves at one time or another, "Am I the person who should make this judgment call?" For the most part, they answer this question with a clear no, and then go on to do their job, presenting the best possible defense and letting the jury decide.

Most people have a hard time accepting the idea that lawyers can and should vigorously defend clients they don't believe in, whom they know or firmly believe to be guilty. As for the argument that the lawyer should not judge the client, some compare it to that advanced by soldiers of the Third Reich that their job was not to judge but to perform their duty. People want to know where is the point beyond which legal technicalities must stop, where adherence to procedure and "the Law" in the abstract must yield to commonly held notions of truth, justice, and decency.

Here's an example of an ethics analysis of a lawyer's conduct in a criminal case, based on a 1987 Michigan state bar ethics opinion. It illustrates the gulf between what the public and the legal system each perceive as "correct" and "ethical" behavior. The issue is whether an attorney who knows the client is guilty should present evidence that, though truthful in itself, misleads the jury into thinking that the client did not commit the crime.

These are the facts: The defendant is charged with robbery. The victim identifies the defendant as the robber, but mistakenly tells the police that the robbery occurred at 10:30 P.M. when it actually occurred at about 8:30. She makes this mistake perhaps because her watch was stolen in the robbery, perhaps because she briefly lost consciousness. The police put the mistaken time in their report.

Meanwhile, the defendant, seeing the wrong time in the police report, admits to his lawyer that he committed the robbery, but at 8:30, not 10:30. The defendant went from the robbery to a bar he frequents. Several of his friends and the bartender can provide him with an alibi for any time after 9:15, over an hour before the victim believes the robbery took place. There is no way for either the victim or the police to know that they have the time wrong. When the victim testifies to the wrong time at trial, what should the lawyer do about presenting the "alibi"?

The Michigan ethics committee's answer was clear: "Go for it!" The committee said that the principle of zealous advocacy required the defense counsel to do everything within the bounds of the law to help the client.

The opinion emphasized the central tenet of the adversary theorem—that the lawyer-client relationship is paramount. This allows clients to be candid with their lawyers. Without this policy, in the long run, "future defendants [might] fail to disclose everything to their lawyer; the result would be that they would receive an inadequate defense." Pointing out that there can be different degrees of guilt, and raising the specter of Dr. Johnson on judging one's client, the committee wrote that "criminal defense counsel are not sent to the jail's interview room to be their client's one person jury."

How does this principle of zealous advocacy apply to the issue of seeking the truth? "It is not the obligation of defense counsel," concluded the opinion, "to correct inaccurate evidence introduced by the prosecution or to ignore truthful evidence that could exculpate his client. . . . Although the tenor of this opinion may appear to risk an unfortunate result to society in the particular situation posed, such an attitude by defense counsel will serve in the long run to preserve the system of criminal justice envisioned by our constitution. . . .

"[Our ethics code] prohibits counsel from using perjured testimony or 'false evidence,' but it is perfectly proper to call to the witness stand those witnesses on behalf of the client who will present truthful testimony. . . . Client indeed was with the witnesses at the hour to which they will testify. The victim's mistake concerning the precise time of the crime results in this windfall defense to the client."

The implication of this Michigan ethics opinion is clear: Truth with a capital *T* is not the goal of the criminal defense lawyer, and it is not always the goal of the criminal justice system, either. The truth of the defendant's guilt is secondary to the lawyer's zealous representation of the client. To many, this seems like justice denied, not justice served. So while much of America is concerned with the actions of Richie and his colleagues, the more fundamental question may be whether we should continue to have a criminal justice system that can put protecting guilty defendants ahead of convicting them.

The system's proponents look beyond its effect on one individual and argue that important constitutional protections are at stake, including some of the most basic of our Bill of Rights: the right to effective assistance of counsel and due process of law. From these constitutional protections have come fundamental social policies that have been part of the fabric of our justice system for hundreds of years. Among the most familiar—and most important—of these policies is that before anyone in our society may be convicted of a crime, the state must prove its case, and do so beyond a reasonable doubt. This is our highest standard of proof, as few things can ever be proven beyond all possible doubt.

Criminal defense lawyers reason, cogently, that their job—their sworn duty of advocacy—is to do anything within the bounds of ethics rules to raise such a doubt in the minds of the jurors. Put another way, truth must be measured not by whether the accused is guilty, but by whether the state has met its constitutional burden of proving that guilt.

There is ample historical basis for our constitutional requirements. Quaker William Penn had been imprisoned again and again in England for his heretical beliefs, which amounted to preaching his religion and arguing that not everyone should have to join the Church of England. On one occasion when a jury voted for Penn's acquittal, the judge ordered the jurors to reconsider and threatened them with imprisonment if they didn't change their vote. Penn fled to America to found the colony of Pennsylvania. In the colonial America of 1735, John Peter Zenger was accused of criminal libel when his newspaper published articles strongly critical of the governor of New York. Zenger had trouble even getting a defense, because the government disbarred his lawyers. He finally imported a Philadelphia lawyer, Andrew Hamilton. Zenger was exonerated when Hamilton convinced a jury that anyone should be free to speak the truth.

It's obvious that the Kirk Hopmans of the world have little in common with Penn and Zenger as innocent victims of an oppressive justice system. But those who toil in our criminal courts argue that in order to protect the Penns and Zengers of the world, we must also protect the Kirk Hopmans, because all people, even Hopman, must be afforded the same due process rights, the same right to freedom, unless a case is proved beyond a reasonable doubt. Justice is truly served, they say, by ensuring that the rights of even the worst of us are protected. The cost of allowing a few guilty people to go free is seen as less than the cost of choosing whose rights "deserve" protection.

Some lawyers make social and economic arguments to bolster their constitutional claims. Almost all of us agree that everyone should have the same rights without regard to what a person can afford. But just as gross inequities remain in our society, they remain in our criminal justice system as well. The vast majority of our criminal defendants are poor. African-Americans continue to be disproportionately represented in our country's jails and prisons. Numerous studies show that for the same class of crime, from petty offenses to murders, blacks get harsher sentences than whites. And law enforcement bias against minority groups in general and black men in particular continues to permeate America's justice system. This was among the most important lessons of the Rodney King case. Without the system's explicit constitutional protections, these racial inequalities would surely increase.

People such as Richie Richewski often take a less theoretical approach in describing why they do what they do. "In order for the state to be put to its proof, people like me are necessary," one criminal defense lawyer told us. "I'm experienced and good at it. But if I'm just going through the motions, am I really putting the state to the test? Our justice system is like the carnival strongman who says, 'Hit me with your hardest punch.' If I don't use my best punches, it defeats the whole purpose of the exercise."

In our interviews with a score of public defenders and private criminal defense lawyers, a composite argument emerges. It goes something like this: "Look, most of the clients we represent have never had much of a chance in life: poor, poorly educated, no intact family. I'm the one person whose job puts me on their side. At the very least, I treat my clients with dignity and respect. And if I don't speak for them, who will? After all, on one side you've got the power of the state, the legal authority of the DA, the police department, the sheriff. On the other side? Just one poor, scared son of a bitch. And me.

"It's only one small step from the use of power to its abuse. Some DAs 'prep' their witnesses by telling them exactly what to say. Cops lie, not all but some; cops plant evidence, not in every case but in a few. When cops lie, it's not usually done to frame an innocent person; it's usually where the client is guilty and the case needs a little shoring up. But that still doesn't justify the abuse of power.

"Please understand: I'm not defending what my client did, except in court. I worry just like everyone else about dangerous people going free. I don't know how I'd react if I got a client off on murder charges and he went out and killed again. Some people ask me why I don't withdraw from a case when I realize my client's guilty. But the system doesn't work like that; judges don't let me out of a case 'just because' my client did it. Besides, what would it accomplish? Put some other sucker in my shoes and encourage my client to come up with a better lie?

"It's tough doing your level best for someone you ordinarily wouldn't want in the same room with you. But if I'm asked to represent someone and I agree, once I sign on, I've got to block out all the pop psychology and give my client the very best I've got to give."

How do such justifications play out in real life? How does a lawyer go about representing a criminal defendant, especially when the lawyer does not believe in the client's innocence?

First, the lawyer has a lot of help available. Techniques designed to make sure the state is "put to its proof" are taught at workshops, practiced at training sessions, polished over time, and applauded in seminars. One common technique is to point the finger at someone, anyone, other than the defendant, even a person or persons unknown (sometimes called the "some-other-dude-done-it defense"). Lawyers learn to use any way possible, within the bounds of the law and ethics, to establish reasonable doubt.

A lawyer who knows a client is guilty cannot ethically allow that client to take the witness stand to claim innocence; that would be perjury. But presenting a false defense can be done without overt lying. Truthful facts can be presented in a misleading way, as the Michigan opinion shows. And since the state must prove its case beyond a reasonable doubt, defense counsel can claim that circumstantial evidence is not sufficient proof of guilt, or argue that an eyewitness identification or scientific evidence is not positive enough to meet that very high standard.

A lawyer's willingness to pull out all the stops for a client is most often tested in two places: cross-examining a witness who the lawyer knows is truthful, and presenting an argument to the jury that the lawyer knows is false. The importance of vigorously cross-examining even a truthful witness has been supported by no less an authority than the United States Supreme Court, which in an opinion by Justice Byron White in the 1967 case of *United States v. Wade* said:

[D]efense counsel has no . . . obligation to ascertain or present the truth. Our system assigns him a different mission. He must . . . defend his client whether he is innocent or guilty. . . . If he can confuse a witness, even a truthful one, or make him appear at a disadvantage, unsure or indecisive, that will be his normal course. Our interest in not convicting the innocent permits counsel to put the State to its proof, to put the State's case in the worst possible light, regardless of what he thinks or knows to be the truth. . . . In this respect, as part of our modified adversary system and as part of the duty imposed on the most honorable defense counsel, we countenance or require conduct which in many instances has little, if any, relation to the search for truth.

Former Chief Justice Warren Burger, a conservative who was certainly no friend of criminal defendants, once described the duty of vigorous cross-examination this way: "A lawyer may never, under any circumstances, knowingly . . . participate in a fraud on the court," but the defense lawyer must use "all legitimate tools available to test the truth of the prosecution's case," even when the witness is known to be telling the truth.

In the abstract, this viewpoint may seem to be praiseworthy. But in the courtroom it can wreak havoc. Take, for example, crimes against the elderly, the people most susceptible to thefts, purse snatchings, even sexual assaults—and often also the weakest witnesses. Linda Fairstein, famed longtime chief of the Sex Crimes Bureau of the Manhattan District Attorney's office, told the *New York Times* some years ago how defense attorneys emphasize elderly witnesses' memory lapses and prey on the slightest mistake "by asking so many detailed questions that will have to result in an 'I don't know' or 'I don't remember' . . . to give the impression of faulty memory, obtuseness and senility." These witnesses are often victimized twice, first by the perpetrator and again by the defense lawyer, through rigorous cross-examination during trial.

One of the most extreme examples of "effective cross-examination" occurred during the trial that followed the infamous Triangle Shirtwaist Factory fire of 1911. The fire had killed over a hundred sweatshop workers, mostly immigrant women, trapped by the flames in a horrible work environment that afforded little chance of escape.

Famed criminal defense lawyer Max D. Steuer defended the factory owners on criminal charges, focusing his defense on the cross-examination of a young survivor of the fire who spoke little English. Because of the witness's poor command of the language, prosecutors had rehearsed her testimony over and over again, making sure she would testify to all the necessary "elements" of the crimes. Back then, cross-examination rules allowed Steuer to force the young woman to repeat her story again and again on the witness stand. When she testified in the exact same words each time, Steuer proved that her testimony had been memorized word for word. This threw the veracity of the entire prosecution case into doubt, and Steuer's clients were acquitted.

Is this, in Chief Justice Burger's words, using "all the legitimate tools available to test the truth of the prosecution's case"? Or is it simply going too far? And how much does this equation change when the lawyer knows the client is guilty?

Several years ago, for the first volume of a new journal on legal ethics, a noted criminal law professor, Harry I. Subin, analyzed a case he had encountered as the director of a law school clinic, and evaluated his conduct in ethical hindsight. The client, charged with rape, had confessed to Subin that his alibi was false and he in fact was guilty. Subin analyzed the state of his client's defense:

> [M]y problem was not that my client's story was false, but that it was not credible. . . . To win, we would therefore have to come up with a better theory than the alibi, avoiding perjury in the process. Thus, the defense would have to be made out without the client testifying. . . .
>
>   There were two possible defenses that could be fabricated. The first was mistaken identity. . . . [But] it seemed doubtful that the mistaken identification ploy would be successful. [¶] The second alternative, consent, was clearly preferable. . . . To prevail, all we would have to do would be to raise a reasonable doubt as to whether he had compelled the woman to have sex with him. The doubt would be based on the scenario that the woman and the defendant had met before, and she voluntarily returned to his apartment. . . .

The consent defense could be made out entirely through cross-examination of the complainant, coupled with argument to the jury about her lack of credibility on the issue of force. I could emphasize the parts of her story that sounded the most curious. . . . [An] allegedly stolen watch was never found, there was no sign of physical violence, and no one heard screaming or any other signs of a struggle.

Professor Subin was never required to put this defense to the test, because his client was offered a plea bargain to a reduced charge. But years later he returned to the "scene of the crime" to reevaluate his conduct: "Should the criminal lawyer be permitted to represent a client by putting forward a defense the lawyer knows is false?"

Subin then cited three methods lawyers use in order to win a case—even if they are "completely at odds with the facts." First, a truthful prosecution witness can be cross-examined to undermine credibility. Second, the defense may present testimony, not false in itself, that is used to discredit truthful evidence or create a false defense. Third, the lawyer may argue all of this to the jury. "To the extent that these techniques of legal truth-subversion have been addressed at all, most authorities have approved them," wrote Subin. "[But i]f there is any redeeming social value in permitting an attorney to do such things, I frankly cannot discern it."

Subin then proposed a new rule of ethics for lawyers in such situations: "It shall be improper for an attorney who knows beyond a reasonable doubt the truth of a fact established in the state's case to attempt to refute that fact through . . . evidence . . . or argument."

In Subin's own case, since his client had confessed, he would have limited his own role as defense lawyer to being a "monitor." He could test the constitutionality of the state's evidence, such as the police's failure to get a search warrant, and test whether the state had proved its case beyond a reasonable doubt. But, he concluded, "I would not cross-examine [the victim], because I would have no good faith basis for impeaching either her testimony or her character, since I 'knew' that she was providing an accurate account of what had occurred."

To date, no jurisdiction in this country has adopted an ethics rule like Professor Subin's. Most legal scholars maintain that such a rule would directly undermine the Fifth and Sixth Amendment principles of due process and effective assistance of counsel, and some consider Subin's theory to be on the fringe of mainstream legal thought. But Subin insists that he simply cannot defend "the utterly arbitrary line we have drawn between deliberately offering perjured testimony and deliberately attempting to create false 'proof' by offering truthful but misleading evidence."

Professor Monroe Freedman is one of the country's best known and most widely read experts on legal ethics. Freedman, like Subin, wonders how the rules of ethics can prohibit perjured testimony on the one hand, while on the other permitting—even requiring—cross-examination of a truthful witness. Indeed, he finds the cross-examination to be worse than the perjury: "In both cases, the lawyer participates in an attempt to free a guilty defendant. In both cases, the lawyer participates in misleading the finder of fact. In the case of the perjured witness, however, the attorney asks only non-leading questions, while in the case of impeachment, the lawyer takes an active, aggressive role, using his professional training and skills, in a one-on-one attack upon the client's victim. The lawyer thereby personally and directly adds to the suffering of the [victim]. In short, under the euphemism of 'testing the truth of the prosecution's case,' the lawyer communicates, to the jury and to the community, the most vicious of lies."

Freedman is offended by those who label cross-examination "good" without considering the consequences. Unlike Subin, however, Freedman, an apostle of the adversary theorem, reluctantly comes to the opposite conclusion: The lawyer must cross-examine this innocent victim to the fullest extent. The alternative is lawyers who either lie to their clients "by impressing upon them a bond of trust that the lawyers do not intend to maintain" or who are "selectively ignorant" of their clients' stories—by saying, in effect, "Don't tell me too much, because if you confess, I won't help you." Given the defense lawyer's sworn obligation under our Constitution, neither of these courses is acceptable to Freedman.

Subin's proposal is as lofty an ideal as the Supreme Court's pronouncements on due process of law. But it is not a realistic solution when applied in actual practice. It's very difficult to defend real clients in real cases with half measures and halfhearted support, particularly when the lawyer's job includes protecting the client's constitutional rights. Besides, evidence rarely falls into neatly wrapped packages labeled "true" and "false." Attorney and law professor John B. Mitchell, writing in the same Georgetown Law School ethics journal that had published Subin's article, tested the practical difficulty of Subin's proposal by trying to present a closing argument that both provided a defense to the accused and avoided resting on falsehoods.

Mitchell hypothesized that he was defending a young woman accused of shoplifting a Christmas tree star. The store manager stopped the defendant when she walked straight through the store and out the door with the star in her hand. When stopped, the woman burst into tears. Just as the manager was about to take her to the store's security office, a small fire broke out in the camera section, and he rushed off to help put it out. When he returned five minutes later, the woman was still sitting where he had left her. Back in the security room, the manager asked her to empty her pockets. He found that the woman had nothing else belonging to the store, but she did have a $10 bill. The star cost $1.79.

Mitchell's fictitious client admitted her guilt to him: "[The star] was so pretty. . . . I would have bought it, but I also wanted to make a special Christmas dinner for Mama and didn't have enough money to do both. . . . But that star . . . I could just see the look in Mama's eyes if she saw that lovely thing on our tree."

Mitchell described how he would defend the case: "I will not assert that facts known by me to be true are false or those known to be false are true. As a defense attorney, I do not have to prove what in fact happened. . . . Thus, in this case I will not claim that my client walked out of the store with innocent intent (a fact which I know is false)." Rather, Mitchell says, he would argue it this way:

> The prosecution claims my client stole an ornament for a Christmas tree. . . . Now, maybe she did. None of us were there. On the other hand, she had $10.00 in her pocket, which was plenty of money with which to pay for the ornament. . . . Also, she didn't try to conceal what she was doing. She walked right out of the store holding it in her hand. Most of us have come close to

innocently doing the same thing. So, maybe she didn't. But then she cried the minute she was stopped. She might have been feeling guilty. So, maybe she did. On the other hand . . . she didn't run away when she was left alone. . . . So, maybe she didn't. The point is that, looking at all the evidence, you're left with 'maybe she intended to steal, maybe she didn't.' But, you knew that before the first witness was even sworn. The prosecution has the burden, and he simply can't carry any burden let alone 'beyond a reasonable doubt' with a maybe she did, maybe she didn't case.

Mitchell defended his argument by noting that he merely made inferences from the evidence that "raise a doubt by persuading the jury to appreciate 'possibilities' other than my client's guilt." He acknowledged that Subin would find this a "false defense," since the lawyer knows all along that the possibilities raised in the argument are not true.

But how realistic is even Mitchell's closing argument? Most criminal defense lawyers feel it doesn't go nearly far enough. They see Subin's "monitoring" and Mitchell's "maybe she did, maybe she didn't" argument as little more than holding up a big sign saying GUILTY with an arrow pointing to the defendant. Subin and Mitchell see the lawyer's role as testing "reasonable doubt." But most criminal defense lawyers believe that the only way to test reasonable doubt is to swing with their best punch, not merely testing the prosecution's case, but attacking it directly as hard as they possibly can. Here's how our composite defense lawyer might argue the Christmas star case:

"Members of the jury, let's look carefully at the evidence the prosecution has presented against Martha. First, she walks out of the store holding the star in her hand. Not in her pocket, not in her purse, not in a bag. In her *hand*. She didn't conceal the star, didn't try to hide it. In fact, that's why she was caught—because she walked right out of the store with the star in plain view, where everyone could see it. That's not how you steal something. That's what happens if you forget you have it. How many of you have ever absentmindedly picked up something and started to leave without paying? Isn't that what this is about?

"Second, when the manager left her alone for five full minutes to deal with the fire, what did Martha do? If she had left, no one would have been the wiser. The manager didn't even have her name. But leaving is what a guilty person would do. Martha sat there and waited for the manager to come back. That's the behavior of someone who had nothing to hide, who knew she had not done anything wrong." The argument would then go on to discuss the money in the defendant's pocket and her crying in similar terms.

To many, this argument may seem tantamount to lying. The judge always tells the jury that argument is just argument, not evidence. But should an argument ever be allowed that overtly attempts to mislead the jury about the truth? Before answering this question, we return to the case of Kirk Hopman.

Epilogue:
The Trial of Kirk Hopman

Richie Richewski came out with both guns blazing in the case of *State v. Kirk Hopman*. His cross-examination of Rowena included the following key portion:

MR. RICHEWSKI: Is this the written agreement to plead guilty that you signed, Ms. Soo?

THE WITNESS: Yes, sir.

MR. RICHEWSKI: Do you see on this form where it has the charges you pled guilty to?

THE WITNESS: Yes, sir.

MR. RICHEWSKI: And that includes that you, quote, "personally committed great bodily injury"?

THE WITNESS: No, I didn't do that, sir.

MR. RICHEWSKI: No, my question is whether you see that on the guilty plea form. Right there [pointing]. Do you see it?

THE WITNESS: Yes, sir.

MR. RICHEWSKI: And you signed that plea form? Right there on the bottom, is that your signature?

THE WITNESS: Yes, sir, that's my signature.

MR. RICHEWSKI: Well, isn't it true, then, that you battered your own child?

THE WITNESS [crying]: No, no, I never did that.

MR. RICHEWSKI: But didn't you admit doing that in this document?

THE WITNESS: I had to. I had to. I had to say it or they wouldn't let me plead guilty.

MR. RICHEWSKI: So you said it so you could plead guilty?

THE WITNESS: Yes, sir.

MR. RICHEWSKI: So you could get probation instead of go to prison, right?

THE WITNESS: Well, I just wanted it to be over.

MR. RICHEWSKI: But Ms. Tang [the DA] did promise you probation if you pled guilty and testified, didn't she?

THE WITNESS: Yes, sir.

MR. RICHEWSKI: Now, Ms. Soo, are you saying that when you signed this plea form, you lied when you said you hit your own child?

THE WITNESS: No, I wasn't lying. They told me I had to sign it.

MR. RICHEWSKI: I'm not asking what "they" told you, Ms. Soo, I'm asking what you admitted in this document. Isn't it true that you admitted right here [pointing], in this sentence, that you personally battered your own child?

THE WITNESS [crying]: Yes.

MR. RICHEWSKI: Except now you say that what it says on this form isn't really true?

THE WITNESS: That's right.

MR. RICHEWSKI: So now you expect the jury to believe you, that you didn't really hit your child, even though eight days ago you swore that you did before a judge right here in this court?

DA TANG: Objection, Your Honor, argumentative question.

THE COURT: Sustained.

In his closing argument, Richie asked: "Members of the jury, do you really believe that a mother would ever admit to hurting her own poor child if she did not truly do it? Do any of you know a mother who would lie in this horrible way? There's simply no proof that Kirk Hopman did this terrible thing, except the testimony of Rowena Soo, a sworn liar who has already admitted that she lied to the court to save her own skin."

Kirk Hopman was convicted only of the lesser crime of reckless endangerment and sentenced to one year in the county jail. After the case, Richie Richewski justified the way he defended Kirk: "Look, I'm charged with the responsibility of representing my clients zealously. To me, within the bounds of the law, there is no such thing as degrees of zeal. Zeal means doing your best, period. I can't be less zealous for Kirk than I am for someone I like better. Or for someone whose crime is not so serious. Or even someone who hasn't admitted guilt like Kirk did. Because the law is the same in each case: A criminal defendant goes free unless and until the state proves guilt beyond a reasonable doubt.

"The bottom line is that my job is to put the state to the test—a true test. The DAs always pull out all the stops in their arguments. If I do a half-assed job, they're not really being put to their proof. In most cases, I'm the reason law enforcement can say that they did their job and did it right. Because they convicted my client despite my best efforts. Not 'going through the motions,' my best efforts."

Richie Richewski is right. Sanitized cross-examinations and reasonable doubt arguments *don't* work; they point the arrow of guilt directly at the defendant. The criminal justice system requires Richie and his colleagues to serve as "mouthpieces" for their clients, even where a client's guilt is clear. So the more important question is not how Richie justifies representing a guilty client, but whether the system itself—based on a Constitution written over two hundred years ago by Founding Fathers who in their wildest dreams could not have envisioned today's America—still works for the twenty-first century.

There's a natural temptation to measure this system by a few individual cases that make headlines—the Simpson trial, the Dan White "Twinkie defense," or those rare occasions when innocent people have been wrongly sent to prison. But a far more accurate measurement is how the system functions as a whole. One look at our ever-expanding prison population shows that people who commit crimes get caught, prosecuted, and convicted. The state has little difficulty meeting its burden of proof in the overwhelming majority of cases. The "adversary theorem" simply does not result in large numbers of guilty defendants getting off through trickery or technicalities.

What about the "moral costs" of Richie Richewski's actions? Richie would claim that these costs are outweighed by the moral benefits: first, to the client he has sworn to protect, by being that client's only defender against a hostile world, and second, to our society, whose greater interests are served when that client is protected, lest we descend the slippery slope of either autocracy or mob rule.

By representing the poor and disadvantaged, the Richie Rich-ewskis of the world compare themselves to Atticus Finch, the hero of Harper Lee's 1960 novel *To Kill a Mockingbird*, who does his best to ensure justice for his falsely accused client when everyone else is against him. There are at least some similarities. Atticus Finch took on his case only partly because he believed in his client's innocence. He also acted because the accused, poor and black, a pariah in the southern town Atticus called home, would otherwise have had no champion, no one to speak for him. What made Atticus a hero was not just that his client was innocent, but that Atticus was willing to stand up to the system, a lone voice testing that system to its fullest.

But what about those who are not disadvantaged—wealthy mobsters or members of a Colombian drug cartel? Many criminal defense lawyers set limits on whom they will represent. For some, it's the accused rapist; for others, the alleged antiabortion terrorist or renegade cop. For many defense lawyers, it's the reputed mob-ster or drug kingpin. But these lawyers all point out that their choice is made when they accept the case, because once they sign on, they must do their best whether or not "accused," "alleged," or "reputed" turns out to mean "guilty."

There's been much public outcry recently about lawyers like Richie. But when members of the public change hats and become clients, they will want, even insist on, a Richie Richewski. They will not want lawyers who will judge them, or base a defense on per-sonal likes or dislikes. They will not want counsel who conclude that since they are guilty the lawyer need only go through the mo-tions. They will want lawyers who give their best in every case to put the state to its proof. And, under our Constitution and our sys-tem of justice, they'd be entitled to nothing less.

PART TWO

POWER AND ITS ABUSE, OR "WE'RE ONLY DOING OUR JOB"

It's easy enough to trace the lineage of the "adversary theorem" in criminal cases. The inquisitorial Star Chamber of sixteenth- and seventeenth-century England intimidated those it accused and severely restricted their rights. Defense lawyers faced imprisonment themselves if they filed motions that the crown decided were frivolous; this was hardly conducive to zealous advocacy. While the Glorious Revolution of 1688 brought the Star Chamber to an end, in the colonies an increasingly unpopular government often tried to deny rights to those accused of acts against the crown. It's not surprising that the new American Constitution offered substantial protections for anyone charged with a crime.

The Bill of Rights, "a social compact . . . to secure the liberty of the people," according to its chief architect, James Madison, embodied these protections. The Constitution had already been ratified; the Bill of Rights became the first ten amendments to the Constitution. It included the Fifth and Sixth Amendment protections with which we've become so familiar: the right not to testify against oneself; the rights to a jury trial, to call witnesses, and to confront one's accusers; the prohibition against double jeopardy; and the right to "due process of law."

Among the most important of these rights is that an accused is entitled to "the Assistance of Counsel for his defence." In the 1932 case of Powell v. Alabama, the Supreme Court defined this right as "effective and substantial" assistance. Under our Constitution, providing effective and substantial assistance is difficult if not impossible unless counsel accepts the adversary theorem and advocates zealously on behalf of the accused. But the concept of zealous advocacy has come to be applied with equal force in civil cases as well. How this came about is something of a mystery, but there is no question that it has occurred: Civil litigators refer to their duty of zealous advocacy as often as their counterparts in criminal law.

James Madison specifically warned about the abuse of power when he presented the Bill of Rights to the First Congress in 1789. He argued that citizens of this new nation needed more protection than in England, where declarations of rights were limited to "rais[ing] a barrier against the power of the Crown." But for the new country, Madison worried less about governmental power than the danger to individual rights from powerful forces within the citizenry—what he termed "the power of the community." To Madison, the Bill of Rights was particularly important because "prescriptions in favor of liberty ought to be levelled against that quarter where the greatest danger lies, namely, that which possesses the highest prerogative of power."

In the world of civil litigation, the "highest prerogative of power" is held by multicity, often international conglomerates that speak for other multicity, international conglomerates. These institutions are modern American law firms, capable of waging litigation wars from outposts across the country and around the world.

CHAPTER 3

Power, Arrogance, and the Survival of the Fittest

Under our discovery system the role of counsel is not to make sure the truth is ascertained but to advance his client's cause by any ethical means. . . . [C]ausing delay and sowing confusion not only are his right but may be his duty. —Chief Justice William Rehnquist of the
United States Supreme Court, in *Walters v.*
National Association of Radiation Survivors, 1985

Discovery is not just a game where all that counts is the ultimate score no matter how unethically the players behaved.
—United States District Court Judge Gladys Kessler,
in *Richardson v. Union Oil of California,* 1996

Esperanza Dejos is thrilled. She has just heard that Butler, Ayers, Reece & Singh, the city's top plaintiffs' employment firm, will take her case. It has been a miserable last five years at Hillsman Oil. Now for the first time she has some hope. She knows her boss harassed her, and she's sure it cost her at least one and probably two promotions. But she is savvy enough to know that taking on a big company like Hillsman on harassment and discrimination charges will not be easy. Any lingering doubts are quickly dispelled when she meets with her new lawyer, Willa Reece. Reece pulls no punches about what to expect: defense lawyers prying into her personal life, fights over every scrap of information her lawyers try to get, and no hope of settlement until the eleventh hour. But despite the grim picture Reece paints, the reality will turn out to be far worse.

Across town, Clancy Garrett, senior partner in the litigation department of 225-lawyer Hardgrave, Dimon & Woodford, prepares for his lunch meeting with Gregory Ngim, a new senior associate the firm just hired. Garrett has taken on the Dejos case. He knows that if Dejos hangs tough, she will almost certainly win. He knows Dejos's boss has a history of "problems with women," since Garrett twice extricated him from lawsuits making similar claims. But he is not about to fold up his tent this early in the advocacy game. The best thing he can do right now for Hillsman Oil is to get Greg on board by giving the new associate what his partners fondly call "The Lecture."

At lunch, Garrett describes how a "real litigator" defends a case. "Greg," he advises, "around here, we simply *do not* give away information. If you can argue with a straight face that you don't understand exactly what the other side means when they ask for something, then object: 'It's ambiguous, it's vague, it's too broad, it's too narrow.' I don't care how you do it, just get it done. If they can't follow through, too bad. And don't worry too much about being sanctioned by the court. Our client will foot the bill for any fine, and most judges won't make it more than a thousand dollars, anyway."

Garrett then explains to Gregory how to go on the offensive. "Remember, the best defense is a good offense. We've got to discourage these employment claims. So we do what I call the 'nuts-and-sluts defense.' Look into the plaintiff's sex life. Find out if there's any potential to argue that she 'asked for it.' If she's not that type, see if she's ever been to a psychologist. We'll use that to show she's not playing with a full deck. That means you've got to get every conceivable piece of information about Dejos, and go to the mat to get it if you need to. Get personal stuff, the kind of stuff that will make her want to forget the whole case. And make sure you get her medical records."

When Gregory asks how often the cases settle, Garrett explains that they settle quite often, but that the firm will "hold out on settlement until we're on the courthouse steps." He takes the opportunity to explain his litigation philosophy: "Our job is to protect our clients, not to dole out money to lightweights who can't stick it out. Litigation is a war of attrition. Our firm has the resources, and our client can back us up. If we fight every case to the nth degree, give no quarter and offer nothing, our opponents will fold nine times out of ten. The tenth time they may roll the dice and go to trial, but even then their chances are not much better than even. And there's always an appeal."

As the lunch check arrives, Garrett reminds Gregory that Greg will be doing most of the discovery work in this case—answering requests for documents, even deposing Dejos. "Do me proud," says Garrett. "Let's see what kind of trial lawyer you can be." Gregory, who left his old firm to get real litigation experience, is excited that he's finally going to get his chance.

●

The most common battleground for zealous advocacy in civil cases is discovery, the pretrial process of gathering information and documents about the other side's case—and the place where most lawyers say cases are usually won or lost. Since the vast majority of cases settle, the nature and extent of the information turned over by one side to the other is crucial to the outcome. Even more important, the battle over discovery can become a war of attrition, waged by the strong to wear down weaker opponents, instead of focusing on the actual exchange of information. When this occurs, it is usually (though not always) the more powerful forces—big law firms, with deep pockets, and their clients, with deeper ones—who wage the discovery war in the name of zealous representation.

Most of the time these battles are invisible to the public, waged in papers that fly back and forth between counsel, in law office conference rooms where sworn depositions are taken, and in empty courtrooms before judges who rule on discovery disputes when the lawyers can't agree. While stories of these battles are often reported in the legal trade press, only infrequently do they surface in the mainstream dailies.

Some of the most common fights over discovery concern interrogatories, or written questions from one side to the other about the case, the parties, and the evidence; motions and requests for documents, or demands for documents held by the other side; and depositions, where witnesses must answer questions under oath about the case. Generally, the rule is that the parties are entitled to information "reasonably calculated to lead to the discovery of admissible evidence" in the case. Often, though, this rule is trumped by tactics that call for delay, denial, obfuscation, refusal to provide and even destruction of documents, and personal attacks on opponents.

To be sure, many lawyers look at discovery wars with disdain and consider them unprofessional. "Your case is your case," taught one well-known West Coast litigator, a mentor to younger lawyers. "You can't change the facts, and you can't change the rules. So if the other side asks, you've got to tell." Many other attorneys, though, believe that the adversary theorem gives them license to put the rules to the toughest possible test; they give no quarter unless absolutely necessary, and point out that this is exactly what their clients want.

Washington, D.C., litigator Mark Dombroff wrote an article in 1989 for the legal trade paper the *National Law Journal* called "Winning Is Everything!" which epitomized this view. Dombroff criticized those who condemn hardball litigation tactics: "It may give you a warm feeling inside to know you're right and that your opponent isn't, but it doesn't win cases." While he reminded lawyers that no one likes an "obnoxious winner," he concluded that "winning for our clients is the only thing that matters so long as we do it within the ground rules." Invoking famed football coach Vince Lombardi, Dombroff closed his article with this slogan: "Let's hear it for winning. It's everything. It's the only thing!"

Dombroff practices what he preaches. In 1994 an ill-fated USAir flight crashed in a thunderstorm near Charlotte, North Carolina, killing thirty-seven of fifty-two passengers, many of them soldiers on leave and their spouses, enticed by the low Fourth of July holiday fares. Three years passed before the lawsuits arising out of the crash saw the inside of a courtroom, thanks to Dombroff, who staved off the inevitable by fighting the discovery of documents all the way to the United States Supreme Court, where he lost. But he bought valuable time for USAir by delaying the case.

Joseph F. Anderson, the federal judge in charge of the USAir cases, was not amused. He rebuked and fined Dombroff, and in early 1997 he called for an FBI inquiry into possible witness tampering. "I am not going to sit back and let someone intimidate a witness in my courtroom," Anderson said after learning of an organized personal attack via e-mail on the character of the plaintiffs' expert witness, a Northwest Airlines pilot. USAir, said the *National Law Journal*, "is showing that it will use every tactic in the book to dodge a liability finding."

Delay coupled with obfuscation can arouse the anger of many a judge, at least on those few occasions when the lawyers get caught. In the late 1980s and early 1990s Suzuki Motors faced hundreds of claims that the design of their Samurai sport utility vehicle was defective, making it prone to roll over. Lawyers defending a Samurai rollover case in Savannah, Georgia, were asked in a written interrogatory whether General Motors had turned down an offer to market the Samurai in the United States because GM had safety concerns. Suzuki's lawyer, Atlanta's Joe Freeman Jr., claimed Suzuki was "unaware of any decision by General Motors not to market the Samurai."

Plaintiffs' attorneys proved this false by subpoenaing GM's own records, which included correspondence between GM and Suzuki showing that GM backed away from marketing the Samurai specifically because of safety problems. Federal judge B. Avent Edenfield also found that a lawyer at Crosby, Heafey, Roach & May, the California firm coordinating all Samurai rollover cases across the country and co-counsel in the Savannah case, already knew about the GM letters.

The managing partner of Crosby, Heafey told two legal affairs reporters that the case was nothing more than "a real discovery battle, typical of the adversarial process." Meanwhile, in the Savannah courtroom, Suzuki's lawyers argued that GM and Suzuki had been discussing a slightly different model than the one in their case. The judge didn't buy it: "Regardless of how tricky the defendants have been in avoiding an overt lie, their actions have had the same result as an outright lie." The judge described the lawyers' actions as a "cover-up" and "part of their overall campaign to obfuscate the truth." He ordered fines for both Freeman and two Crosby, Heafey lawyers, and also ordered that Suzuki and its counsel pay for the plaintiffs' costs of conducting discovery, which they put at almost $200,000.

When obfuscating the truth combines with altering or destroying documents, there is no credible argument to justify such actions. A wrongful death complaint in federal court in Washington, D.C., accused Union Oil of California (Unocal) with being responsible for toxic levels of benzene in a cleaning solvent. In 1995 Unocal responded to written interrogatories by saying that their product contained no more than 11 parts per million of benzene, when in fact their own test results at their Beaumont, Texas, refinery showed almost two hundred times that level—2,100 parts per million. Unocal's lawyers had simply not included the Beaumont test results in the documents they gave the plaintiffs. The lawyers blamed a paralegal for altering the documents and said it was an isolated mistake, but Judge Gladys Kessler excoriated them:

> [T]his Court does not believe for one moment that a legal assistant with seven years experience, who has worked on at least 20 benzene cases, would take it upon herself to alter documents, withhold information, and give false responses in verified court documents unless she had reason to believe that she was acting with either tacit or overt approval from her superiors.

Noting that the paralegal had been neither demoted nor formally reprimanded, and had actually received a raise, Judge Kessler concluded that "[d]iscovery is not just a game where all that counts is the ultimate score no matter how unethically the players behaved."

Chemical giant Du Pont ran into trouble in at least three states, Florida, Hawaii, and Georgia, over charges that its fungicide Benlate was tainted with herbicide, and that the company and its lawyers concealed test results that would have helped prove this. A Florida judge wrote in 1996 that Du Pont had intentionally mislabeled documents, delayed producing them, and even destroyed them, and called the company's conduct "atrocious." Later that same year, a Hawaii judge criticized Du Pont's legal staff and its Washington, D.C., law firm, Crowell & Moring, for abusive litigation tactics and misconduct, and fined the company $1.5 million for withholding test data.

In Atlanta, Judge J. Robert Elliott went a step further. In 1993 Elliott presided over a trial between Du Pont and a group of growers who claimed that their crops were damaged by herbicide after they used Benlate. After six weeks of trial and on the eve of verdict, the growers, afraid they were about to lose, settled their case. But the growers charged that Du Pont and its Atlanta-based lawyers, Alston & Bird, had withheld evidence of soil tests on the growers' own lands that showed the presence of herbicide. Had they been given these test results—documents they were entitled to in discovery— they never would have settled, the growers said.

After a weeklong hearing Judge Elliott found that Du Pont and its lawyers had colluded to misrepresent test results to the growers. Calling it the worst case of discovery abuse he had ever seen, Elliott hit Du Pont and the law firm jointly with a $114 million penalty, saying he would forgive $100 million if Du Pont published full-page ads in major newspapers admitting wrongdoing. Du Pont declined the judge's offer and appealed. The federal appeals court reversed the sanctions order but offered little comfort to Du Pont or its lawyers; it based its reversal on the fact that more due process rights were required because "Du Pont and its counsel may very well have engaged in criminal acts." So serious were the charges that Judge Joel F. Dubina wrote that he assumed "the appropriate U.S. Attorney" would be considering a criminal investigation of both Du Pont and Alston & Bird.

Why do lawyers think that they can hide documents, lie about it, and get away with it? The reason, in part, is the adversary theorem, run amok to the point where some lawyers believe that anything they do on behalf of the client is justified if it is not clearly illegal and if their chances of being caught are low enough to be worth the risk. But a large part of this attitude is due to changes in American law practice in the last twenty years. America's largest law firms have increased enormously in both size and strength. The bigger and stronger law firms grow, the more insular and arrogant they become. Discovery abuses are buried deep inside the walls of the firm, with little accountability and even less public scrutiny. Perhaps more important, the more law firms become business conglomerates, the more they distance themselves from the basic precepts of professional ethics that are supposed to govern their conduct.

It is impossible to quantify the extent to which the abuses described in this and other chapters are attributable to what we call the "con-glomeratization" of the American law firm. But there is a definite relationship. *The National Law Journal,* one of the country's two major legal trade publications, began publishing detailed statistics on the nation's largest law firms in the late 1970s. By the mid-1980s the *American Lawyer,* the other major trade journal, had begun listing so-called white-shoe firms by average profit per part-ner. Firms once happy turning reasonable profits began competing to be bigger, more profitable, and more national and even interna-tional in scope. Others that had traditionally worked on corporate transactions added litigation departments to become full-service shops. When the recession of the late 1980s hit, many firms, now bloated by overexpansion, found themselves desperate to keep their clients. Large clients who insisted on winning at all costs were able to put even more pressure on law firms to go to any lengths to keep their business.

By the mid-1990s the race to be bigger, better, and more power-ful was back. Firms again expanded their areas of practice to cover every conceivable client need. Law firm mergers became far more common. Not long ago, a beginning lawyer could expect to stay with one firm for an entire career. Not any longer. Mergers and "lat-eral transfers"—associates and partners who move from one firm to another, and specialty departments that move en masse from one law firm to the highest-bidding competitor—have undermined the concept of firm loyalty. Paralleling this has been a marked change in the loyalty of large clients. The result is that the manic competi-tion for clients grows side by side with increasing law firm expan-sion.

In the early 1960s only a few dozen law firms had more than fifty lawyers; thirty years later, firms of that size numbered over five hundred. In 1978 only one American law firm had over three hun-dred lawyers, and fifteen had over two hundred. By 1996, 161 firms had at least two hundred lawyers. In the late seventies most of the hundred largest firms had a single office in a single large city, with an occasional outpost elsewhere in the same state. In 1997 the largest firm, Baker & McKenzie, had nine domestic offices and forty-seven in foreign countries from Saudi Arabia and Vietnam to

Kazakhstan. Thirty other firms had over five hundred lawyers and averaged a dozen offices worldwide.

Not surprisingly, the law firms mentioned in this chapter are almost all on the *National Law Journal*'s list of America's two hundred largest: Alston & Bird with 389 lawyers, Crowell & Moring with 238, and Crosby, Heafey, Roach & May with a relatively cozy 195. When Du Pont and Alston & Bird chose counsel to appeal the Georgia sanctions order, they chose 505-lawyer Kirkland & Ellis.

As the size and scope of the nation's largest law firms increased, so did their concentration of power, leading to what many see as the death of the law as a profession. The efforts of many law firms to use discovery not as a means to an end but as a profit center underscores this feeling. Many stories like this one circulate in trade journals or on the Internet: A senior corporate counsel interested in moving back to private practice suggested to the senior partner of a large law firm that he would bring with him case-settling skills that could help avoid years of unnecessary discovery. But the partner explained clearly and bluntly what a terrible idea this was, because it would interfere with the firm's principal moneymaker—discovery battles.

Discovery isn't the only area where the big business of law firms makes itself felt. Under long-standing ethics rules, each client hiring a lawyer retains that lawyer's entire firm. As firms became larger and spread out around the globe, the chances of them representing clients whose legal interests conflict increased dramatically. But the ethics rules of every jurisdiction make it clear that firms can't represent conflicting clients without all clients' consent. These rules often do little to deter law firms from signing on big clients, however. Rather, they pressure clients for consent and lobby bar associations for exceptions to the usual conflict of interest rules for corporate deal making, real estate transactions, estate planning, entertainment law—whatever area the firm practices in. The rules, they argue, should apply everywhere else, just not to them.

In the mid-1980s the American Bar Association, the nation's largest organization of lawyers, began studying whether the law could still survive as a profession rather than a business. The ABA issued several reports, including one in 1996 from its Professionalism

Committee, articulating several "prevalent themes" as reasons for the decline of professionalism. Among the themes: the "perceived excesses of the adversarial process"; the change of law to a business, making lawyers feel their practices are "incompatible with personal values and goals"; and the "change in the traditional concept of lawyers serving the public good."

Lawrence J. Fox is the former managing partner of one of those big firm conglomerates, Philadelphia's 223-lawyer Drinker, Biddle & Reath, and the 1996–97 chair of the ABA's Ethics Committee. Fox, long an outspoken opponent of the increase in cutthroat tactics and the accompanying loss of professionalism, has put it this way: The typical law firm has changed "from a collegial collection of dedicated professionals . . . to a business enterprise that, frankly, has lost its soul."

The soul of a law firm is in jeopardy when it wages campaigns of semantic subterfuge and wars of attrition. The soul of the legal system is in trouble when a firm's seemingly unconscionable conduct is supported by the leading lights of the bar, and the firm itself seems unaffected even when punished by its state's highest court.

Bogle & Gates, one of the Pacific Northwest's largest law firms, is a place known for its hardball litigation tactics. With over two hundred lawyers, it too is on the list of the nation's largest firms. In 1986 it began representing the drug company Fisons in a case filed by the parents of a three-year-old girl named Jennifer, who was permanently brain-damaged from a dose of theophylline, the active ingredient in Fisons's Somophyllin Oral Liquid. The parents also sued the girl's pediatrician for prescribing the drug. Theophylline can be toxic when given to children who are suffering from a viral infection, as Jennifer was. Though Fisons knew of this problem, the pediatrician did not, because the company had never warned him. The doctor filed a counterclaim against Fisons, saying he never would have prescribed the drug had he been told.

During the discovery process Jennifer's lawyers requested "all documents pertaining to any warning letters including 'Dear Doctor' letters or warning correspondence to the medical profession regarding the use of the drug Somophyllin Oral Liquid." The pediatrician's lawyers asked Fisons for "any letters sent by your company to physicians concerning theophylline toxicity in children." The law firm knew of at least two documents fitting these descriptions: a 1981 letter addressed "Dear Doctor" on the subject of "Theophylline and Viral Infections" that was sent to two thousand physicians, but not Jennifer's doctor, and a 1985 memo warning of an "'epidemic' of theophylline toxicity." But Bogle & Gates advised Fisons not to produce either document.

Eventually, with no proof that Fisons had misled him, the doctor settled with Jennifer's parents. They fought on against Fisons for four years. Then in March 1990 the pediatrician's lawyer received in the mail an extraordinary document from an anonymous source—a copy of the 1981 "Dear Doctor" letter. A month later, with this document now the cornerstone of Jennifer's case, Fisons settled with Jennifer's parents for $6.9 million. The pediatrician, having kept his cross-complaint against Fisons alive, and furious about the deceit, went on the offensive against both the drug company and its lawyers for damaging his reputation and withholding vital documents.

Incredibly, rather than conceding it had made an error of judgment, Bogle & Gates's lawyers arrogantly defended its decision. They argued that Bogle had truthfully answered the doctor's request for documents because the lawyers had limited their response to information about Fisons's *brand name*, Somophyllin Oral Liquid, even though the request referred to theophylline itself. As for the "Dear Doctor" letter, Bogle argued that it had interpreted this request as being limited to the "term of art referring to a warning letter mailed at the FDA's request to all physicians" and not merely to *any* letter addressed "Dear Doctor." The patent absurdity of this position—what investigative reporter Stuart Taylor later called a "surreptitious, self-serving semantic gambit"—would be laughable had it not been taken so seriously by so many.

At trial the pediatrician won a million-dollar verdict against Fisons, and the judge tacked on an award of $450,000 to cover his attorneys' fees. But the judge refused to order Bogle & Gates to pay for discovery abuse, finding that Bogle's conduct was "consistent with the customary and accepted litigation practices in the bar of this community and this state." Perhaps he was swayed when Bogle produced the sworn declarations of fourteen experts, including perhaps the country's most eminent ethics expert, Geoffrey Hazard, two past presidents of the Washington state bar, and leading lights of the trial bar, all of whom said Bogle had acted appropriately.

Typical of the experts' declarations was this from a legal ethics professor at the University of Puget Sound: " 'Practitioners' see discovery as a part of, not an exception to, the adversary system. . . . Tendentious, narrow, and literal positions with regard to discovery are, in my opinion, both typical and expected." "All experienced lawyers do some ducking and dodging," argued Bogle's outside counsel. Three of Bogle's fourteen experts even argued that the principle of zealous advocacy *required* that the law firm not provide the documents.

On appeal, the Washington Supreme Court unanimously reversed the trial court on the discovery issue. "It appears clear," wrote Chief Justice James Anderson, "that no conceivable discovery request could have been made by the doctor that would have uncovered the relevant documents." The higher court then sent a loud message, ordering the case sent back to the trial court with instructions to punish Bogle in an amount "severe enough to deter these attorneys and others" from engaging in such conduct again.

That a state's highest court had gone this far to punish a law firm in discovery "scare[d] the heck out of a lot of people," said Washington law professor Robert Aronson, one of the two experts to side with the physician. Bogle agreed to pay $325,000, made a public admission of its mistake, and said it had "taken steps to ensure that all attorneys at Bogle & Gates understand that the rules . . . must be complied with in letter and spirit." Some lawyers may have been scared, but apparently not those at Bogle & Gates. Despite Bogle's claim that it sent a copy of the Fisons decision to every litigator in the firm, and despite mandatory training for all its trial lawyers, less than two years after the Fisons opinion litigators from Bogle & Gates were in trouble again.

This time Bogle & Gates represented Subaru of America on charges that the driver's seatbacks in Subaru's Justy could collapse backward when hit from the rear, potentially causing grave injury. In the view of federal Judge Robert Bryan, Bogle obfuscated, stonewalled, and "gave answers that were just plain wrong." In one request, the plaintiffs had asked for National Highway Traffic Safety

Administration records that showed the collapse of driver's seatbacks from a rear-impact "force" of 30 miles per hour. Bogle's response was that the request was "vague, confusing and unintelligible. . . . Specifically, 30 miles per hour is a velocity, not a force, and due to this confusion of technical terms, no meaningful response can be given." Judge Bryan called this "lawyer hokum," and forced Bogle to pay the other side's attorneys' fees.

Why the repeat performance? Because even with an anonymous informant providing the smoking-gun memo in the Fisons case, Bogle & Gates almost got away with it. It's impossible to gauge how many other times it conducted discovery this way *without* getting caught. Even in the Fisons case, while Bogle's reputation may have been sullied, its pocketbook was left largely untouched; $325,000 was undoubtedly a small fraction of the fees it had charged. Besides, all the memos and training programs sent around the firm can't outweigh the fact that the two lawyers primarily responsible for the Fisons discovery remained with the firm in good standing. The younger one was even promoted to partner.

Ethics rules say lawyers may not "unlawfully obstruct another party's access to evidence or unlawfully alter, destroy or conceal [anything] having potential evidentiary value." Many local, state, and federal court rules have the same requirement. But no rule couched in general language can address every type of discovery abuse, and rules without teeth—and penalties that don't go well beyond mere money—are unlikely to deter lawyers who know that the chances of being caught are slight.

Lawyers will continue to argue that obligations to their clients require them to give discovery rules the most narrow interpretation possible and that throwing roadblocks in opposing counsel's path is merely part of being a zealous advocate. But zealous advocacy is no longer emphasized in most ethics codes. One of the nine principal canons in the American Bar Association's Model Code, first passed in 1970, was "A Lawyer Should Represent a Client Zealously Within the Bounds of the Law." The word *zeal* or *zealous* is mentioned nine times in the code, usually exhorting a lawyer to act zealously.

In 1983, though, the ABA passed a substantially different set of standards, the Model Rules of Professional Conduct. Under these rules, now the primary source for the regulations in over forty states, the word *zeal* appears only three times, twice to admonish the lawyer to balance zeal with other duties. The new rules replaced the duty to act "zealously" with the duty of "diligence." The comment on diligence says: "A lawyer should act with commitment and dedication to the interests of the client and with zeal in advocacy upon the client's behalf. However, a lawyer is not bound to press for every advantage that might be realized for a client." Yet lawyers—and many courts—continue to talk and write about "zealous advocacy."

To some lawyers, the solution to this dilemma has been to develop "civility codes" that define, but don't mandate, acceptable lawyer behavior. These codes, now adopted in many states and localities, are by their very nature advisory only. If they had the force of law, they would no longer be codes of conduct but rules of discipline. While they may make lawyers feel better about themselves, civility codes also create an impossible tension between the way a lawyer wants to behave—or *claims* to want to behave—and what that same lawyer argues is a higher duty to fight for the client. As one attorney put it during an on-line discussion with colleagues, "When the client asks you to do things that are not 'civil,' but are also not clearly unethical, is that too much to ask? Can you point to a rule that says you can't be a jerk?"

Viewed realistically, civility is something that comes from within each individual lawyer. One attorney—a partner in another firm on the list of the nation's largest—told us he simply will not engage in "scorched-earth" or mean-spirited discovery. He believes that the long-term interests of his client—especially when it comes to his fees—are best served when he responds to reasonable discovery requests by providing reasonable information. For those clients who still want a "jerk," he and they "agree to disagree," and they are served by others within his firm.

A far better solution than civility is to fight power with power through the judicial use of issue sanctions. Issue sanctions can be ordered by a judge where one side's breach of the discovery rules is sufficiently great. These sanctions mean that the judge decides contested issues in the case against the side that engaged in the discovery abuse. For example, in the Washington, D.C., case where

Unocal withheld benzene test results, the judge ruled that Unocal was forbidden to claim that its product contained lower benzene levels, while the plaintiff *could* present evidence that Unocal altered and suppressed the tests. The judge in the Georgia Suzuki Samurai case entered a judgment against Suzuki on liability, leaving the company to fight only about what the damages should be. This extreme sanction, authorized by a United States Supreme Court case, was upheld after Suzuki's appeal.

In contrast to sanctions that merely cost money, issues sanctions work because they have a direct effect on the outcome of a case—an outcome adverse to the party hiding the discovery. Most judges are reluctant to use such extreme remedies. But unless members of the bench are willing to do more than just complain about what they see, the deterrent to future abuses simply won't be great enough. Discovery is such a high-stakes game—and such a vital profit center for corporate law firms—that monetary sanctions even in the hundreds of thousands of dollars are too often seen by powerful firms and their clients as simply the cost of doing business, even when that business is shady and unethical.

To many, discovery abuse can't possibly get worse than obfuscation, lying, or the overt destruction of documents. To others, that is just the beginning. In the hands of the arrogant and powerful, the war of attrition can turn to personal attack.

A. H. Robins Company's Dalkon Shield intrauterine device caused women to die or become gravely ill from pelvic inflammatory disease, children to be born with serious birth defects, and fetuses to be miscarried in unprecedented numbers. For many women, using this particular IUD meant they would never be able to bear children. Still, from the early 1970s until the 1990s Robins waged a war of attrition against the tens of thousands of women who filed complaints against the company.

Despite discovery orders that dated from the mid-1970s, as late as February 1984 a Minnesota federal magistrate wrote that "an impenetrable wall has been erected around the A. H. Robins Company." An order from a St. Paul federal judge barring the destruction of any Dalkon Shield–related documents didn't stop one San Francisco attorney who represented Robins in over a hundred cases. He shipped twenty boxes of documents to his new home in Indiana in 1983, then destroyed them when he moved again a few months later.

But Robins's lawyers saved their worst offenses for their destructive and unwarranted personal attacks on the women who sued. One Iowa mother who lost her ovaries and uterus was grilled about her sexual relations before her marriage, ten full years before she began wearing a Dalkon Shield. Another woman was cross-examined about the kind of fabric used in the crotch of her pantyhose. She prefaced her answer by observing that the question sounded "more like an obscene phone call." A Boston woman was asked whether she had oral or anal intercourse or used marital aids, and if so, how often. Addressing Robins's CEO, chief of research and development, and general counsel in his Minneapolis courtroom in 1984, federal Judge Miles W. Lord lambasted this conduct:

> [W]hen the time came for these women to make their claims against your company, you attacked their characters. You inquired into their sexual practices and into the identity of their sex partners. You exposed these women—and ruined families and reputations and careers—in order to intimidate those who would raise their voices against you. You introduced issues that had no relationship whatsoever to the fact that you planted in the bodies of these women instruments of death.

•

Perhaps the most effective form of personal attack is the SLAPP suit. Named by two University of Denver faculty members, sociology professor Penelope Canan and law professor George Pring, SLAPP stands for Strategic Lawsuit Against Public Participation. These lawsuits are designed to intimidate people from seeking their day in court or requesting relief from a government agency, or from simply protesting and speaking out publicly about their concerns.

The Denver professors defined some common characteristics of SLAPP suits: they are filed by those with deep pockets, and seek large awards against those with limited resources; they are designed to be expensive to defend; they charge defamation or business interference—complaints that directly attack people's free speech rights; and they usually have little or no merit. About 80 to 85 percent of these lawsuits eventually fail, but often the damage has already been done because of the time and money spent by defendants and the chilling effect the suits have on the free speech of both the defendants and others.

Another common element of many, though by no means all, SLAPP suits is the plaintiff's willingness to drop its suit if the defendants "apologize and retract everything." Those were the words of Guess? Inc.'s general counsel, who hired high-profile lawyer Daniel Petrocelli, Fred Goldman's lawyer in the O.J. Simpson civil trial, to sue two groups of women for publicly criticizing the Los Angeles jeans company's labor practices. According to LA investigative reporter Steve Lowery, Guess? "sues at the drop of a stitch," especially when its reputation is attacked. Part of the reason for this suit: a book reading attended by thirty people in the back room of a Santa Monica bookstore. Several women read from their work, including a poem about the infamous Triangle Shirtwaist Factory fire, and a University of California sociology professor made a pitch for unionizing Guess?. The suit is still pending.

Interestingly, Guess? *didn't* sue *Fortune* magazine, which had written a highly critical piece in October 1996 accusing Guess? of threatening employees, bribing IRS officials, even selling counterfeit Snoopy T-shirts. But *Fortune*, itself part of a formidable corporation, would be much harder to SLAPP.

Special real estate projects, especially those using land to build on or dump waste, are frequently the focus of SLAPP suits:

- After the Rhode Island Department of Environmental Management asked for public comment on a set of groundwater guidelines, Nancy Hsu Fleming wrote the agency that the new rules would allow a private landfill near her home to continue to contaminate the water. The landfill company insisted Fleming retract her letter. When she refused, she was sued for defamation and interference with business. But Fleming, a naturalized citizen born in Taiwan, remembered her citizenship studies in American history. She wrote back to the landfill's lawyers, citing her constitutional right under the First Amendment to petition the government: "In this instance, I am petitioning state government to close and clean up your client's dump." When the trial court refused to dismiss the case against her, Fleming appealed to the Rhode Island Supreme Court and got her dismissal.

- A Minnesota land developer sued two middle-class Minneapolis women who posted signs in front of their homes criticizing a development on wetlands the women wanted to protect. The developer described them as ringleaders of a movement, which the women—dubbed the "Notorious Sign-Building Two" by the Minneapolis *Star Tribune*—denied. But they refused to identify any of their supporters for fear they too would be in jeopardy. "I'm in awe that all this is happening," said one. "I don't think I'm all that dangerous." The lawsuit against them is ongoing.

- In 1988 Carolina Solite Corporation began burning hazardous waste instead of coal. Joann Almond, a self-described "little old country grandma," soon noticed a dusty film on her vegetables and those of others who lived near the Solite plant. When Almond spoke out about Solite's burning of waste, the company engaged her in a series of legal battles, culminating in 1997 with its effort to get an injunction to stop her from speaking out against Solite's air emission permit. The injunction was denied, and Almond was still talking: "We're country people, and we're not used to being put in situations like this. But if somebody's got to bear it, I will."

SLAPP suits can reach well beyond local disputes about local politics. When combined with discovery abuses, they create a double nightmare for those being SLAPPed. The Center for Auto Safety, a nonprofit consumer group founded by Ralph Nader and Consumers Union, has long believed that General Motors trucks with side-mounted gas tanks are dangerous, because when hit from the side they tend to explode in flames. The center heard of a GM plan to conceal documents about the fires in its vehicles. According to Clarence Ditlow, the center's director, the plan called for groups of young lawyers from private firms hired by GM—nicknamed the "fire babies"—to search GM's records for damaging documents and destroy or bury them. One engineer, deposed on videotape, told how six file cabinets of documents were sent to the "chopper-upper." The center also got information from one of the "fire babies" himself, who bragged to a colleague about what he had done. Among the missing documents: minutes from GM board meetings during the period the side-mounted gas tank design was first considered.

The center went public with the story, and Ditlow called on the Department of Justice to investigate, in effect petitioning the government as Nancy Hsu Fleming had. GM SLAPPed back, and Ditlow, the center, and Nader himself found themselves the defendants in a lawsuit. GM, though, was too smart to sue directly; a direct lawsuit would have made GM's own records discoverable in the center's effort to prove the truth of its statements. Instead, outside counsel Eugene Grace, alleged to be one of the coordinators of the "fire babies" project, filed the suit. This made it far more difficult for the defendants. GM was not a party to the case, so its documents were not subject to ordinary discovery. When the center tried to get Grace's records, he refused on the basis that GM had an attorney-client privilege to keep the records secret.

The SLAPP suit itself then became a discovery war of attrition, with Grace's and GM's lawyers fighting on all fronts. Depositions often were attended by four separate lawyers for the Grace/GM side: Grace's attorney, GM's in-house lawyer, an outside lawyer hired by GM, and a lawyer hired by GM to represent the person being deposed. Eventually the case was resolved by the insurance company, as it turned out the company had written policies for both sides. Meanwhile, Ditlow, Nader, and the Center for Auto Safety had run up $700,000 in legal fees.

A dozen or so states have jumped on the anti-SLAPP bandwagon with legislation designed to protect the victims of SLAPP suits. Professors Canan and Pring even drafted a model statute. In the states with stronger anti-SLAPP laws, the SLAPP victims can bring a motion early in the case, before expenses go through the roof, to force the SLAPPer to present evidence that it has a reasonable chance to win. A few lawyers, such as Mark Goldowitz, of Oakland, California, specialize in writing anti-SLAPP motions. Goldowitz won one case against the California branch of the Church of Scientology that went all the way to the Supreme Court.

Anti-SLAPP legislation—and the court decisions that further define what is and is not a SLAPP—are clearly still in the formative stages. New York lawyer Michael Stokes, who helped draft early anti-SLAPP laws, came to believe that SLAPPs have become "another weapon in the arsenal of wealthy defendants in defeating the claims of their lesser-financed opponents." Though California has one of the stronger anti-SLAPP statutes, some lawyers complain that Goliaths as well as Davids claim to be victims of SLAPPs, so that what was supposed to be a shield has turned into a sword.

The rules of ethics do little to provide a basis for disciplining an attorney who files a SLAPP. While lawyers are prohibited from filing a "frivolous" claim, almost no one is actually disciplined for this. Adding teeth to anti-SLAPP laws, through significant disciplinary sanctions for lawyers guilty of filing them, would be a step in the right direction. At the same time, lawmakers must work out the kinks in anti-SLAPP legislation, so that those needing protection for exercising their rights to free speech and to freely petition government over matters of public concern are the ones who really get it.

The problem with regulating SLAPPs typifies the general problem of regulating abusive power tactics. Those lawyers—and clients— with deep pockets and large litigation war chests will ordinarily find ways to beat the system unless the penalties for their conduct are sufficiently severe to convince them that they are risking more than they can gain. To date, our legal system has done little to get that message across.

Epilogue:
Resolving the Dejos Case

Three years went by after Clancy Garrett and Gregory Ngim had lunch and discussed Esperanza Dejos's harassment case. The case finally settled three days before trial. Esperanza got more money than she thought she would, but wondered if it was worth it. She found Gregory Ngim, the lawyer who did most of the work for Hillsman, disgusting. He kept her in deposition for seven days, asking questions so personal that she would have been uncomfortable if they had been asked by her own doctor. Still, Willa Reece insisted that she answer the questions and stick with it. If Willa hadn't insisted, Esperanza would have given up years ago. Mostly she hung in there because her lawyer did. Three times Willa went to the appeals court to get orders requiring Hillsman to provide documents, and three times she won. But if Esperanza had it to do all over again, she wasn't sure she would.

As for Gregory Ngim, he made partner soon after the Dejos case settled. Sure, Dejos made out well, because she was lucky to have lawyers strong enough to withstand his attacks. But in several other cases where the plaintiffs' facts were just as good, Greg had been able to wear them down and get them to take a small fraction of what the case was worth. He was learning what Clancy Garrett had meant by the "war of attrition." He loved it. He loved the battle, he loved winning, and he loved the power he felt when the other side blinked and settled for less. Clancy Garrett had taught him well.

CHAPTER 4

A Gun to the Head of
the Junior Attorney

Many associates feel like they suffer from something similar to battered spouse syndrome. They keep getting beaten up by partners, but blame themselves and keep going back for more.

> —Anonymous lawyer in 1994 replying to a survey
> conducted by the trade publication *American Lawyer*

Every attorney who has billed time knows that hourly billing creates rich opportunities for fraud.

> —Professor William Ross, whose surveys of lawyers
> uncovered widespread admissions of
> unethical billing practices

It has been a difficult eighteen months for Sharon Chau since coming to Swenson & DeLuca, and now she finds herself faced with the Reynolds case. Midway through her second year, Sharon has recently been spending a lot of time thinking about why she joined the firm. Not that it's a bad place; they have a solid litigation and real estate practice, and when the firm branched out into environmental work, Sharon was recruited from the regional counsel's office of the Environmental Protection Administration, where she'd worked for three years. Almost immediately she became the firm's resident expert on hazardous substances and toxic torts.

At first Sharon was excited about working at Swenson. The

money was great—a base salary of $85,000 per year, much more than she made at the EPA, plus a year-end $10,000 bonus if she billed over the expected 1,950 hours. But while the firm assured her that it worked both sides of the environmental street, so far Sharon has spent 90 percent of her time defending companies against environmental claims, and only 10 percent working for proenvironmental interests. She finds herself defending some of the same companies she helped prosecute at the EPA. Then there's the billable hours requirement. Sharon had never worked so hard, but she still fell a hundred hours short of her billing quota in her first year at Swenson.

This year she has barely managed to keep up on her hours, thanks largely to the advice of her old law school friend Billy Frieden, a sixth-year associate at Swenson who helped show Sharon the ropes of law firm life. First, Billy told her, never turn down work: "The worst thing you can do is look like you're not overwhelmed all the time. That's what they hired you for, and that's what they expect."

Billy also educated Sharon in the "fine art" of billing, the "tricks of the trade" that help desperate associates trolling for billable hours to meet their quotas. He taught her how to bill for any and all time spent on a case: "If I'm standing in the shower thinking about the Jones case, that's billable time—'strategizing client's case' or 'evaluating trial tactics' is the way I put it." He showed her how to bill twice for the same research by updating old memoranda and opinion letters while charging for the time as if she'd done the work from scratch. "After all, they're hiring us for our expertise. Yours is in environmental regulation. There's a value to what you do. If the first time you research a particular point it takes ten hours to do the memo, the second client gets a bargain if you only bill five, even if it takes you just half an hour to update it."

When Regina Dern, one of the firm's real estate partners, asks for Sharon's help on an environmental issue, Sharon doesn't hesitate, remembering Billy's rule about "trolling for work" and his oft-repeated admonition that "you *never* say no to a partner." One of Regina's best clients is Reynolds Realty, a real estate development firm owned primarily by its president, George Reynolds. Reynolds owns a building that had been leased for years to a company whose business used extensive quantities of a chemical called Thorzac. The company recently went bankrupt, and now Reynolds is looking to sell the building. There's a potential buyer, but Reynolds is reluctant to say anything about the Thorzac because he's afraid the buyer might back out. While Thorzac hasn't been defined as a toxic substance by the state, some people consider it to be hazardous waste. Regina asks Sharon to research Thorzac and write a memorandum about whether it's toxic.

Sharon researches Thorzac and comes to the clear conclusion that it is indeed a toxic waste. Although the state hasn't yet made this determination, Sharon is certain that the state EPA will agree with her analysis as soon as it looks at the issue. Thorzac's toxicity was clearly shown in two of the four studies Sharon finds. One of the studies that didn't find Thorzac toxic was an early inconclusive effort, and the other was sponsored by a grant from the chemical's manufacturer.

Sharon puts her findings in a memo to Regina concluding that the firm should advise Reynolds to disclose the Thorzac. Regina asks her to come to a meeting with Reynolds the next day. After Sharon describes her findings to Reynolds and tells him that not disclosing hazardous waste could make him liable for civil and criminal penalties, Reynolds bluntly makes his position clear.

"I know all that," he barks, "but how can you be sure? Look, I need to sell this property, and I've got a buyer waiting to take title. I need your letter saying that Thorzac is not hazardous; I paid a lot for this place, and if I lose this buyer, it may not be worth spit. So don't waste my time, and get down to work."

After Reynolds leaves, Sharon meets with Regina. Regina is not receptive to Sharon's doubts. "Look, Reynolds is sitting on four million dollars here. They need to sell this parcel."

"I understand that, Regina, but I don't know how anyone could write an opinion letter saying Thorzac is not hazardous."

"Nonsense," Regina replies. "We can't base our opinion on two studies out of four, especially when the state hasn't ruled. If that's all you've got, I have no problem with an opinion letter saying Thorzac is not now a hazardous substance. And by the way, I want *you* to sign the letter. You're the toxic expert around here—you worked for the EPA, not me. That's why we got you involved."

Great, thinks Sharon. *I'm finally on track with my billable hours, and now in the one case that could give me a little cushion, I've got to write an opinion letter that's simply wrong for a client I can't stand.*

•

The typical American lawyer believes that the adversary theorem works when a law firm represents whoever asks it, and the firm's lawyers do their level best to zealously represent those clients.

In 1975 a group of law students picketed the offices of Lloyd Cutler, a leading Washington, D.C., lawyer. Cutler represented General Motors and had successfully lobbied Congress on GM's behalf to postpone automobile safety regulations. Among the lawyers rising to Cutler's defense was Simon H. Rifkind, long the leader of one of New York's most well known firms, and a staunch believer in the adversary theorem. " 'How could you represent so-and-so?' is a question frequently put to me," he said in a speech to the New York City bar. "As you know, there are fashions in untouchability. One season it is a sharecropper in Mississippi, the next season it is a multi-million share corporation in Detroit. From the viewpoint of the adversary system, the applicable principle is the same."

Rifkind strongly criticized the picketing students. "Had they mastered the meaning of the adversary system they would have known that their conduct was subversive of the central tenet of the profession they were about to enter. . . . [They] have not taken account of the operation of the adversary process. The utility of that process is that it relieves the lawyer of the need, or indeed the right, to be his client's judge and thereby frees him to be the more effective advocate and champion."

In the 1990s Cutler and his firm, Wilmer, Cutler & Pickering, were again in the news, first when Cutler, now one of Washington's senior statesmen, agreed to became President Clinton's chief White House counsel after the previous counsel resigned under a cloud of Whitewater controversy. Not long after, Wilmer, Cutler agreed to represent clients in a matter more controversial than anything it ever did for GM. Credit Suisse and other Swiss banks were accused in a class action case of denying payments to the survivors of Holocaust victims. Credit Suisse in particular had been widely accused of stealing gold belonging to those who died in concentration camps.

Despite the horrific implications of this conduct, accepting Credit Suisse and two of the other banks as clients was a routine matter for Wilmer, Cutler; the firm's "new business" committee approved it, and the new clients then simply appeared on the periodic "new business" memo that the firm circulates to all its lawyers.

New York's Cravath, Swaine & Moore also took Credit Suisse as a client, although it took pains to claim its role would be advisory only. Cravath has about a thousand employees, about a third of whom are Jewish. Although the firm insisted that it was simply providing strategic advice to help the bank determine its proper course of conduct, twelve associates—junior attorneys who were not partners in the firm—challenged the decision in a written memorandum. The partner in charge of the representation admitted that these objectors "felt very strongly that the bank acted improperly in some of the vilest acts in memory and should not be represented" but overruled the associates' objections. Still, it was Cravath's associates, not the partners who brought in the case, who would do the bulk of the day-to-day work defending Credit Suisse.

It is impossible to prove what motivated Cravath and Wilmer, Cutler to take on such reprehensible clients. Everyone, Credit Suisse no less than the worst criminal defendant, is entitled to representation. But unlike the typical criminal defendant, the Swiss banks can and will pay whatever they must to get the best possible counsel. And unlike the typical criminal defense lawyer, an associate in a large firm is given no say in deciding what clients the firm will represent.

The overriding reality is that large law firms have become big businesses first and associations of professionals second. When influential law firms lobby against the public interest on behalf of powerful clients, the lawyers do so as "a matter of personal choice, not professional compulsion," according to Mark Green, the elected ombudsman for New York City. Green wrote those words in attacking Wilmer, Cutler back in 1975, when he was an early "Nader Raider." He said that lawyers like Cutler should "make a judgment about the likely impact on the public" of their representation, and insisted they be held morally responsible for the help they give such clients. The same should be true today.

Indeed, many lawyers expressed similar sentiments about Wilmer, Cutler and Cravath, Swaine's representation of Credit Suisse. "I don't have to stop just because [a client] has the correct fare," said William Kunstler associate Ronald Kuby, distinguishing himself from a taxi driver.

His was hardly the only voice of protest. On Counsel Connect, *The American Lawyer*'s on-line service, lawyers across the country debated the issues in a far-ranging discussion. One argued that those who took on a case had to be willing to "identify themselves fully with it," citing Stephen Vincent Benét's famous story of Daniel Webster's representation of Jabez Stone, in which Webster realized that trying to save Stone's soul might cost him his own. Professor Monroe Freedman noted that we often lionize lawyers who take on unpopular causes, but we should "also celebrate the lawyers who turn down clients for reasons of conscience."

Meanwhile, another Washington, D.C., law firm took an approach very different from that of Wilmer, Cutler. Arent, Fox, Kintner, Plotkin & Kahn was asked to represent one of the European insurance companies accused of wrongfully denying life insurance claims of relatives of people who had died in the Holocaust. The plaintiffs charged that when they tried to collect on the policies, the companies denied their claims for reasons such as not having original policies or proper death certificates, impossibilities given the realities of the death camps. Instead of approving the client, the Arent, Fox partners held a firmwide meeting open to all who wanted to attend. After a vigorous debate at the meeting, the firm's management committee unanimously turned down the case.

What is remarkable about Arent, Fox's action is not that it occurred, but that it is so unusual. The economics of large modern American law firms virtually require a conscious decision to take almost any client that walks, crawls, or gets chased through the door, in order to maintain profitability. According to reports in the *American Lawyer* and the *National Law Journal*, in recent years 370-lawyer Cravath, one of the richest firms in the country, has grossed more than $2,500,000 a year per partner, and had average *profits* per partner of over $1 million. 250-lawyer Wilmer, Cutler has grossed over $1 million per partner, and netted half a million per partner.

"I am certain any lawyer at one of our large firms could make do with five percent less," admonishes William Reece Smith Jr., former president of the American Bar Association and senior partner at Carlton Fields, one of Florida's largest firms. Smith chaired the ABA committee that issued a 1996 report studying how to revitalize professionalism in the law.

Most legal legwork is done by the firm's lawyer-employees, the associates. On one hand, these young men and women are very fortunate. They are extraordinarily well paid—$85,000 for a twenty-four- or twenty-five-year-old beginning attorney at Cravath in New York, and $74,000 at Wilmer, Cutler in slightly less pricey D.C. On the other hand, most associates have little control over their lives. Many feel they have the worst of both worlds: no power to decide whom they represent, but the clear expectation that they will summon all the zeal necessary to further the interests of clients they may find repugnant.

Just like the criminal defense attorney, once a young associate gets assigned a case, that lawyer will be required to represent the client as zealously as possible, at least if the firm's partners are to be satisfied. New York University professor Stephen Gillers, a leading ethics authority, describes what an associate must do to make it in this environment: "Lawyers are told to do whatever will work best if it is legal and won't result in discipline or some similar sanction. This is what zealous advocacy means. . . . The client's autonomy and right to achieve his objectives through the law demand no less. . . . What about the lawyer's personal ethics? In the view of many law firms, there's no such thing once you've accepted the client."

When Sharon Chau begins her evaluation of how to draft the Reynolds opinion letter, she must take all these considerations into account. She will also undoubtedly give a lot of thought to the remaining $40,000 she owes in student loans, and her two young dependent children. Making the morally right decision under these circumstances can be a daunting task.

Perhaps the biggest pressure Sharon faces, and probably the most influential factor in the development of any big firm associate, is the billable hour. At her firm, Sharon is expected to spend 1,950 hours per year that are actually billed to clients. This excludes hours spent on educational seminars, business development, and other pursuits not directly billable. Sharon's starting salary is $75,000; the firm bills clients for her time at $150 per hour, making her worth almost $300,000 to the firm in billable time. Even after accounting for health insurance and other benefits and the cost of support staff, the Sharon Chaus of the legal world are major profit centers for their firms.

The billable hour began as a reform that helped law firms justify the value of their services, and helped clients understand what they were paying for. Until the 1960s, lawyers often sent bills for work completed that simply stated the amount—"For professional services rendered: $500" or "Preparation of *Smith v. Jones* documents: $1,500." Clients usually paid, with no questions asked. Some state bars even suggested billing rates that fixed prices for certain legal services, until the United States Supreme Court outlawed the practice in 1975 because it violated antitrust laws.

With the rise in consumer consciousness in the 1960s, clients wanted more information about what they were paying for. The use of automated accounting systems in the fifties and sixties, and the computerized billing that followed, enabled law firms to identify case name, time spent, task performed, and the lawyers responsible both for bringing in and performing the work. Firms soon found it easy to track how much was billed for each case simply by assigning a dollar value to each lawyer, and computing the time they spent on each matter. Clients found it easier to understand what they were paying for.

But the obvious advantages of the billable hour soon paled next to the ways in which it came to be abused. Today, this "reform" has too often become a tool used *against* clients. When discovery battles become long, drawn-out wars of attrition, lawyers bill more time. When trials that thirty years ago would have taken two weeks drag on for four months, lawyers run up six- and even seven-figure tabs. Law firms use the "pillar of zealous representation" to justify these strategies, said a 1995 article in the *ABA Journal*, the principal periodical of the American Bar Association: "If hourly billing is the financial engine of most law firms, the duty of zealous representation . . . is the gas pedal." As one understandably anonymous Washington,

D.C., lawyer told his subordinate, "If you want to make it in this firm, you've got to learn how to . . . bill them, and then you bill them again and, if you can, bill them again." Or, as Cumberland (Alabama) Law School professor William Ross put it, lawyers have developed a "fetish for accumulation of billable hours."

It's sometimes easy to pick out the most extreme examples and claim they are proof of widespread abuse. But there are so many anecdotal accounts of incredible billing abuses that it is hard to choose among them. Perhaps the most well known recent case is that of Webster Hubbell, a former chair of the Arkansas bar's ethics committee and a partner at Little Rock's prestigious Rose Law Firm, who went from number three in the Clinton Justice Department to prison. Hubbell was convicted of stealing $394,000 from his clients and his own law firm by billing for time he never worked, and claiming that personal expenses—including purchases at Victoria's Secret and a fur salon—were business-related.

Hubbell is hardly alone. Another flagrant example of gross billing abuse involved a prominent Chicago lawyer in a large and prestigious firm who averaged 5,941 billable hours per year over four years. That's an average of sixteen hours and twenty minutes per day, 365 days a year. The lawyer claimed to have never taken a day off in four years. But every lawyer must remain current on the law, go to firm meetings, and stay in touch with clients to keep and develop business. It's impossible to convert every second into time that can be billed to a client. Carl T. Bogus, a longtime Philadelphia practitioner who recently turned to teaching law, calculated that if this lawyer met "the standard assumption" that at most, only 70 percent of work time can be turned into time billed to a client, "this lawyer needed to work 23.3 hours per day, 365 days a year, leaving just enough time for a round-trip commute home but not enough time to enter the house." Yet the lawyer's partners remained silent until an anonymous source furnished reporters with the lawyer's billing sheets.

Billing abuses are by no means limited to excesses at our largest firms. A Kansas attorney at a small firm reportedly charged the State Workers' Compensation Fund an average of thirty-three hours a day for one ten-day period. An auditing expert uncovered a southern California lawyer who had billed a single client for fifty-hour workdays and a New Orleans firm that routinely billed four hours for letters a single sentence long.

Despite these extreme cases, lawyers—with the notable exception of the high-visibility Hubbell, whose prosecution stemmed from the Whitewater investigation—are rarely punished for billing abuses. Raleigh bankruptcy attorney Mark Kirby was indicted in federal court on sixteen counts of billing fraud. Among other offenses, he billed ninety hours in one day. Between June 1990 and July 1991 Kirby billed a total of 13,000 hours, even though that thirteen-month period, calculated at twenty-four hours a day, seven days a week, was only 9,500 hours long. Yet Kirby's trial resulted in a hung jury. His defense: Everybody does it.

Kirby eventually pled guilty to one count and was sentenced to fifteen months. Hubbell received twenty-one months in prison, though one former Arkansas Supreme Court judge argued it was unfair to single out Hubbell when billing fraud is so common and so rarely prosecuted. Indeed, the justification that "everybody does it" is widely used in the legal community. "The problem is not so much the behavior of one lawyer," says Professor Bogus, "as it is the conduct of the firm." If attorneys believe that they can ethically "multitask" by billing two, three, or more clients for the same hour, or bill for the "value" of their services, even when that value vastly exceeds the time the work actually takes, lawyers like Kirby will continue to be the inevitable consequence.

In 1991 Professor Ross surveyed 280 lawyers in private practice and 80 who worked in-house for companies. The results were shocking. Seven out of eight practicing lawyers said that it was ethical to bill a client for "recycled" work originally done for another client. Half said they had billed two different clients for work performed during the same time period, such as dictating a memo for one client while traveling for another. Just as shocking was what lawyers concluded about their colleagues' billing practices, with 55 percent saying that lawyers occasionally or frequently "pad" their hours, and 64 percent saying they were personally aware of lawyers who had padded their bills. The in-house lawyers surveyed were even more clear: Over 80 percent felt that the billable hour influenced how much time the outside lawyers they hired spent on a case, and 74 percent felt that the billable hour significantly decreased lawyers' incentives to work efficiently.

"You *can* handle a case aggressively and efficiently at the same time," says San Francisco lawyer and billing expert William Gwire, who often consults with clients suspicious of their lawyers' bills. "I think the issue can be summed up in one simple sentence: Is the firm acting in the best interest of the client—putting the client's interests ahead of its own?" When they do, lawyers bill honestly and fairly. When they don't, they overbill and often get away with it. As Professor Ross says, "Overbilling is the perfect crime because it's awfully hard to detect."

Detection is made more difficult because so many lawyers turn a blind eye toward their colleagues' dishonesty. Catholic University professor Lisa Lerman talked to many lawyers uncomfortable with partners who cheated, "but they go along with it because they see it as professional suicide to do anything about it." And the bigger the firm, the deeper the abuses can be buried.

Law firms routinely use many different techniques to keep their billable hours high. One of the simplest and most prevalent is double billing. For example, a lawyer travels by plane for one client and while airborne works on another client's file. The lawyer bills both clients hourly, reasoning that since Client A has to pay even if the lawyer watches a movie, A shouldn't complain if the movie turns out to be *Ishtar* and the lawyer opts to work on Client B's case instead. Nor should B complain, since the lawyer is focusing completely on B's file. But in the end, the lawyer has still charged two different hourly clients a total of six, seven, or eight hours for a four-hour flight. Unless the lawyer splits the hourly rate between the two clients, this legal alchemy makes eight billable hours out of a four-hour period. The American Bar Association has written an opinion that says it is simply unethical for a lawyer to charge a total of more than one hour for an hour's time, unless the clients consent. But clients are rarely asked permission, and unless the clients know each other, it's difficult for them to catch the lawyer in the act.

The plane scenario at least makes some sense, particularly

if one client is paying a flat rate for the lawyer's travel. But some lawyers have taken double billing to illogical extremes. In certain types of courts—family law, probate, worker's compensation, bankruptcy—it's often possible to schedule several routine case appearances on the same day's court calendar. Lawyers may be able to make three or four brief court appearances in half an hour. If attorneys charge a minimum of one hour for any court appearance, they can bill three or four hours in thirty minutes. Other lawyers—particularly those with high-volume practices—bill several different clients for their time traveling to court appearances, and bill yet another client for the memo they dictate as they drive.

Another creative version of double billing is what lawyers call "value billing," or billing what the lawyer considers to be the "reasonable value of the services" regardless of the time it takes to complete the work. This means that if a lawyer has already researched or written a memo on a particular issue, this work can be recycled and a "discounted" hourly rate charged. For example, if it took thirty hours to do the work the first time, the second client might be charged "only" fifteen or twenty, even though the recycling and updating took just one or two hours. Professor Lerman was shocked when one lawyer bragged to her that if a client asked him a question and he already knew the answer, he would beef up his reply in a nice letter and bill the client ten hours.

Some attorneys, like the ones charging hour minimums for each court appearance, perform magic by changing minutes into hours. A lawyer who charges a quarter-hour minimum for any work done, instead of a tenth, or six minutes, has much in common with the phone company that bills by the minute instead of every six seconds. Billing these extra few minutes makes little difference on long jobs, but has an enormous effect on brief tasks. A lawyer might leave two or three voice-mail messages during the course of a day trying to reach opposing counsel; charging a tenth of an hour for that is certainly justified. But other lawyers may leave one voice mail message at 9:00 A.M., another at noon, and a third at 3:30 P.M., give each message a different "time entry," and charge a full fifteen minutes for each call. Those three messages, perhaps three or four minutes of work, are now "worth" three-quarters of an hour. Multiply this by many similar routine tasks done every day, and it becomes clear how some lawyers are able to bill more than twenty-four hours in a single day.

Many law firms pass on to their clients as many overhead expenses as possible. It's not uncommon for a firm to charge $2 a page for faxes and 25¢ per photocopy, despite the fact that a copy costs about two cents a page and even commercial vendors charge no more than a few pennies. But some firms see the copying and fax rooms as profit centers. Large law firms routinely add surcharges for on-line computer research, telephone calls, even regular secretarial help. One client was amazed to discover that the initials HVAC on his invoice meant that he was being charged for his "share" of the firm's heating and air-conditioning bill. Thomas Barr, a senior partner at Cravath, Swaine & Moore, bluntly told the *National Law Journal* in 1992 that charging costs to clients was "a shell game": "If you tell me you won't pay for one cost, then I will charge you more for another cost." Again, an ABA ethics opinion has made it clear that marking up the actual cost of services is unethical unless the client consents. In fact, the ABA says a law firm is required to pass on any cost savings to its clients.

When lawyers' attitudes about billing are coupled with the big-business mentality of most large firms, the pressures on associates like Sharon Chau to meet their billable hour requirements any way they can—even if it means cheating—are enormous. Billing expert Gwire says that "when you set the bar too high, you are just motivating people to cheat." Gwire, a former associate and partner in a big firm, says, "I know what I had to do for eighteen hundred legitimate hours a year and still maintain my practice, do the business development, and meet the other firm requirements. You kill yourself. It's six or six and a half days a week, nine to ten hours a day, and I was only able to do that for two to three months at a stretch. So people who bill twenty-two hundred hours, year in and year out, I don't know how they are doing it except by lying." Gwire says that when law firms make billable hours the principal performance criterion, they send a clear message: "Never mind the quality of your work."

When associates don't bill enough, they quickly hear about it from law firm higher-ups. "I was constantly dragged on the carpet for not billing enough hours," Richard Gordon, a Harvard Law instructor, told the *Rocky Mountain News*. "I was told, and this is a direct quote, 'When you're taking a dump, you're always thinking about a client.'"

When new associates come to a firm, they are immediately taught how to bill time, even before they learn how to prepare a brief. Some firms even put on "billing seminars" designed to teach new recruits how to make their time acceptable to clients. A lawyer of our acquaintance recalls this advice from her firm's managing partner: Clients get suspicious of time on the exact hour, so bill in uneven increments instead, 3.1 hours rather than 3.0; bill at least a half hour for any court document, even if it's generated off the computer by the secretary, because "that's what the client will pay."

Young lawyers often get conflicting messages. A junior associate at a large New York firm describes a rigorous law firm orientation program in which entering associates are warned that cheating on bills can be criminal. But, given its billable hour requirement, the firm also communicates another message: "Bill!" "We have stage voice and sotto voce," says the associate.

Associates pay rapt attention to what they are told because they know that their paychecks, indeed their jobs, depend on billing. Firms often soft-pedal their billable hour requirements when recruiting new associates, and some claim to have no "formal" minimums, but they strongly enforce billing quotas once lawyers join the ranks. And while most firms claim that they require between 1,850 and 2,000 hours per year, that figure is the bare minimum. The star performers, those on the partnership express, are expected to do far more.

The lawyers who survive in their law firm's environment are those who are able to acclimate themselves to the firm's "culture." Each firm's culture is unique; firms look for a niche, a way to set themselves apart from the crowd. Billing is only one way in which this culture is defined. A firm's culture combines its personality, its traditions, and its core values. These core values may include policies about the kinds of clients the firm takes, or how the firm acts toward its opponents. These values also include what commitment the firm has to the community in which it "lives" and how much the firm focuses on making more money, as opposed to "quality-of-life" issues—everything from part-time partnerships to parental leave policies.

Ultimately a firm shows its culture and values by how it behaves, both in public and behind closed doors. What the firm's partners say, and how they act, are the most important cues young associates have. How the partners approach their clientele, whom they are willing to accept as clients when a lot of money is at stake, and how far they are willing to go to zealously represent their clientele all help define law firm culture.

The firm also defines its culture by the way it treats its associates. Many firms simply place no real value on their younger lawyers except as profitable engines to be run into the ground. Some seem to make little effort to convince associates to stay the course to partner, according to Joel Henning, a vice president at the legal consulting firm Hildebrandt, Inc. "It's kind of like paying millions for a thoroughbred racehorse, then putting it in a dilapidated stable and feeding it lousy food," Henning told the *Washington Post*.

"Did you read that some of the big U.S. firms are moving into China?" says one law associate to another in a June 1997 edition of the trade cartoon *J.D.* "Incredible!" says his colleague. "You're talking about an unscrupulous autocracy that relies on slave labor and . . . limits families to one child. The masses are mere cogs in a great wheel, serving out their days with little hope of advancement until the ruling elite decides they have become expendable! And," continues the second associate, "I hear China's pretty bad too."

Law firms often give little or no feedback to their new attorneys. Annual reviews often last a mere thirty minutes. Associates dread them, knowing they will get little insight into the quality of their work but a lot of talk about billing—how many hours they billed to clients, and how many their partners had to "write down" for their inefficiency before the bill could be sent out. Many firms fear that an associate who is told to improve will leave and go elsewhere, costing the firm a trained billing machine, while a rising star must be kept from presuming a partnership is in the offing someday. In today's modern law businesses, a partnership offer must never seem secure.

Law firms do make efforts of varying kinds to inculcate their young lawyers with the firm's core values. But too often the posh dinners for "summer associates"—the law student interns who form the recruitment pool for permanent jobs—are little more than opportunities to wine and dine while the firm delivers its best PR pitch. Law firms promote retreats and annual meetings as a chance for all firm employees to "bond." Instead, these events are often expensive weekends where drinking, playing golf, and poker form the social schedule, and the business meeting focuses on the firm's financial health and the development of new business. There is generally little opportunity to consider or create new directions or philosophies, or any goals loftier than the bottom line.

Some firms provide training for young associates from more senior lawyers or outside consultants to teach how things are done. Some have senior partners who serve as real role models for associates and take their mentoring role seriously. This training and mentoring, when it goes beyond bottom-line values, can be of enormous help to the new lawyer. But increasingly, partners are worried so much about themselves and their own billing quotas that meaningful help for associates is the exception, not the rule.

Not long ago most partners were worker bees, toiling on cases brought in by the firm's few "rainmakers," the partners who developed the bulk of the firm's business. But things changed in the late 1980s, when the excesses of the "Me Generation" began to catch up with the modern American law firm. Partners were no longer paid based on seniority, but on what came to be called—as only lawyers could put it—an "eat-what-you-kill" mentality: Partners kept more of the work they brought in for themselves, so the more they brought in, the more they and their "team" of associates could bill, and the more they got paid. Increasingly, law firms enticed lateral transfers—partners in other firms—who could bring with them a large "book of business." These lawyers often brought their own associates, creating intrafirm rivalries over who would get to do the work.

Other firms merged, consolidating in efforts to expand markets, branch out into new practice areas, or become full-service firms ready to meet all the needs of any large corporation. But as was once said about mergers, "You may be able to swallow a turkey whole, but can you digest it?" Initially, blinded by the thought of gold at the end of the rainbow, firms merged without considering their different firm cultures and core values. As often as not, these mergers failed or resulted in widespread defections among dissatisfied attorneys. New partners resented "old boys" who were technically competent but whom they considered overpaid. Old partners were suspicious of the new lawyers' claims about their books of business and resentful of new partners who seemed to be selling themselves to the highest bidder.

Lawrence Fox, the former ABA Ethics Committee chair who has written often about law firm culture, has said that lateral transfers and mergers may be the most negative influence on the development of a healthy, ethical, and moral law firm environment. He also points out this double bind: As attorneys' loyalties to their law firms decreased, so too has the loyalty of clients toward the firms they hire.

When law firms become revolving doors in which values and traditions give way to free-market economics and the question "What have you done for me lately?" the associate, at the bottom of the food chain, usually feels the pressure the most. Lawyers have one of the highest alcoholism rates of any group in the country. Many simply work too hard; half of those surveyed in 1990 reported working over two hundred hours per month. The number of lawyers in private practice who said they were "very satisfied" dropped 20 percent in the six-year period from 1984 to 1990. To be sure, there are exceptions—law firms whose core values include the welfare of their employees and their community as well as the bottom line. But for many of the Sharon Chaus of the legal world, their reality is a large firm with small-minded values.

Changing the way of life at the modern American law firm will not be easy. For many, including Fox, former ABA president Smith, and billing expert Gwire, the solution seems simple: The law must return to being a profession, not a business. As Gwire puts it, "Sure, lawyers should make a decent living, but we are not in the business of making money; we are in the business of helping people." This "solution," simple in theory, is elusive when one tries to implement it. Smith's ABA Committee on Professionalism spent years studying the issue without being able to draft clear, concise prescriptions for change.

A better solution may come from clients themselves. Clients no longer stick loyally by their old law firms the way families used to keep their family physician. In 1996 a Task Force on Lawyer Business Ethics published a statement of principles emphasizing billing ethics. Increasingly, large corporations use in-house lawyers and outside auditors to scrutinize their outside counsel's fees. Big companies now hire several firms, rather than just one or two. The firm that doesn't measure up will be fired; the firm that cheats on its bill will be audited, even sued.

Institutional clients have also fought back by requesting innovative billing methods, and many lawyers, not wanting to lose these clients, are willing to go along. Some clients have agreed and even sought to pay lawyers on a percentage basis, a payment method that used to be reserved for those who couldn't afford hourly fees. Other lawyers and clients have agreed on task or "value" billing, where the law firm is paid a specific amount for the task it's hired to complete, and some insurance companies now insist on paying flat fees for routine cases. These billing methods have long been staples of smaller firms with individual clients, who want to know "exactly what I'm looking at," whether it's fees for a will or living trust, an uncontested divorce, or a drunk driving defense.

With law firms still growing larger and new lawyers continuing to spill out of law schools in enormous numbers, the legal marketplace of the millennium will be a buyer's market. Clients willing to take control of their legal business will be able to dictate how they will pay for legal services. While this is easier for institutional clients such as banks and insurance companies, it is also well within the ability of the average individual, who can price-shop, insist on value for service, and require reasonable protections like clearly written fee contracts and assurances of malpractice liability coverage. For the Sharon Chaus of the world, the more difficult issue is whether, in this competitive marketplace, clients will also be able to insist that their lawyers provide legal services that include doing something the attorney feels is clearly wrong.

Epilogue:
The Reynolds Opinion Letter

Sharon spent the first half of the weekend trying to reach her boss, Paul Holly, the partner in charge of the environmental group. She hoped that Holly would intercede with Regina Dern on Sharon's behalf. Paul might have been willing to explain to Regina, partner to partner, why Sharon was so troubled by writing the opinion letter. But Holly was on a backpacking vacation, totally unreachable. Sharon spent the second half of the weekend trying to write a letter that would satisfy both George Reynolds and her own desire to do honest work. This too proved impossible. She simply could not reconcile her views with the opinion Reynolds wanted. And every time she drafted the letter by qualifying her opinion or balancing the conflicting reports, she realized it would fall far short of what Reynolds Realty thought it needed to close the sale.

By Sunday night Sharon was distraught. She had decided she would not draft a letter that expressed her professional opinion if she could not honestly stand behind it. But she knew that if she told that to Regina Dern on Monday morning, it could cost her her job. Then, on the way to work Monday, Sharon had an idea.

Sharon started talking as she walked into Regina's office: "Regina, I'll give you the letter George wants if it's still what *you* want, but I think it could hurt the firm." When Regina asked what she meant, Sharon began: "You know that I think it's a sure thing the state will eventually say Thorzac's hazardous."

"I thought you understood your personal beliefs are not the issue here," snapped Regina.

"I understand that," continued Sharon, "but if the state does rule on Thorzac anytime soon, and I'm right—which I'm sure I am—then the buyer is going to go after Reynolds Realty, maybe even sue. And Reynolds is going to wave our letter around and say they relied on *us*. If Reynolds gets sued, we're going to be next."

"So you think George is getting our letter just to cover his ass?" asked Regina.

"Yes," replied Sharon, "but you know him best. What do you think?"

"Okay, rewrite it giving both sides," ordered Regina, "but do it quick; we've got to get this to Reynolds today."

"I thought you might want to go that way," said Sharon, "so I drafted the letter both ways."

"Great," said Regina, now beginning to thaw. "And don't worry about George. I'll deal with him; I'll just tell him this is as good as it's going to get."

Sharon left work that day with renewed confidence. She'd learned a lot in the last few days. She had not compromised her ethics; she'd never written the letter Regina wanted, but she managed to avoid having to produce it. Sharon also recognized with some amusement that after she had explained to Regina how the law firm might be at risk, Regina had swung 180 degrees from her insistence that the client get whatever he wanted. Meanwhile, Sharon had billed a hefty chunk of legitimate hours. She was starting to think she might just learn how to walk the tightrope from junior attorney to partner.

CHAPTER 5

Blowing the Whistle in
Corporate America

An artificial being, invisible, intangible, and existing only in law.
> —Chief Justice John Marshall of the
> United States Supreme Court, describing
> corporations in an 1819 opinion

The accumulation of corporate wrongs is, in my mind, a manifestation of individual sin.
> —Federal Judge Miles W. Lord, addressing the
> president and general counsel of
> A. H. Robins in his courtroom, 1984

Ask not with whom the buck stops, it stops with thee.
> —Maryland law professor David Luban,
> discussing a lawyer's moral obligation to "blow the whistle"
> if necessary to protect the public safety

Jesse Valencia has worked for National Motor Corporation for seventeen years. He came to NMC right after college with an engineering degree, and eventually applied for a pilot program that sent him to law school at night at NMC's expense while he continued his engineering job during the day. After he passed the bar, he joined the Office of General Counsel, the company's in-house law department. After two promotions, Jesse was named senior assistant general counsel three years ago, and given the job as principal legal officer to the company's Vehicle Reliability Committee (VRC).

The VRC is composed mostly of upper-level engineers and middle-management executives. It is chaired by company vice president Joseph "Buck" Packard, part of the senior management team, and functions as the company's in-house safety board.

Jesse loves his job working with the VRC. He has always been concerned with safety—he's well aware that cars are inherently dangerous—and this job gives him the opportunity to combine that concern with his engineering background. Much of his job involves reviewing the work of other engineers—design plans, proving grounds tests, crash studies—with an engineer's eye and then making sure NMC vehicles meet all industry and government safety requirements. He's proud to work for National Motor and proud of his record with the company, where he's developed a reputation as both a loyal employee and an advocate for vehicle safety.

One afternoon Angela Jackson, one of the company's internal auditors, calls Jesse and asks for an appointment right away. Auditors are responsible for reviewing whether other corporate departments are doing their work properly. Jackson has a particularly important job: She is one of National's auditors assigned to review engineering protocols that directly affect product safety. She occasionally reports informally to Jesse, mostly to keep him advised of ongoing safety-related issues that engineering is working on. On this occasion, though, Angela clearly has a more urgent matter.

Angela tells Jesse that she was doing a routine review of the model-year changes for the Luxor II, one of NMC's most popular cars. "So I sit in on a design engineering meeting where they're talking about the 'climatic problem,'" says Angela. "You know part of my job is to ask a lot of questions, so I'm asking, 'What climatic problem?' Well, here's the story." Angela repeats what she's learned: Recent controlled proving grounds tests for the new model changes have shown that under certain climatic conditions, defective brake fluid distribution systems can cause complete brake failure in all of the two million Luxor IIs on the road.

"I haven't seen *anything* on this," says Valencia, clearly upset. The thing he likes least is a safety issue he doesn't know about.

"I think they just found out and they're still writing the report," says Angela.

"Well, you'd better stay involved and get a memo directly to me. Put it in a 'magic report' in case this turns into a big deal, so we can control the situation." They both understand that a "magic report" is created specifically for NMC's legal department, so that the company can guard the information as an attorney-client confidential communication. "And Angela," concludes Valencia, "get on top of this from soup to nuts: likelihood and frequency of failure, cost of retrofit, the works. And do it quickly."

Within two weeks Jackson has followed the safety issue through the company's product line designers, climatic engineers, statisticians, cost analysis group, and actuarial department. She addresses her completed report with preliminary findings directly to Valencia as a memo, and puts CONFIDENTIAL—ATTORNEY-CLIENT COMMUNICATION on the cover sheet, as she'd been taught.

The report explains that between the estimates of the climate experts and statisticians, the chance of complete brake failure is slight but significant: enough to cause about one accident per every 120,000 vehicles per year, or approximately sixteen accidents annually. Partial brake failures were harder to estimate, except that they would be more frequent than complete failures. No one could compute precisely how many of these accidents would result in a fatality or serious injury, but everyone agreed that serious accidents would occur. The economic analysis was no less worrisome: an estimated repair cost of $145 per car, or $290 million for a complete recall. And the design team for the new model year hadn't yet gotten a "fix" in place for next year's cars.

As soon as he gets Angela's report, Jesse calls Buck Packard and asks for an emergency Vehicle Reliability Committee meeting. The next morning Jesse presents the situation to the VRC. He tells the committee members that he believes it's a "controlled situation," meaning that the only documentation is in the form of protected communications to Valencia as company attorney. But he makes his advice clear: "We must fix the new models to correct this problem, and as soon as we can get accurate verification on Jackson's numbers, we may have to recall these cars."

Three weeks later the VRC has its regular monthly meeting. The Luxor II brake problem is not on the agenda. Valencia asks Packard what's going on, and he's told that Packard has taken charge of the situation himself. "The data's not in yet," Packard tells

Jesse. "These things take time, so be patient." Two more VRC meetings go by without discussion of the Luxor II. Packard repeatedly tells Valencia the problem is "being dealt with," but Jesse is starting to feel that he's been taken out of the loop. He calls Angela Jackson to find out what she knows. Angela tells him that all she's heard is that her original estimates on both the number of accidents and the cost of repair were "very close."

By now Jesse is having serious concerns about what's being done. He hasn't heard a whisper of a Luxor II brake safety report, or seen anything on design changes for the new model year. The new models will be in dealer showrooms in two months, and sales are expected to average fifty thousand vehicles a month. And so far it looks as if the new vehicles will have the old brake defect.

·

About 10 percent of America's lawyers—80,000 to 100,000 of them—work "in-house," as both employees of their clients and as attorneys, providing these clients with a full range of legal services. These lawyers are in an unenviable position. They face pressures that even the lowest-ranking law firm associate never has to confront. Most feel they have far more in common with other corporate employees than with other lawyers—their pay, bonuses, stock options, and promotions are all determined directly by their client. They can never "fire" a client without quitting their job.

Even if Jesse Valencia is that rare lawyer who believes he has a moral obligation to protect innocent victims by disclosing the truth about his company's dangerous product, he will find it impossible to ignore the enormous costs of acting on this imperative. He will be fired. He will have great difficulty finding another job. His version of events will likely be denied by his employer and his former coworkers, and he will be called a liar. He may even face bar disciplinary charges for revealing the confidences and secrets of his client.

We saw in Chapter Three how outside lawyers hired by A. H. Robins stonewalled the efforts of plaintiffs to discover relevant documents about the defective Dalkon Shield intrauterine device. What happened within the walls of Robins's own corporate legal offices was even worse, according to Roger Tuttle, a Robins in-house lawyer who by the early 1980s had left to teach law—and legal ethics—at Oral Roberts University in Tulsa. In 1984, over Robins's attorneys' vehement objections and their efforts to get an injunction, Tuttle gave four days of sworn testimony in a deposition taken by plaintiffs' lawyers in Minnesota. The lawyers were trying to piece together how essential documents proving Robins's knowledge of the dangers of the Dalkon Shield had been concealed for over a decade.

In 1974 Robins had faced an increasing number of lawsuits and mounting evidence that women were being hurt and fetuses spontaneously aborted by the Dalkon Shield. In June 1974 Robins removed the device from the American market (though, incredibly, it continued for years to sell it abroad). Later that year the Food and Drug Administration held its first round of hearings on the safety of the Dalkon Shield. Early in 1975, according to his testimony, Tuttle received an extraordinary request from Robins's highest-ranking lawyer and Tuttle's boss, general counsel and corporate vice president William A. Forrest.

Forrest ordered Tuttle to oversee the destruction of "troublesome" documents—those that pointed to the dangers of the Dalkon Shield and to Robins's early knowledge of those dangers. Tuttle, in turn, not wanting to do the dirty work and as a "sop to my conscience," ordered his subordinates to do the job. They complied by destroying hundreds of documents in the forced-air furnace Robins used to burn contaminated drugs. Forrest and those acting under Tuttle's direction all categorically denied Tuttle's charges. Yet, given what else is known about Robins's sad behavior, it is difficult to believe that Tuttle would lie about his own complicity in such a serious cover-up. " 'Do it,' " Tuttle said Forrest told him, "and I saluted."

Had these documents become public, tens of thousands of women with the IUDs still in place would have learned of their danger, been able to remove them before further damage was done, and, of course, sue Robins. At his deposition, Tuttle was asked by the plaintiffs' lawyers about these women and what, if anything, was done to warn them. Nothing, he said, nor was anything disclosed to the FDA or a group of independent doctors who were then evaluating the IUD. To an extent Tuttle could have justified the destruction, because there was no outstanding discovery order requiring the production of these specific documents. Still, Tuttle admitted full responsibility at his deposition: He was well aware of the implications of the documents as evidence, and acknowledged that destroying them was both legally and morally wrong.

Why would a seemingly honest man, one with strong religious convictions, participate in a cover-up that harmed so many unsuspecting victims? Because, as he put it at his deposition, he "personally lacked the courage to throw down the gauntlet," knowing that his job was at stake. "[W]ith a wife and two young children, I'll have to confess to you that I lacked the courage to do then what I know today was the right thing."

Tuttle didn't forsake his morals entirely. Instead of destroying everything he was asked to, he selected the "most damaging of the documents" and saved copies, hiding them in the basement of his home. He turned these over at the time of his deposition. A few months later, all of the Minnesota Dalkon Shield cases were settled, in no small measure due to the information provided or corroborated by Roger Tuttle.

The efforts by Robins's attorneys to prevent Roger Tuttle's testimony were based on the theory that Tuttle had been a Robins lawyer and couldn't say anything about the document destruction because of his attorney-client relationship with his former employer. This argument rests on the idea that a corporation, though it's not an individual, has the same right to rely on the attorney-client privilege—its ability to keep confidential what it tells its lawyer—as any ordinary person. This is a vitally important concept to any corporation. If it can successfully argue that various internal communications were made *to its lawyers*, like the "magic report" Jackson wrote Valencia, a wide range of corporate sins—or at least the evidence of those sins—could be hidden behind the protection of the privilege.

The attorney-client privilege is hardly a new concept. Most commentators believe its origins go back to ancient Rome, where slaves doing their masters' business were prohibited by law from disclosing their masters' secrets. In Elizabethan England, the concept was refined to apply to clients who disclosed matters to those acting as attorneys. Until the beginning of the twentieth century, no one questioned that this privilege was personal—a matter of privacy available to protect the autonomy and dignity of the individual speaking in confidence. Confidential communications were entrusted by the individual to the lawyer acting as "fiduciary," or protector, of the client's secrets.

While there are strong historical and social bases for the individual's right to this privilege, these bases did not apply to corporations. The entire idea of a personal right to speak to a lawyer in strictest confidence simply doesn't fit the corporate model. Any information told a corporation lawyer is provided not by the company itself but by individuals, such as employees, or groups, like a board of directors, who speak on behalf of the corporation. But the "artificial, invisible, intangible" entity, as Chief Justice John Marshall described a corporation, would have to hold the privilege, not the individual who speaks to the lawyer.

How, then, did American corporations come to enjoy the right to an attorney-client privilege? Almost, it appears, by accident. In 1895 a Pennsylvania state court, without analyzing or even seriously considering the issue, said that the Pennsylvania Railroad was entitled to keep documents "within the privilege accorded to communications made to counsel." In 1915 the United States Supreme Court, while ruling on another issue, referred in passing to the attorney-client privilege in another case involving railroads, once America's most powerful institution. But just nine years earlier the Supreme Court had made it clear that corporations were *not* entitled to all the legal privileges of individuals, rejecting a corporation's claim that it was entitled to use the privilege against self-incrimination.

Not until 1963, relatively recent history, was a corporation's right to keep information confidential clearly established. Chicago federal judge William J. Campbell ruled in what is called the *Radiant Burners* case that corporations were *not* entitled to hold a privilege that was "historically and fundamentally personal in nature," something that could only "be claimed by natural individuals." Who, among all the corporate employees, Campbell wondered, would be able to claim that the privilege applied to them? And he pointed out other dangers: "Where corporations are involved, with their large number of agents, masses of documents and frequent dealings with lawyers, the zone of silence grows large." He felt that this zone of silence, and the temptation for corporations to "insulate all

RICHARD ZITRIN AND CAROL M. LANGFORD   101

their activities by discussing them with legal advisors," combined to interfere with the rights of anyone seeking information from a corporation.

The chief judge of the federal appeals court, John Hastings, did not share Judge Campbell's view of this risk. "Certainly," he wrote in overturning Campbell's decision, "the privilege would never be available to allow a corporation to funnel its papers and documents into the hands of its lawyers for custodial purposes and thereby avoid disclosure." Hastings, unfortunately, has been proven wrong by what has occurred since. When the Supreme Court, without ever directly addressing the issue, declined to review Hastings's opinion, it threw the door wide open for corporations to hide whatever secrets they could under the attorney-client privilege.

Nowhere has this protective shield been more widely and successfully used than in the tobacco industry. From the mid-1950s through the late 1990s tobacco companies compiled an extraordinary record of denying the public access to information on the dangerous and addictive properties of smoking, while at the same time claiming that no one had ever proven these dangers.

In order to deny litigants access to its research, the industry did its best to fight a war of attrition over every piece of discovery. "To paraphrase General Patton, the way we won these cases was not by spending all of Reynolds's money, but by making that other son of a bitch spend all of his," said R. J. Reynolds general counsel J. Michael Jordan to his fellow tobacco industry lawyers in 1988. But that technique alone was not enough. So the industry took pains to place all damaging documents—especially those relating to industry research projects—under the umbrella of the attorney-client privilege.

Sensitive documents should be "prepared . . . in anticipation of litigation" to be covered by the privilege, advised Brown & Williamson's in-house counsel J. Kendrick Wells. A 1979 Wells memo recommended routing all research projects through the company's lawyers in an effort to make all the information confidential attorney-client communications. Writing a memo to lawyers after the fact about a research project might make the *memo* privileged, without hiding the existence of the project itself. So, Wells wrote in 1984, "direct lawyer involvement is needed in all [company] activities pertaining to smoking and health, from conception through every step of the activity." In this way, the company could argue that the project's entire existence was protected from disclosure.

The tobacco companies perfected this technique. As early as 1968 the Washington, D.C., law firm of Arnold & Porter, working as outside counsel for tobacco interests, suggested a survey to prove that most Americans were already aware of the dangers of smoking. But in case the results came out the wrong way, the lawyers suggested that *they* directly commission and receive the survey. "Should the results prove unfavorable," said the memo, "there will be nothing in the [survey takers'] records to subpoena." The information would be harder to discover "if the survey were in an attorney's files."

Documents finally uncovered in a 1992 New Jersey case against four tobacco giants described the Council for Tobacco Research (CTR) and its "special projects" unit, supervised by lawyers rather than scientists. Lawyers were given decision-making authority over both the hiring and firing of scientific employees and the selection of research projects to be pursued. H. Lee Sarokin, the judge who presided over two New Jersey tobacco cases, quoted one CTR memo as acknowledging that it had been set up as "an industry 'shield' . . . a front," and another CTR participant as saying, "When we started CTR Special Projects, the idea was that the scientific director of CTR would review a project. If he liked it, it was a CTR special project. If he did not like it, then it became a lawyers' special project. . . . We wanted to protect it under the lawyers. We did not want it out in the open."

Five years after Judge Sarokin wrote his opinion, the floodgates of information finally opened. In December 1997 Minnesota judge Kenneth J. Fitzpatrick ordered the public release of 865 tobacco company documents that the industry had tried to hide behind the attorney-client privilege. Fitzpatrick charged Big Tobacco with a "conspiracy of silence and suppression of scientific research" by its improper claim that the research involved "communications between attorney and client." In late April 1998, after the Supreme Court refused to reverse Fitzpatrick's order, the House Commerce Committee released thirty-nine thousand formerly secret tobacco documents. A few days later the New York State Attorney General went to court to dissolve the nonprofit charter of the Council for Tobacco Research on the grounds it was a fraudulent tobacco front, not an independent research institute. By early May the tobacco defendants had settled the Minnesota case for $6.6 billion.

Overseeing Big Tobacco's efforts, pulling the strings from its secret sanctum sanctorum, according to several lawyers and scientists interviewed for a June 1998 *Business Week* article, was the Committee of Counsel, which began life in 1958 as a group of lawyers known as the "Secret Six" before growing to well over a dozen in-house and outside tobacco attorneys. The committee has been accused by many health advocates of essentially running the industry, reporting directly to each company's president, and institutionalizing the industry's opposition to researching safer cigarettes.

The documents disclosed in Minnesota and Washington lend strong support to these contentions. According to the committee's own minutes, the group's lawyers understood that the rule was "advocacy primary and science secondary." It was to this committee that Arnold & Porter made its secret survey suggestion. And when the industry faced a demand in 1981 from the federal Department of Health and Human Services to provide a list of cigarette ingredients, the Kansas City law firm of Shook, Hardy & Bacon, which held a seat on the committee, recommended that the industry test whether any particular additive caused "adverse results" and then "remove the additive, and destroy the data."

Other documents reveal how scientists routinely sought approval from lawyers for research requests—and amended them as counsel required. Some projects were simply vetoed by the attorneys, such as a study of how tobacco damages a body cell's genetic structure, because the results might help the "other side" or the "enemy." Lawyers suppressed a mid-1970s research effort of a scientist who believed he had found a way to remove carbon monoxide from cigarettes. And as far back as 1953 lawyers prevented circulation of a "volume of material which 'indicted' cigarette smoking" as unhealthy. As Minnesota attorney general Hubert H. Humphrey III concluded, "Tobacco lawyers, not scientists, were the gatekeepers controlling research on smoking and health."

.

Merely including lawyers in business matters isn't enough to create an attorney-client privilege unless the lawyers are actually giving *legal* advice. But that doesn't prevent companies from trying. Often just the company's *claim* of the attorney-client privilege is enough for the other side to fold rather than fight the issue at great length and expense. This makes the mere claim of privilege another weapon in discovery wars of attrition.

Once it became firmly established in the *Radiant Burners* case, the corporate attorney-client privilege gradually broadened. A 1970 case decided that the privilege applied to almost every corporate employee whose discussion with the lawyer concerned legal advice on corporate affairs. That same year, a Washington, D.C., federal court held that the minutes of a hospital's meetings investigating the death of a patient could remain confidential so that the hospital would feel free to conduct a candid inquiry.

Finally, in 1981, the Supreme Court spoke. The federal government was investigating possible illegal payments by Upjohn, the drug company, to foreign governments. Upjohn had its general counsel's office conduct an internal investigation. The lawyers interviewed and reviewed questionnaires from Upjohn employees around the world. The government subpoenaed the investigation files. But Upjohn argued that even low-level employees far removed from the group that ran the company could be protected by the attorney-client umbrella *if* they communicated with the company's lawyers about "actions within the scope of their employment." The Supreme Court agreed, extending the corporate privilege to *all* employees who learn things during their work that the corporate lawyers need to know.

Since the *Upjohn* case, some in-house counsel have sought to broaden corporate confidentiality even more. While courts haven't all agreed, these ideas have gained a foothold. "Document retention policies" have been developed by many corporations, ostensibly to provide guidelines for how long old documents must be kept. Too often, though, these retention policies serve instead as tools for the destruction of documents that show wrongdoing. Limiting the time documents must be retained is particularly self-serving for those companies whose products have a long incubation period before they do harm, such as cigarettes and asbestos.

Another relatively new concept is a corporate "self-evaluative privilege" that would apply when a company undertakes a "self-audit," or a voluntary review and analysis of its own behavior. Supposedly these self-audits are conducted for the purpose of improving corporate behavior. The theory behind keeping them confidential is that they foster a free flow of candid information about corporate behavior and, ultimately, corporate compliance with required standards. But such a privilege would enable corporations to hide their bad acts behind these self-audits. And there's not that large a gulf between protecting self-audits and claiming that the proving grounds safety and crash tests conducted by an auto company's engineers fall under the self-evaluation umbrella.

The extent of corporate attorney-client confidentiality is important not just because it defines what a lawyer can protect in litigation. It also directly affects the situation confronting Jesse Valencia: What should a lawyer do when it comes to telling the truth about his corporation's dangerous product? The answer to this question, according to the American Bar Association Model Rules of Professional Conduct approved in 1983, is that in-house corporate counsel have much less leeway to prevent their employers from hurting the public than criminal defense lawyers have to stop a client about to commit a dangerous crime.

The ABA's rule governing individual clients says that an attorney is released from the bonds of confidentiality when the lawyer reasonably believes it is necessary to reveal information in order to prevent a client from committing a crime "likely to result in imminent death or substantial bodily harm." But the rule for corporate attorneys gives them a much more complicated course to follow: If a lawyer believes the company is violating the law in a way that could cause "substantial injury to the *organization*," counsel "shall proceed as is reasonably necessary in the best interest of the organization." But the best interests of the organization—including making a profit or increasing stock value—often bear little relationship to the best interests of society.

In its rule commentary the ABA tells corporate lawyers to pay attention to other rules, including the general rule on confidentiality and its exceptions. But the corporate rule is set up to make whistle-blowing a virtual impossibility, even in cases of the most egregious and dangerous conduct. Attorneys may ask that the dangerous situation be reevaluated or that a separate legal opinion be obtained. In particularly serious cases, lawyers can refer the issue to "higher authority in the organization." But "any measures taken shall be designed to minimize disruption of the organization and the risk of revealing information to persons outside the organization." In other words, whatever happens, knowledge of the danger will never leave the company's four walls.

If, as seems likely, the lawyer's efforts fail to change the corporation's position, then—and only then—may the lawyer move to the ultimate "remedy," which is to resign. The problem, of course, is that while this resignation may be the ultimate act for the lawyer-employee, it is meaningless to the outside world. Regulatory agencies and the public are left completely in the dark. At least, as Hofstra University ethics professor Monroe Freedman has pointed out, the lawyer for an individual who is in the course of committing a crime can withdraw from the case right away. Meanwhile, the corporate lawyer is spending months asking for reconsideration, another opinion, and higher authority while "the criminal and fraudulent activity continues unabated."

How did the American Bar Association rules come to such a state of affairs? According to a number of law professors who have examined the issue, it came down to politics. When the ABA's Kutak Commission, named after its chair, Omaha attorney Robert Kutak, rewrote the ethics rules in 1980, the first draft of the corporate rule said that if the corporation's "highest authority" refused to act legally, the lawyer could "disclos[e] client confidences to the extent necessary." Corporate lawyers screamed their objections.

Fifteen months later, under pressure from these corporate counsel, the Kutak Commission drafted a second version of the rule. This "first final draft" also allowed for the possibility of corporate counsel blowing the whistle, but was significantly watered down. It no longer mentioned "disclosing client confidences," but instead made only vague reference to the possibility of "revealing information relating to the representation." This information could be revealed only if the attorney believed that "the highest authority" had acted to further its own "personal or financial interests." The issue of a corporate cover-up of a dangerous condition was simply not addressed.

But even this was not acceptable to the organized corporate bar, which took the position that unless there was *no* mention of even the possibility of whistle-blowing, these lawyers would vote against the entire new set of rules. Kutak and his allies were fighting a battle already lost. The final draft of the corporate counsel rule was virtually turned inside out, from being consumer-protective to one that strained to shield organizational wrongdoing.

In 1982 the European Court of Justice decided that no European Community country could allow in-house lawyers to maintain confidential communications with their employers. This rule respected the laws of Italy, France, Belgium, and Luxembourg, which do not permit in-house attorneys even to be members of the bar, because they consider it impossible for them to be both employees and independent, objective lawyers.

In contrast, in 1981 the United States, through the *Upjohn* case, moved in the opposite direction. The corporate attorney-client privilege, seemingly fashioned out of whole cloth, had established itself in the nation's highest court. And by 1983, thanks to the lobbying efforts of corporate counsel, the ABA, the country's largest, most powerful group of lawyers, had made corporate attorney-client protections even stronger than those given to criminal defendants under the Constitution.

What is the consequence of a corporate attorney-client privilege that knows virtually no limits? Take the saga of the Ford Pinto. The Pinto was an inexpensive subcompact car developed in the late 1960s, designed to be made cheaply and sold cheaply. It met those goals, but in one respect the Pinto was too cheap: It had a gas tank that was not sufficiently protected in rear-end accidents. A rear-end impact could pierce the tank at speeds as low as 21 miles per hour, allowing a gasoline leak that any spark could ignite into a fire or explosion.

Pinto engineers had known of the gas tank problem since 1968, and Ford officials had debated what to do since 1970. Ford general counsel working with the Pinto and involved in reviewing the company documents "definitely knew" about the situation, according to one Ford executive. Yet despite estimates that a gas tank repair would cost only $5 to $11 per car, Ford did nothing to recall cars already on the road or to build a safer system. In fact, they did just the opposite: In 1970 and 1971 Ford officials set out to convince the National Highway Traffic Safety Administration (NHTSA) to postpone its proposed minimum safety standards, including those on fuel tank safety. They succeeded; in 1973, NHTSA ruled that the new standards would not go into effect until 1977. Thus not only did Ford fail to fix its existing vehicles, but it continued producing Pintos without adequate firewall protection right up until the 1977 models, when the NHTSA regulations went into effect.

By 1977, though, word of the Pinto's problems had managed to surface. A *Mother Jones* magazine article about the defective gas tanks caused a large stir. In the case of Richard Grimshaw, who had been horribly burned at age thirteen in a 1972 California crash, the boy's lawyers discovered an extraordinary document. Ford officials had written a report computing the "costs and benefits" of improving gas tank safety.

At $11 per car for 12.5 million vehicles, the report predicted that it would be far more costly to fix the problem than to leave the defective gas tanks in place and pay the burn victims and the families of those who died. Ford estimated that failure to add a safety device would result in 180 deaths and 180 serious burn cases. Valuing deaths at $200,000 each and burns at $67,000, Ford figured it would pay out roughly $50 million, much less than the $137 million cost of fixing the gas tanks. Early in 1978 a jury awarded Richard Grimshaw $125 million in punitive damages alone—an amount the jury thought would be enough to teach Ford a lesson, and quite close to the total cost of correcting the defect.

Although the trial judge set aside all but a few million dollars of the punitive damages award, the *Grimshaw* case and the cost-benefit memo shocked the public into a new awareness of the automotive industry. Many people at Ford had been in a position to blow the whistle on Ford's refusal to fix its faulty gas tanks: engineers, internal safety board members, high-level executives, *and* lawyers.

The Pinto case thus became a cause célèbre in legal circles as well as in Detroit. Some justified Ford's actions, noting that everybody, from armies to governments to most industries, puts a cost on human life. University of California, Los Angeles law professor Gary T. Schwartz argued that cars, like power lawn mowers, airplanes, or even ladders and knives, are inherently dangerous products. No car, said Schwartz, was perfectly safe, and consumers pay for safety. The Pinto, an inexpensive car, was never expected to be the safest.

But as Professor David Luban wrote, "[T]he Pinto did not represent a safety-versus-price trade-off. It represented a blunder." Luban, a philosopher who is on the law faculty at Georgetown, was right: The Pinto cost-benefit report measured not safety versus price but the cost of recalling a car that had known, unintended safety defects.

Luban pointedly focused on Ford's lawyers: Setting aside any duty Ford's engineers and executives might have had to "blow the whistle" on the defective car, what was the obligation of Ford's in-house counsel? He concluded that once the lawyers had failed to convince Ford to change its course, they "should have alerted the public to the menace of the Pinto." Why lawyers rather than other responsible executives or scientists? "Ask not with whom the buck stops," wrote Luban, "it stops with thee."

To encourage those who might find themselves in a situation like Jesse Valencia's, Luban argued that the ABA rules would allow for "preventive whistle-blowing" in the Pinto case. But this argument is a tough sell. First, the rule requires that a *criminal* act be prevented, though Luban found this irrelevant from a moral standpoint: "It is the actions themselves rather than their legal classification that give rise to the need for whistle-blowing."

Second, the rule requires that the act result in *imminent* death or bodily harm. Here corporations are given another layer of protection. A criminal defendant threatening to kill a witness, or an angry divorce client who threatens to kill a spouse, signals that there's danger of an imminent but by no means inevitable harm. The lawyer might dissuade the client, or the client may simply calm down. But for Jesse Valencia, while the harm caused by the Luxor II defect is not imminent—it may be weeks or even a month before climatic conditions cause a brake failure—it is inevitable. This results in a rule that, in Professor Freedman's words, "gives significantly broader protection to the confidences and secrets of corporate clients than to those of unincorporated individuals."

Clearly lawyers are but one cog in the corporate wheel. Where a corporation sells a dangerous product, almost always some company scientists, designers, safety analysts, and senior executives will know. They too have the ability either to convince the corporation to fix the problem or to blow the whistle if necessary. Most modern corporations have developed staffs of internal auditors like Angela Jackson, whose job includes doing an honest evaluation of the dangers of company products. Auditors, many of whom are designated the corporate "ethics officer," are no higher than middle management in rank, giving them little power to convince higher-ups to change their way of doing business. If auditors are not themselves the ethics officers, they often report to a separate ethics officer who is also an attorney in the corporate law department; that makes their report of wrongdoing arguably privileged information.

Neither proving grounds engineers, nor internal auditors, nor staff attorneys in the office of general counsel are likely to feel anything less than extreme pressure should they even think about blowing the whistle on their employer. The stakes are very high—loss of job, and often loss of career. But there are ways to help them. "You *can* legislate morality," says Michael Josephson, a lawyer who heads a nonprofit ethics institute that works with businesses, lawyers, government agencies, and the press. Indeed, in the last twenty years, there has been an enormous increase in both regulations and benefits designed to motivate corporations to do the right thing.

Many corporations face increasingly stringent governmental oversight. Companies in a number of industries, such as banking, must file compliance certificates, which affirm that there are no violations of law. Often these certificates must be filed by the person at the top, the CEO. NHTSA safety requirements have been stiffened several times since the days of the Pinto, and proof of compliance, not just paperwork, is required. Perhaps the most stringent compliance rules are those that regulate companies creating pollution or disposing of toxic waste. An entire area of practice that barely existed a generation ago, environmental law, has developed around these standards.

Companies caught violating governmental regulations are subject to civil lawsuits and, increasingly, criminal penalties that can include large fines. In 1991 the federal government approved the Organizational Sentencing Guidelines, which determine how corporate criminal penalties should be measured. The guidelines work like a criminal defendant's rap sheet. "Points" are added and penalties go up for a company's bad behavior: prior offenses, violations of injunctions, or high-level approval of illegal behavior. But points can be subtracted for a company's good efforts. If companies accept responsibility and report their own violations, they pay lower fines. If they have an effective compliance program in place—one that prevents and uncovers violations of law—they get lighter sentences. These mitigating sentencing "points" can be used by in-house counsel to encourage their employers to disclose their own mistakes.

The increased regulation and the sentencing guidelines have led to an explosion in the number of companies that have ethics officers. According to a 1992 survey, about a third of these are higher-level in-house counsel. A corporate Ethics Officers Association, created in 1992, is growing quickly, as is the association of internal auditors. People like Michael Josephson have been called in to do independent "ethics audits," creating ethics plans and committees, doing training programs on how to behave ethically, and even in some cases setting up confidential whistle-blowing hot lines. Many ethics officers have taken on another job—"compliance officer," the person whose job it is to make sure that government regulations are met.

According to Josephson, though, compliance is the easy issue, while ethics asks a tougher question: "What does virtue require of us?" It is clearly part of a lawyer's job to advise a client of the moral costs of the client's behavior. Josephson argues that in-house counsel should advise a corporation that virtue is its own reward. Some corporate decision makers will be sympathetic to this message. For others, it's a matter of the carrot and the stick: While regulation forces compliance, an increasing number of "good-guy" corporate awards have been designed to give virtue a helping hand by encouraging businesses to be socially responsible. The payoff is their public image.

It can be difficult to measure a good public image against the bottom line. But a corporate general counsel looking to convince a company to behave responsibly can use both good-guy awards and bad-guy sanctions—governmental punishment and the potential for bad publicity—as persuasive ammunition. If the public cares about a corporation's behavior—Nike, Guess?, and Kathie Lee Gifford's apparel lines are well-known examples—corporations will sit up and take notice. The Environmental Protection Agency also uses publicity: an annual "Toxics Release Inventory," available both online and in hard copy, is widely credited for increasing corporate compliance. Encouraged, the EPA in 1997 announced plans to make public the pollution emissions profiles of hundreds of factories in the oil, metals, auto, and paper industries.

In-house counsel can also argue that the true cost of hiding the truth, especially about dangerous products, is far higher than many corporate executives estimate. Business public relations expert James E. Lukaszewski manages "litigation visibility." His view is that the less visibility, the better. That means it's almost always in a company's best interests to settle cases quickly. But Lukaszewski also urges corporations to adopt strategies that reduce the risk of litigation: acting quickly to help victims, speaking with compassion and being "neighborly," and taking the long view by recognizing that "organizations are usually guilty of something." Most of these ideas come down to the straightforward notion of taking responsibility.

For Jesse Valencia, the issue is ultimately the same: taking responsibility. Merely advising corporate higher-ups to recall the Luxor II may result in Valencia's dismissal. If it doesn't, Valencia, having made all his arguments and seen them fail, will have few options. If he decides to go public, he will have little in the way of a safety net.

Many states now have statutes that protect whistle-blowers, allowing them to sue their companies for "retaliatory discharge," or being fired for speaking out about corporate concealments or dangerous conduct. But in-house lawyers remain bound by the attorney-client privilege and the narrow exceptions to the rule of confidentiality. In most states it's unclear to what extent whistle-blowing statutes apply to lawyers. And there is a second, catch-22 problem: Even where lawyers might be allowed to leak enough information to protect the public, they, unlike other employees, can't sue for retaliatory discharge if their suit requires them to reveal *additional* confidential information, either to prove they were justified in speaking out or that speaking out was the true reason they were fired.

Donald J. Willy was an in-house attorney for Coastal Corporation in Texas who said he was fired in 1984 for refusing to make false statements in environmental audits and for advocating stronger corporate environmental cleanup measures. Willy went to federal court, which said he had no right to sue for retaliatory discharge. He took his case to state court in Texas, where a judge awarded him $500,000. But a Texas Court of Appeals decision in 1996, twelve years after his termination, gave Willy his catch-22: He could sue for retaliatory discharge, but only if he could do it without violating his oath of confidentiality to Coastal. The appeals court found that he couldn't make his case without revealing confidences, and reversed his award.

In 1991 Massachusetts attorney Jefferson Davis Stewart III was fired as in-house counsel for GTE's lighting subsidiaries for what he says was an effort to persuade management that the companies needed to issue public safety warnings about certain dangerous products and deal properly with toxic wastes. That same year California lawyer Andrew Rose was fired from General Dynamics Corporation after thirteen years because, he said, he called attention to a number of improper and illegal practices of his employer. Both states' highest courts sided with the lawyers, at least in theory, deciding that they could sue for retaliatory discharge. After all, as the Massachusetts court put it, the fact that the employee is a lawyer "does not diminish the public interest" in being safe. But both courts then presented the attorneys with the same catch-22: Their usual duty of confidentiality to their client/employers was un-changed, and they would not be allowed to prove their cases by using privileged information. Only New Jersey treats in-house lawyers in the same way as any other whistle-blowing employee.

Ironically, this leaves in-house corporate counsel, whose clients have scant historical grounds for confidentiality, with a most diffi-cult path to follow in order to disclose even grave wrongdoing. In contrast, criminal defense lawyers, whose clients' claims of confi-dentiality are unquestioned, long-standing, and well documented, have the clear ability to expose any serious future harm threatened by their clients. A 1994 survey of New Jersey lawyers, most of whom practiced in the volatile areas of criminal defense and domestic rela-tions, discloses a further irony: Unlike their brothers and sisters in the corporate bar, lawyers for individuals are overwhelmingly will-ing to strongly dissuade their clients from acting wrongfully *and* are successful at doing so. For corporate counsel, as the Willy, Rose, and Stewart cases show, the mere effort to dissuade the client may well be enough to get the lawyer fired.

Eighty-eight percent of the lawyers surveyed in New Jersey said they would disclose information to save someone from death or se-rious injury. But these attorneys were considering particular harms to particular people. When a client says, "I'm going to kill that wit-ness," or "My ex-wife is really going to get it this time," the threat-ened harm is not only substantial but *personal*. When a corporation continues to conduct business in a way that will inevitably injure or even kill scores of people, the harm remains abstract—anonymous people being harmed by anonymous, unspecified events. That ab-straction, coupled with the dire consequences for in-house counsel who have the temerity to speak out, may explain why more corpo-rate counsel don't put themselves at risk.

The New Jersey survey confirmed that almost all the lawyers who had found it necessary to disclose their client's conduct to save someone from harm did so *not* because of their state's unusually broad ethics rule, but because of their personal responsibility to a victim who had both a face and a name. The fact that a specific vic-tim is not known creates an understandable emotional distance. But if anything, harm to anonymous victims of defective products is far more likely than to the intended victim of an individual who may, at the last moment, relent.

After seeing A. H. Robins and its attorneys hide the Dalkon Shield's defects for years, Miles W. Lord, the federal judge who presided over two hundred Minnesota cases involving the dangerous IUD, gave a speech to his local Council of Churches in which he graphically confronted the issue of corporate conscience. "In the olden days," intoned Judge Lord, "if you killed somebody, if you produced something that would hurt somebody, you were stopped. . . . Not today. Today we have cost-benefit analysis, [but] when you put a price on the priceless, all is lost." Lord appreciated the irony that society applauds the efforts to "crack down on criminals who are making our country a less safe place" while we use a different standard to measure corporate criminality that can be even more harmful. "Almost any corporate president or official would walk miles to help a little child who is hungry or injured," said Lord. "But he or she could then walk back to the office and approve a plan that would dump tons of poison into the drinking water of that same child."

Lawyers—officers of the court, as they often describe themselves—should and must do better than that, even at the risk of their own jobs. And the public should be able to expect more. How much more? Michael Josephson would hold lawyers to the standard a son demands of his father in Arthur Miller's play *All My Sons*. The father is one of those responsible for putting defective airplanes in the air during the war. He pleads with his surviving son that he was no worse than half the country. "Why am *I* bad?" the father implores. "*I* know you're no worse than most men," says the son, "but I thought you were better."

Epilogue:
Blowing the Whistle

With only six weeks to go until the new model year, at Jesse Valencia's insistence, Buck Packard agreed to put the Luxor II brake safety issue on the next Vehicle Reliability Committee agenda. At the VRC meeting a week later, Packard distributed a one-page summary report from a specially appointed Luxor II subcommittee. The report did not refer to Angela Jackson's memo or cite any other statistics, but instead referred vaguely to the subcommittee's "thorough evaluation."

"After careful consideration," the report read, "we have determined that the danger of brake failure accidents is not substantial, and that no recall is required. We understand that an in-service fix will be available three months into the new model year. While the brake condition clearly does not warrant holding up the new model year, the fix can be implemented in vehicle assembly as soon as it is ready for in-service application."

Valencia was furious. This was all news to him; he had never even heard of the subcommittee, and it certainly sounded as if there was no new statistical evidence. He asked Packard directly whether Jackson's estimates had been proven wrong, and Buck replied that "that's no longer the issue." Jesse demanded that the full committee reconsider the subcommittee's report, only to be told by Packard that the subcommittee, with the VRC's blessing, had already submitted its findings straight to the board of directors.

That night it seemed to Jesse that it was time to consider taking this issue himself to the corporation's highest authority, the board. Before doing anything, though, he went to see chief general counsel Theodore Vandiver the next morning to seek his advice. He held Vandiver in high esteem—a mentor who had recommended him for the VRC position and had always encouraged his strong belief in safety. To his surprise, Vandiver seemed to know all about the Luxor brake problems. "Look, Jesse," Vandiver told him. "The train has left the station on this one; the decision's made. Let it be and they'll fix it as soon as they can."

Valencia agonized for three more days before sending his own report to the board. He began it by saying, "I consider it my duty to you, my client, to make sure you have all essential information relating to a seriously dangerous condition in one of our vehicles." He included his own narrative and a copy of Angela Jackson's memo. He closed with a recommendation that the board act "to prevent further harm to the public and to National Motor by retrofitting and/or recalling all Luxor IIs to ensure the safety of our products." The next day Jesse Valencia was fired.

For several weeks Valencia debated filing a retaliatory discharge suit against NMC, but finally he decided against it. He knew the uphill fight he would face. Not only had his state's courts never allowed such a suit by an in-house attorney, but he would have to use confidential information to prove his case—information that he himself was responsible for making confidential when he told Angela Jackson to write him a "magic report."

Three months later, on the train to his new office, where he had opened up his own practice, Jesse read a newspaper story about a major accident on the interstate, apparently caused when an NMC Luxor II slammed into several other vehicles. The Luxor driver claimed to have totally lost her brakes. One person was dead and four more were in the hospital. That night's TV coverage had pictures of the accident and an interview with the distraught Luxor driver. The following day Jesse did something he'd been thinking about for some time: He sent his board memo and Angela's "magic report" to the National Highway Traffic Safety Administration, with a cover letter stating where he could be reached.

A year later he'd been subpoenaed by plaintiffs' lawyers in eighteen Luxor II cases. He'd had to hire his own attorney to help determine whether he could, or should, testify. His efforts to start his own private practice were a shambles. And NMC had filed a disciplinary charge against him for violating client confidences.

PART THREE

GREED AND DECEIT, OR "EVERYBODY'S DOING IT"

The adversary system is not the exclusive domain of large, powerful law firms and moneyed corporations any more than it is the private property of the criminal defense lawyer. Practitioners who work in small firms—plaintiffs' personal injury lawyers, employment rights advocates, and attorneys who represent small businesses, tenants, and parties in domestic cases—all operate by the "adversary theorem", and use it to their own advantage. Many who view themselves as Davids battling Goliath see the adversary theorem as a way to level an uneven battlefield. While powerful firms can use their superior resources to great effect in the adversary contest, there are many tactics that any lawyer can use on an equal opportunity basis.

In trial, lawyers of all stripes have the chance to try their most imaginative courtroom tactics. Insurance lawyers from both sides swarm around accident scenes like bees to honey. More ominously, opposing lawyers make secret deals to conceal dangerous conditions caused by one side in return for the other side's silence—all to the public's detriment. And any lawyer willing to do so can lie or mislead on behalf of a client, or even assist the client's fraud, while pointing to the adversary theorem as a defense. Davids and Goliaths even engage in collusive settlements, some of which benefit the lawyers on both sides far more than the clients. "Everybody's doing it" is hardly an excuse, but unfortunately, it's too often offered as a justification.

CHAPTER 6

Insurance Lawyers:
Chasing Ambulances and
Chasing Money

Everybody else in America solicits business without shame. So do I.
> —Richard French, Ohio personal injury attorney

I consider this emotional rape. My profession is better than that.
> —Attorney Richard Kessler, who lost his wife in a
> 1996 plane crash, commenting on the solicitations
> he received from lawyers right after the crash

I'm usually there *before* the ambulance.
> —Melvin Belli, after being accused of
> being an ambulance chaser

Attorney Sam Hammond does not have the best reputation among the other lawyers in Highland City. It is hard to tell whether this is because of the "undignified" way in which he gets his cases or simple jealousy. Sam has made a great deal of money as a plaintiffs' personal injury attorney. He advertises extensively on late-night TV, telling his audience that there's "no case too big, no case too small, for Sam Hammond to handle." He runs large display ads in every yellow pages in the metropolitan area, and even has an Internet home page and a full-time law clerk who surfs the Net looking for potential cases.

Most of his cases are small ones—fender benders and slip-and-falls in supermarkets or retail stores. But the plaintiffs in these cases are unlikely to ever see Hammond himself after their first trip to his office. Client intake will be turned over to a paralegal, and the case assigned to one of Hammond's fleet of young associates.

He gets his share of big cases, too, usually in bus and airplane crashes, where his "investigators" have been known to get to the accident scene before the police. When asked why he engages in ambulance chasing, Sam vociferously defends himself, arguing that he "helps victims get the money they deserve." He contends that he's "the only check on big insurance companies screwing the little guy. They know I'll be there to teach them a lesson."

Insurance adjusters unanimously see Hammond as a shameless huckster after nothing but money. When Hammond lands a big case and handles it himself, he can be a formidable foe, and insurance companies consider him the bane of their existence. So when there's a mass transit accident or a multicar crash on the interstate with serious injuries, the insurers will try every means possible to get to the victims before he does. On the smaller cases, though, they'd just as soon face Hammond's firm as most others, since his associates have a reputation for settling these claims without ever filing a complaint in court. That saves the law firm a great deal of time but nets the clients a lot less money—hardly the "lesson" Hammond claims he wants to teach the insurance industry.

•

More lawsuits are filed per capita in the United States than in any other country on earth. While best estimates show that personal injury and other tort cases are but a small fraction of the total, and less than 10 percent of the civil cases filed, these lawsuits have become a focus of public and media attention. Some people are repelled by lawyers swarming around airline crashes or toxic accidents like gnats on a summer evening. Others are offended by late-night TV ads that look more like used-car sales pitches than offers of public service from highly educated professionals. Still others, protesting what they feel are unjust verdicts, from whiplash cases to suits involving elderly women burned by hot coffee, have taken up the banner of "tort reform," where the loser pays for the costs of suit, "pain and suffering" recoveries are limited, and contingency fees are substantially reduced.

All these people have one thing in common: They are sick of the American system of tort litigation, and they want to see it change. But the stereotypical image of the ambulance chaser is just the beginning, not the end, of the story.

Ambulance chasers exist; of that there is little doubt, though in fact they may be as likely to get their cases by cultivating hospital personnel, funeral home directors, and tow truck drivers. The term itself dates from the turn of the last century, when the car whiplash cases of today were more likely to be claims of "railway spine," the injury allegedly caused by the sudden movement of trains. Stories of sleazy plaintiffs' lawyers and their disreputable clients include one woman capable of dislocating her bones and hemorrhaging at will and another who made so many claims in the early 1900s for slips on a banana peel that she earned the moniker "Banana Anna." The hardships of the Great Depression brought people willing to mutilate themselves, even to the point of "accidental" amputation.

Rings of accident fakers and injury chasers operate on a far more sophisticated level today. A 1997 Brooklyn grand jury indicted eight lawyers, two physicians, three medics, and four ambulance-chasing henchmen in the lawyers' employ. The ring was caught in part because one of its members had posted a $200 reward for each referral on an on-line bulletin board for paramedics. The Brooklyn bar reacted by saying all personal injury lawyers do it; those arrested were not even "small fish," but "guppies."

Today, "ambulance chaser" has a different meaning than when the term was coined. The term was originally a disparagement based on elitism and ethnic stereotype. The law has long been the province of the elite. In thirteenth-century England, the Inns of Court began as places where wealthy young men could learn the law and practice their profession as a public service. Fees were honoraria, given voluntarily by grateful clients. In the States, lawyers were willing enough to collect fees, but the elitist attitude remained well into the twentieth century. The American Bar Association, formed in 1878, limited its membership, in the words of one of its founders, to "leading men or those of high promise."

Powerful Philadelphia lawyer Henry Drinker personified the racism and elitism of the organized bar of a hundred years ago. Drinker felt so threatened by the idea that lawyers would lose professional status through creeping diversity—such as "Russian Jew boys" and other riffraff "up out of the gutter" invading the province of gentlemen—that he took matters into his own hands. As chair of the ABA Committee on Professional Ethics for over a decade, he became a leading advocate of the Pennsylvania Preceptor Plan, a program designed to keep the bar clean by denying membership to lawyers from different ethnic backgrounds and lower social strata.

Overall, this plan worked rather well, though in 1912 the ABA inadvertently conferred membership on three black lawyers. Prodded by a few of its more enlightened members, the group was persuaded not to rescind the three memberships when it learned of its "mistake," but merely to make sure it didn't happen again. The ABA quickly passed a resolution stating that "the settled practice of the Association has been to elect only white men as members."

In 1908, the year its first ethics code was drafted as thirty-two canons of conduct, the ABA was thus a "professional protective organization" that existed to "preserve its own exclusiveness," according to legal historian Jerold S. Auerbach. Its members were more interested in protecting lawyers who represented moneyed interests than the millions who formed the constituency for the progressive politicians of the time. The stimulus for the ABA's canons came less from a desire to control the conduct of its members than from a speech critical of the profession given at Harvard in 1905 by the country's number-one progressive, President Theodore Roosevelt. Roosevelt criticized corporate lawyers who made their living advising clients on ways to evade regulatory control. But the ABA's canons more closely reflected the concerns of wealthy "gentlemen" practitioners than the views of the president or his constituency.

Several early canons addressed issues such as advertising, soliciting cases, and fees. In part, these regulations were needed to control the free-for-all mentality in which lawyers could do anything to "buy" a case. But these regulations stemmed more from the fact that the organized bar, mostly lawyers whose client base emanated from their social and big-business connections, wanted to restrict other lawyers who had to hustle for business. This ensured that the balance of power in the profession remained securely in the hands of those who had held it throughout most of the nineteenth century.

Canon 28 of the 1908 ABA canons reflects this dual purpose:

> It is unprofessional for a lawyer to volunteer advice to bring a lawsuit. . . . Stirring up strife and litigation is not only unprofessional, but it is indictable at common law. It is disreputable to hunt up defects in titles or other causes of action and inform thereof in order to be employed to bring suit or collect judgment, or to breed litigation by seeking out those with claims for personal injuries or those having any other grounds of action in order to secure them as clients, or to employ agents or runners for like purposes.

Those left out of the ABA had limited alternatives. Organizations like St. Louis's predominantly African-American Mound City Bar Association, founded in 1922, gave minority lawyers a home of their own. Since most avenues of corporate practice were not open to those excluded from the ABA and similarly "elite" local organizations, personal injury became one of the staples of these small-firm, independent lawyers.

Soliciting cases through contacts within their community was part of the job for many personal injury lawyers of all ethnic stripes. This solicitation was difficult for bar associations to detect, prove, and punish. But bans on advertising—far easier to identify, and much easier to prevent—were much more successful. Lawyer ads came to a virtual halt for the first three-quarters of the century.

The advertising ban reached its extremes in the late 1960s and early 1970s, corresponding, interestingly enough, with the rise of the consumer movement. When the California bar suspended Melvin Belli for thirty days for the offense of "self-aggrandizing" after he was profiled in one of Dewar's celebrity ads for its scotch, many felt he was being singled out because of his high-profile personal injury practice. When Jacoby & Meyers was reprimanded by the bar for calling itself a "legal clinic" instead of a law firm, the courts rejected the sanction, noting that "clinic" was actually a more accurate description than "law firm."

Finally, in 1977, the United States Supreme Court held that

Arizona's Legal Clinic of Bates & O'Steen could publish its fee schedule in the local newspaper because the ad was constitutionally protected commercial free speech. Describing antiadvertising regulation as an "anachronism" and a "rule of etiquette," not ethics, Justice Harry Blackmun wrote that "the historical foundation for the advertising restraint has crumbled." Though Blackmun tempered his decision by saying that "false, deceptive, or misleading" advertising could still be punished, the advertising floodgates opened.

It seemed to matter little that the Bates & O'Steen ad was pristine—the scales of justice accompanying a straightforward fee schedule ("Change of Name—$95.00 plus $20.00 court filing fee"). Nor did it matter that the very next year, the Supreme Court upheld the indefinite suspension of Albert Ohralik, an Ohio lawyer who signed up two teenage girls to personal injury contingency fee contracts, the first one by going to her hospital room while she was still in traction, and the second by pressuring her with the decision of the first and refusing to let her change her mind the very next day.

None of this history of regulation, even if it involves the worst elitism or even racism, excuses the egregious conduct of personal injury lawyers who take advantage of injured people and their families at times when they are most vulnerable. The 1996 crashes of ValuJet Flight 592 and TWA Flight 800 brought out the worst in ambulance-chasing personal injury lawyers.

After a ValuJet DC-9 slammed to earth in the Florida Everglades, dozens of lawyers sent promotional brochures to the Miami hotel housing many of the victims' families. Some sent flowers, and at least one firm offered attractive young women to chauffeur the bereaved. Some lawyers literally hid behind potted plants in the hotel lobby in their efforts to get families to sign on the dotted line. "The vultures are circling," said the sister of one victim, "just when people are trying to grieve." "I'd like to get through the funeral at least," said the father of the victim of another mass disaster. "When the time comes, we'll select an attorney, but not from these guys," said the relative of a family killed in the ValuJet crash. "That's where attorneys get the reputation for being sleazy."

None of this fazes Ohio plaintiffs' lawyer Richard H. French. He not only acknowledges doing mass mailings to victims' families within a week of an air crash, but insists that he provides a public service by informing them of their rights. "I'm very, very sorry if and when I distress people," French told the *Boston Herald*. "But I think the service I offer to the victims of the crash is a good enough service that it's worth upsetting someone once in awhile." French seems to think the publicity is good for business. He even read his typical letter on the air for National Public Radio's *All Things Considered* after the TWA Flight 800 crash:

> Dear Family of—insert the name here. Please accept my deepest condolences for the tragic death of—insert the name here—in an air crash. I am sure this must be an extremely difficult time for all of you. I would be pleased to offer any assistance that I can from a legal standpoint, with no obligation for an initial consultation. . . . If you have a few spare minutes, please call me collect so that we might further discuss this matter. Very truly yours.

"Everybody else in America solicits business without shame. So do I," French told ABC's *Nightline*.

The portrait of the American personal injury lawyer emerges with a far more complex personality than the accounts of these airline disasters might suggest. A few personal injury lawyers make enormous sums of money from their contingency fees, while many others make a comfortable living. But they often face long battles against better-financed opponents, usually insurance companies. They must believe in their clients' causes, because they have to lay out the entire costs of the suit in advance—costs that can run into hundreds of thousands of dollars, particularly in product liability or complex mass disaster cases. Many of these lawyers do the work not just for the money, but with a genuinely held belief that their clients, harmed through the fault of another, often burdened by medical bills and loss of earnings that cause severe financial hardship, are entitled to be fairly compensated. For every headline-making case, there are literally thousands of ordinary people who have suffered harm and must now look to powerful insurance companies for compensation. Their lawyers understandably see themselves as defenders of what one called the "little folk."

It's also true that many of the most successful of these lawyers have egos as large as their verdicts, a charge that Chicago's Phil Corboy readily admits. Corboy, now in his seventies, has handled his share of airline cases, but his most visible case was his lawsuit against Johnson & Johnson over contaminated Tylenol capsules that were tampered with and caused several deaths. Corboy claims to have handled over 250 cases worth a million dollars or more, but he'd rather be remembered as a fighter for average people who also soothed his clients in times of need. His clients consider him both sympathetic and empathic. In 1976 his youngest son was killed in a car accident, making it easier to believe him when he says that he "would never tell you, 'I know how you feel.' All tragedy is personal."

At the other end of the spectrum from the dedicated professional is the sleazy lawyer making money off the misfortunes of clients who wind up with little to show for their troubles. While this image has been fostered by the insurance industry and by some in the media, and carries a vestige of Henry Drinker's elitism, there are too many lawyers who fit the description. Here are some of their offenses:

- Overcharging clients, either by demanding fees that are simply too high or by charging more than some services are worth. A California attorney who calls himself the "People's Lawyer" in his TV ads was twice disciplined by the bar, most recently in 1997, for, among other offenses, charging up to 50 percent of a case's value to "advise" clients about cases in small claims court, where no lawyers are allowed and the court provides advisors for free.

- Running "injury mills," which take on a high volume of clients, most with modest cases—fender benders and slip-and-falls—and then settle them quickly for a fraction of their value. Insurance claims adjusters love to see these lawyers on the other side because the quick settlements save their companies money. The lawyers do it because they can make more money settling quickly with little effort and going on to the next case, even though their clients would do much better if a lawsuit was filed, discovery conducted, and depositions taken.

- "Inventive" fee agreements and accounting practices. Some

lawyers calculate the fees they charge clients on the gross recovery and take expenses only out of the client's share. When
these expenses include paying back health care providers for
the costs of care, the client can be left with little or nothing.

• Equally inventive use of local leaders in immigrant commu-
nities as "paralegals," whose employment by the law firm is
trumpeted in the community's native-language newspapers,
accompanied by photographs of both the leader and the
lawyer. This brings in the cases but doesn't answer questions
such as whether the lawyer speaks the clients' language or
whether the attorney is sharing fees with the nonlawyer
"paralegal," a violation of the ethics rules of every state.

It's hard to figure where Houston's John O'Quinn fits in this picture. On one hand, he is one of the most successful personal injury
lawyers in the country. He's won awards worth billions of dollars.
He has been an aggressive leader in breast implant litigation, successful enough to be used as a poster boy for tort reform by both
Forbes magazine and the *Wall Street Journal*. Ordinarily, that kind
of publicity earns accolades from a lawyer's brothers and sisters in
the plaintiffs' bar. But the reaction to O'Quinn has been decidedly
mixed. Several national organizations of trial lawyers have rejected
his membership, according to the trade paper *Texas Lawyer*, and
even his own state's trial lawyers' association has stopped asking
him to speak at seminars.

The most likely reason is the controversy over how O'Quinn
gets his cases. In late 1996 the Texas bar charged O'Quinn with
using nonlawyer "accident runners" and a sometimes-suspended
longtime associate to solicit cases arising out of the 1994 USAir
crash near Charlotte. In April 1997 O'Quinn was indicted in South
Carolina on misdemeanor counts based on the same charges.
O'Quinn has had this kind of trouble before. In 1987 the Texas bar
brought a disciplinary action against him for using eight "runners"
to solicit over a hundred cases. He got off almost scot-free, with a
reprimand, one hundred hours of community service, and payment
of the bar's investigative costs.

O'Quinn defends his actions on free speech grounds, arguing
that if he didn't sign up the families of USAir victims, they would be

at the mercy of the airline's lawyers. "Nobody has ever accused me of not doing a good job for a client," he told the New Orleans *Times-Picayune* in 1994. Some observers agree with this perspective, arguing that if accident victims get the benefit of a high-profile winner like O'Quinn instead of a lesser lawyer, they are better off. "[I]f the lawyer did a helluva job, even if he ran the case—even if he paid $10,000 to get it—and he ends up getting $10 million for the client, where's your victim?" one Texas lawyer and volunteer bar prosecutor asked *Texas Lawyer*. The only harm he saw was to the lawyers who *didn't* get the case.

The United States Supreme Court does not agree with this view. In 1995, by a 5-to-4 vote, it approved a Florida ethics rule that prevents lawyers from soliciting clients within the first thirty days after an accident. The Florida rule goes well beyond banning lawyers from accosting clients in hotel lobbies or sending "runners" into the neighborhood—acts that are already prohibited in every state, whether the prohibition is enforced or not. Rather, Florida's rule was specifically designed to prevent *mail* solicitations.

Since the Supreme Court's decision, several other states have considered or approved similar bans. But plaintiffs' lawyers and many ethics experts see a serious problem with these prohibitions: They give the insurance industry free rein to solicit accident victims themselves—not to represent them, but to get cheap settlements, or even avoid a lawsuit altogether.

Insurance companies are among the very few organizations in America, other than law firms, that are in the business of litigating cases. While litigation is not their sole business—they have to advertise and sell insurance first—any company selling liability insurance knows that inevitably a significant percentage of its claims will wind up in court. The more they can avoid this, the more money they save.

Take a recent San Francisco Bay Area case. A baby was badly burned while in the care of her adult cousin. Negligence and liability were clear—a dangerous condition in the cousin's kitchen. Shortly after the accident, the little girl's parents got a call from the claims adjuster for the cousin's insurance company, Civil Service Employees' Insurance. He told the girl's parents that if they settled the claim without a lawsuit, they could avoid having to sue their own relative. He spoke of his concern for the child, and also shared his Christian beliefs with the girl's mother, whose beliefs were similar. He sent a thousand dollars right away to help defray the parents' immediate expenses. He kept on calling, and was always friendly. The girl's father thought he was "a great guy." But this "great guy" got the parents to settle for less than the company knew was the value of the case, in part by hiring a lawyer loyal to the insurer to help nail the settlement down and then appear in court on the child's "behalf."

When the claims man said he would get the parents a lawyer to help at no cost to them, they were more than willing to talk. The attorney met with them and helped work out the details of the settlement. He even complained to an annuity company that the payments the girl was supposed to receive each month were not large enough; the annuity company recomputed the numbers and agreed. The lawyer then prepared a petition to present to the court for approval of the settlement, a necessary step any time a minor is involved. Curiously, although the lawyer put his and his law firm's names on the petition, he left blank the place where the lawyers state whom they represent. Still, the lawyer made it clear to both the parents and the girl's doctor that he was presenting the matter on behalf of the child.

The parents, understandably concerned about the condition of their little girl, took the lawyer at his word. But they later found out that the insurance company had held money back—money it knew it would have to pay if the girl had her own lawyer. They learned this almost by accident, when the mother called the lawyer to get his help after the court hearing and the lawyer refused, admitting that he actually worked for the insurance company.

This couple was lucky; they sought another attorney and successfully sued both the insurance company and the lawyer for representing themselves falsely. But most are not so fortunate. In his deposition, this particular insurance lawyer testified that he had done the same thing "dozens and dozens of times," and presumably had gotten away with it on each occasion.

Years ago in Pennsylvania, another child, five-year-old Ernest Gunn, fared much worse. After the boy was seriously injured in a car accident, a claims adjuster from the driver's insurance company visited the boy's mother at home and told her that she didn't need a lawyer because the insurance company would pay as soon as the boy was no longer under a doctor's care. During the next two years the adjuster stayed in touch regularly with Mrs. Gunn. But when Ernest stopped being treated, the adjuster suddenly was unavailable. Mrs. Gunn finally went to a lawyer, but it was too late to sue, as the statute of limitations had already run out. The Pennsylvania court refused to allow the boy's lawsuit, and developed a rule that said a plaintiff had to show *"clear* cases of fraud [or] deception" before a statute of limitations could be extended because of the actions of an insurance company.

The Gunn case and the rule that came from it occurred in the 1960s. Thirty years later, little has changed in Pennsylvania. After the Florida antisolicitation rule was upheld, Pennsylvania's bar gave tentative approval to a Florida-style ban on mailed solicitations by plaintiffs' lawyers. Some wanted to create a two-way street by voiding any insurance settlements made in the same thirty-day period, but there was little interest and not enough votes. Once again the effect was to shield the actions of insurance companies.

In Texas, where John O'Quinn now faces charges, new antisolicitation rules include potential criminal prosecution. But Texas's rules also apply only to plaintiffs' lawyers, not lawyers from the insurance industry. Some years ago a Texas state bar president, a partner in the prestigious firm of Fulbright & Jaworski, organized a "truth squad" to go to accident scenes to warn victims and their families that plaintiffs' lawyers were forbidden from soliciting their business at the scene. These efforts were widely publicized as reforms, until the self-serving nature of the truth squad was discovered: The bar leader's law firm represented insurance companies and airlines that were potential defendants.

Richard Kessler is a lawyer. He is also a victim—he lost his wife in the ValuJet Everglades crash. Within five days of the tragedy he began receiving solicitations from plaintiffs' lawyers asking for his business, including overnight letters with graphic pictures of the crash that caused him to relive his wife's death. "It was awful," he later reported. The experience made him feel "totally offended" and "emotionally attacked." But while he thinks there should be a ban on solicitations by plaintiffs' lawyers, he is convinced it must apply to insurance companies and their lawyers with equal force. Both sides use "coercive tactics, scare tactics," he told National Public Radio's *All Things Considered*, "so you have both sides taking advantage of people who have been brutalized and brutalizing them again." His solution: a freeze on *all* sides, to "make it a level playing field" while allowing the bereaved a private time to grieve.

Kessler is right. Solicitations that compound a bereaved's grief are inexcusable—unless they are the only way to protect against insurance companies and their lawyers getting the jump on the victims. There is simply too much evidence that insurance companies focus on the bottom line first, and that they would use a thirty-day window of opportunity to do almost anything within their power to resolve cases on their own terms.

Shortly after the Supreme Court's decision upholding Florida's thirty-day ban, the insurance company Allstate began aggressive efforts to convince claimants to settle before lawyers got involved. The company started sending letters and brochures entitled "Do I Need a Lawyer?" Allstate encouraged claims representatives to get out into the field, monitor police reports, and visit accident sites, all in order to try to settle claims fast.

Allstate told accident victims that even if they took a little bit less directly from the company, they would wind up with more because they wouldn't have to pay lawyers' contingency fees. Victims were also told that a 1992 study by the Insurance Research Council showed people who settle directly with the insurance company get their money quicker. What they weren't told is that a 1994 study by the same council, an insurance industry organ, found that car accident settlements averaged $14,700 for those represented by lawyers, but only $4,100 for those without counsel. That difference is more than enough to pay for contingency fees and, for most, well worth the wait.

At first Allstate was the only company acting this aggressively, but in early 1997 Liberty Mutual also started sending out letters. Plaintiffs' trial lawyers began to complain, and at least one state attorney general started an investigation into whether the insurers were giving legal advice to the accident victims, and whether these efforts were misleading. Still, the insurers showed no signs of stopping their programs. Clearly, these programs were not created without careful crafting from the insurance companies' own attorneys.

More than almost anyone, Bob Manning understands the damage that can be done by insurance companies and their lawyers. When the *New York Times* put his story on its front page in mid-1997, he was still waiting to receive insurance benefits for an accident that occurred in 1962. He is paralyzed from the neck down after being electrocuted while descending a utility pole and falling to the pavement headfirst. The New York State Workers' Compensation Board has twice granted Manning awards—one for $1.2 million—but the insurance company, Utilities Mutual, refused to pay. The problem centers on Manning's need for around-the-clock medical care, much of which he gets from his wife, a registered nurse. Despite precedents for paying a qualified spouse and the decision of a five-judge appellate court panel ordering Utilities Mutual to pay, the insurer's lawyer, Philip J. Rooney, claimed he still had several new grounds for appeal.

In 1988 the insurance company offered to settle, but only if it could dictate the terms. When Manning and his lawyers rejected the offer, the insurer wrote saying it would renew litigation, and that Manning "can forget about any clean, clear-cut disposition of this problem case." In the years since, Manning hovered on the edge of bankruptcy, to the point where the appeals court found he could no longer afford physical therapy and that his health was deteriorating as a result. "I understand what's going on," Manning said in May 1997. "The company knows that if I don't get the medical care I need I will die sooner." Not true, said insurance lawyer Rooney, who claimed that while he had "great sympathy" for Manning, his client was "not obligated to make any payments at all" until receiving a ruling from the highest state court.

The day Manning's story appeared in the *Times*, Governor George E. Pataki called the case "a disgrace" and Utilities Mutual's assertions "ridiculous," and the state's attorney general sent a letter to the insurance company saying that the appeals had been exhausted and it was time to pay. Soon after, Manning's former employer, Mohawk Power, publicly asked the insurance company to pay the worker's compensation claim, which it did. The power of the press and New York's highest officials was greater than the ability of an insurer and its lawyer to continue to delay. But Manning's further claims for his special medical needs are still pending.

Unfortunately, the Manning case hardly stands alone. Insurance companies, with the advice and consent of their lawyers, too often refuse to pay claims if they think that stonewalling is a viable financial risk. In one recent case a monastery burned to the ground. The insurer said it would pay only the actual out-of-pocket cost it took to build it. This would amount to almost nothing, since the monastery had been built with volunteer labor and donated materials. When a member of the order asked how they could rebuild with just a small fraction of the money needed, the insurance adjuster replied, "Pray to God for a miracle." Instead the monastery hired an insurance consultant familiar with the intricacies of insurance policies to advocate on its behalf; eventually the insurer paid the full replacement cost.

Insurers can be expected to rely on all possible arguments in their efforts to avoid paying claims. One of the most volatile areas is health insurance. Typical is the claim of a Florida girl suffering from a facial disfigurement that caused her to ask her mother, "Why did God make me like this?" Her mother argued that, disfigured, her daughter couldn't function as a normal child or be accepted by society. But insurers argue that disfigurements are "cosmetic"—and thus not covered—unless they affect "a body function, not functioning in society," in the words of Florida Blue Cross's medical director. The girl finally got insurance to cover several surgeries, but only when her lawyer proved the girl's sight was endangered. Other children with equally damaging disfigurements have not fared nearly as well.

Insurers make money not just by refusing payments but by delaying them. About half the states now have review boards where people can appeal denials of insurance by HMOs. But these reviews take time, and relief can often come too late. When claims are denied or deferred, few people have the resources to fight back. "If you got your house burned down, you can't afford to wait a year and a half," said one New York state senator who cosponsored reform legislation.

When the San Francisco lawyer who went to court on behalf of the burned baby was asked at his deposition whom he had represented, he sounded puzzled. He denied, despite his actions, that it was the little girl. He knew the insurance company was paying his bill. He had never met the people who had the homeowners' policy—the cousins at whose home the girl was burned. But the cousins were the ones who would be named as defendants in a lawsuit. He concluded, after some agonizing, that he represented *both* the insurance company *and* these policyholders, though he had never even spoken to them.

Lawyers who defend people under their insurance policies are in a difficult and unusual situation. For many, it feels like the insurance company is the client: It retains them, decides which cases— and how many—to send to the law firm, and, under most policies, decides whether to settle and for how much. The person the lawyer takes to lunch and treats like a client is the insurance company's claims manager, who doles out repeat business, not the individual policyholder who has only one case. Yet policyholders pay their premiums not just for coverage, but also so that they'll be well represented by counsel if they're ever sued. In any individual case, these policyholders are the clients—the ones who are served with process, named as parties in a lawsuit, deposed, and sworn as witnesses at trial—and the ones entitled to the lawyer's loyal and zealous representation.

While insurance counsel have to report to the company so that it can decide what action to take on a case, such as whether to settle and for how much, most states follow the view that the lawyer's primary duty is to represent the policyholder, the individual defendant in the case. But almost any alliance between insurer and insured will be an uneasy one. The insurer's goal is usually to resolve the case as inexpensively as possible. The policyholder's goals may be very different: to spend the least possible time, have minimal disruption of his or her life, and avoid the trauma of being deposed or sitting through trial. This puts insurance lawyers in the middle. It's hard for them to escape the feeling that they work for the insurer, especially when they have an ongoing relationship that may stretch over hundreds or even thousands of cases. So in 1996 a group of insurance industry lawyers set out to change the rules to give the insurance company a status at least equal to the policyholder's.

For most of this century, a group called the ALI, or American Law Institute, has drafted summaries of laws called "Restatements." In the mid-1990s it was at work on one called the "Restatement of the Law Governing Lawyers." The three-thousand-member ALI is hardly a cross-section of the legal profession, much less the general public. It's made up largely of law professors, judges, and private practitioners from large firms; it's predominantly white, male, and middle-aged. There is little or no input from nonlawyers. While the ALI may be little known to the public, its restatements carry considerable weight with many judges in many states.

By 1996, the restatement on lawyering—a several-hundred-page document in all—already had been through close to a dozen drafts. In a single paragraph the ALI accepted the prevailing view that an insurance defense lawyer owes a paramount duty to the policyholder, even if the insurer chooses the lawyer. Ordinarily, the purpose of the restatement is to do exactly that—*restate* the law as it is, not legislate new changes. But the insurance lawyers saw an opportunity; they wanted that paragraph changed. So they waged an intense, well-orchestrated lobbying campaign to change the ALI's mind.

First, lawyers wrote articles and position papers in various journals expressing their views. Primary among them was Professor Charles Silver of the University of Texas, a recognized expert on insurance law whose work has been funded by two insurance industry organizations. Then other lawyers, led by William T. Barker of Chicago, waged a lobbying campaign to get the "reporters," the law professors who do most of the actual drafting for the ALI, to consider the proinsurer view. Next, in what many lawyers considered an unprecedented effort, Barker and others lobbied individual ALI members to adopt the insurance company position at a spring 1996 meeting of the group in Washington, D.C. Since only 10 percent of the members—about three hundred people—usually attend meetings, changing just a few votes could affect the outcome. There was "a little get-out-the-vote aspect to this," Barker later admitted.

At the Washington meeting, the insurance lawyers got what

they wanted—a change in the restatement's draft to language they had suggested. Policyholders would no longer be considered their primary client. But many questioned both these lawyers' motives and their methods. Some ALI members reported being pressured by their insurance company clients to vote a particular way. Others agreed with Professor Monroe Freedman, who criticized the effort to change the ALI from a group that objectively reports the law to one that makes changes in the law itself. "You cannot contract out of the ethics rules," said Freedman, bemoaning what he called "self-interested lobbying." ALI member Donald Vish of Louisville put it more simply: "I was lobbied. I was appalled."

Clearly, all the posturing and positioning from both lawyers and insurance companies comes at the sacrifice of the rights of the individual—whether victim or policyholder. Sometimes clients seem like little more than pawns in a high-stakes game being played by others. This must change. While the primary objective of insurance companies may be to make money for shareholders, and lawyers have the right to earn a decent living, neither of these goals should interfere with a more important goal—the public policy that the rights of individuals dealing with the insurance system be protected *and respected* by both sides.

One idea that *won't* accomplish this is so-called tort reform. While tort reform advocates cite the vast numbers of cases clogging our courts, the overwhelming majority of court filings are traffic citations, and the second largest group is criminal cases. The most recent statistics from the National Center for State Courts show that tort cases make up less than 3 percent of all non-traffic-related filings, and are well under 10 percent of all the civil cases filed. There are almost four times as many domestic relations cases as tort claims. Tort reform covers everything from cutting contingency fees to making the loser pay all court costs. But the only purpose served by these "reforms" is to deny access to the courts not just to the poor, but to average people who simply can't afford to pay a lawyer by the hour or to be stuck with the other side's costs if they file but lose a legitimate case.

As for the tug-of-war between plaintiffs' attorneys and insurance lawyers, it too often appears that both sides are operating under what Michael Josephson, head of the Josephson Ethics Institute, calls "the doctrine of relative filth": "If I'm not acting as badly as you, then what I'm doing is okay." To avoid the spread of such compromised ethics, organizations like the American Law Institute must make sure that they are truly representative not just of the profession but of the people they serve, and must avoid being swayed by partisan politics more suited to pork-barrel lobbying than to documenting the existing law. Finally, bar regulatory agencies must make sure that neither side in this war can get away with behavior that jeopardizes the individuals caught in the war zone of insurance litigation.

Epilogue:
Disciplining Sam Hammond

Sam Hammond practiced for twenty years before finally being suspended by the state bar. Over the years, thirteen of Hammond's former clients had complained to the bar that he had not given them adequate representation. All these complaints involved small cases handled by a member of his staff; all were resolved by dismissing the charges, the bar finding that while the lawyering might not have been the best, it was not clearly incompetent, either.

Ultimately, Hammond was disciplined for three incidents, all involving "runners" soliciting clients in the neighborhoods near toxic spills. In all three cases the complaints came not from clients but from other plaintiffs' lawyers. The suspension lasted six months. Meanwhile, Hammond brought in a law partner and his firm continued to operate; only the face on his ads had changed.

CHAPTER 7

All the Court's a Stage,
and All the Lawyers Players:
Leading and Misleading the Jury

Litigation, n. A machine which you go into as a pig and come out of as a
sausage.   —Ambrose Bierce, *The Devil's Dictionary,* 1911

We are putting everything but the evidence on trial.
        —Milwaukee DA E. Michael McCann in 1995,
            complaining about the overabundance of litigation strategies

I think we can safely stop trying to treat jurors like congenital idiots.
        —Arizona judge Michael Brown, who has
            implemented changes in the jury system
            that have jurors more involved during trial

Abraham Dennison is one of the most successful trial lawyers in Port City. McCabe & Dennison has eighteen lawyers, who handle a wide range of litigation for everyone from wealthy divorce clients and executives charged with white-collar crimes to large corporations that need defending in messy environmental cleanup cases or lawsuits over injuries caused by defective products. Many of Dennison's own clients are among the social elite of town, and Dennison himself is the president of the local country club. The club serves him well for happy-hour rainmaking, or business development, as well as for playing $100 Nassaus on the city's most exclusive course.

Although Dennison is smoother than silk out of the court-room, in court he takes on a bumbling, aw-shucks persona. He explains to clients and friends that this creates juror sympathy by giving jurors the impression he's just a "hick from the sticks." He wears off-the-rack clothes instead of the Italian designer suits he wears to the symphony. He rarely objects without hesitating, starting over, and making a little speech, which he privately calls "my Jimmy Stewart method." Instead of "Objection, irrelevant," Dennison is inclined to say "I'm sorry, Your Honor, but I don't under . . . I can't put my finger on why . . . I just can't figure out why that question has anything to do with this case." Dennison's persona has earned from his courthouse colleagues the sarcastic sobriquet "Honest Abe."

Dennison also tries to mask the sophistication of his clients, in-sisting that they too dress down in court by wearing discount-store clothes rather than the expensive outfits they favor. He's even bought subway and bus passes for clients and then placed them conspicuously in his clients' pockets or handbags.

In a rare criminal case, Dennison was hired by a wealthy friend to represent his son, who had been accused of rape. Dennison knew that the jury would be acutely aware of the cross-racial nature of the alleged assault—Dennison's client was white, the alleged victim Chinese-American. In order to defuse this, Dennison recruited an attractive Chinese-American woman from his trial practice class at the local law school to act as his law clerk during the trial. He emphasized to her the importance of being friendly to the defen-dant during the course of the trial—"complete," as he put it, "with touching."

Dennison tells his young associates that one of the most im-portant tricks of the trade is "selecting a biased jury. Let's get rid of the notion right now that you want a fair and unbiased jury in every case. Nonsense! You want a jury biased in favor of your client. That wins cases." In one recent case Dennison defended two wealthy immigrants from Mexico City in a breach-of-contract ac-tion brought by a real estate sales company. He did his best to keep Mexican-Americans off the jury: "To win, we needed to keep alive in the minds of the jurors the stereotype of the poor Mexican farm worker. We didn't want to risk having anyone on the jury who could dispel the stereotype."

Dennison justifies these practices as "trial tactics" necessary to ensure winning verdicts. "My clients don't pay me big money to lose," Dennison says. "They're not here to be bled dry by greedy lawyers. The best defense is a good offense, especially if it's subtle enough to convey my message to the jury without me saying a word. After all," he reasons, "a trial is nothing if not theater, and I've always enjoyed good theater."

．

Only a tiny percentage of cases go to trial, but it's during those trials that people give lawyers their closest scrutiny. Yet almost all trial lawyers will admit, at least in their more candid moments, that their job is not presenting the truth in any objective or absolute sense, but their client's version of it. This, they will tell you, is what the adversary system is all about: "spinning" the truth and only then letting the jury decide.

In one sense, the courtroom during trial is the great equalizer— the ultimate level battlefield. All the money paid for pretrial discovery and investigation, all the parties' wealth, or the lack of it, may not be worth a damn in the midst of battle. There, lawyers fight on their own, using their abilities to think, talk, and act quickly on their feet. The great trial lawyer has two objectives: to control the courtroom as a director controls a movie set, and to play the starring role as an actor who can also improvise. Usually trial techniques are designed to make the lawyer more persuasive about the facts of the case, the hard evidence. But sometimes, like the snake oil salesmen of long ago, lawyers like Abe Dennison put on a show for jurors in an attempt to distract them from the real issues.

It's impossible to take the theater completely out of the courtroom. Anyone who's ever watched *Perry Mason*, *L.A. Law*, or *The Practice*— or even the O.J. Simpson, William Kennedy Smith, or Lorena Bobbitt trials on Court TV—expects lawyers to do more than just provide a dry recitation of the facts. Indeed, after Smith was acquitted in his 1991 Florida rape trial, the *Orlando Sentinel Tribune* gave out "Oscars," including one to the "robotic" prosecutor Moira Lasch for her performance, in which she not only read her questions verbatim but "displayed precious little passion." Other awards included "Best Actor" (a tie between Smith and the alleged victim), and even "Best Costume," won again by Smith, the wealthy Kennedy scion who was dressed like a "rejected model from a discount-store catalog." Had a "Best Director" award been given, defense attorney Roy Black undoubtedly would have won. "As TV movies go," concluded reporter Michael Blumfield, "it was an awfully good one. I can't wait for the book."

As actors, the best trial lawyers all recognize that a little bit of humanity can be a great asset in the courtroom. If Abe Dennison thinks that adopting an aw-shucks demeanor will help him relate to the jury, who's to say he can't? John O'Quinn, the breast implant litigator whom insurance companies love to hate, cultivates a "down-home" presence in trial in a conscious effort to appeal to jurors. "He could probably say 'polydimethyl siloxane' [the main ingredient in implants] in his sleep," Dow Chemical lawyer Richard Josephson told *Forbes* magazine, "but in the courtroom he kept calling it 'that stuff.'" This role playing tends to set its own limits: how far a lawyer can go without alienating the jury with something that rings false. When the best trial lawyers teach their techniques to others, one of the points they constantly emphasize is that "you've got to be yourself."

Many trial counsel agree that clothes makes the lawyer, and some agree that, like Abe Dennison, lawyers should avoid fancy dress. "If the unstated accusation is that your client is a rich pig," attorney Jack S. Hoffinger told the *New York Times*, "do you as a lawyer want to come in and look like a rich lawyer?" Post-trial conversations with jurors often reveal that they not only pay close attention to what the lawyers wear, right down to suit and tie coordination, but talk about it amongst themselves, since they are admonished by the judge *not* to talk about the case. Women's attire especially comes in for close scrutiny. When Marcia Clark wore a short red suit one day at the Simpson trial, the suit's color and skirt length got more play in the media than the day's testimony.

Those who teach trial techniques—psychologists, sociologists, and yes, acting coaches, as well as lawyers—often emphasize another point: the art of storytelling. Lawyers learn how to create a clear "image" of the case. They open their arguments with that image—"This is a tale of greed" or "This is the story of a woman who had no choice"—not unlike the sound-bite arguments we hear on *The Practice*. The more graphic the image, the better. Famed New York law professor Irving Younger, who traveled the country teaching the "Ten Commandments of Cross-Examination," explained "demonstrative evidence" this way: "If your client loses a leg in an accident, don't tell the jury about it. Get the leg! And when the time comes, bring it to court and *show them the leg!*"

It's no coincidence that when trial lawyers talk about their triumphs, their tales are called "war stories." Both words say volumes about how litigators think. Often, lawyers describe the tricks they've used as if they're trophies on display. Roger Dodd can hardly contain his pride telling a war story whose point is another lesson often taught budding trial attorneys: how to create an atmosphere or mood—even an aroma—in the courtroom.

Dodd was defending a woman who had killed a man in a barroom fight in full view of other patrons. She plunged a steak knife into the man's chest with enough force to bend the knife 45 degrees. Dodd says he managed to get admitted into evidence a tape of the rap song that was playing on the jukebox, the neon Michelob beer sign that provided the only lighting, and even an open can of beer to convey the stale smell of the bar. In closing argument, Dodd then re-created the barroom as closely as he could in the courtroom. He turned on the Michelob sign and played the rap song tape. He placed the stale can of beer on the jury rail. He told the jury that it was beyond his control to darken the room or to "raise the temperature in this room to the temperature [my client] had felt for two weeks." Then he asked to jurors to close their eyes to simulate darkness.

Dodd reports gleefully that his client was acquitted. "Our closing was a direct appeal to the jury's emotions," he says. "We were admonished [by the judge] to be ashamed of ourselves." While Dodd's glee at putting one over on the jury may not be appreciated by many, few judges would do more than scold him.

At least Dodd tied his techniques to the evidence in the case. The irony is that many of the most effective techniques of trial lawyers are those that *don't* directly relate to the facts of the case. The O.J.

Simpson murder trial brought us a chief prosecutor who wore an angel pin to signify solidarity with the family of one of the victims, and a defense lawyer who "sanitized" Simpson's home before a jury visit by replacing pictures of his girlfriend with portraits of Simpson's mother. But diverting the jury's attention away from the evidence is hardly new.

This story is attributed to Clarence Darrow: Back in the early part of this century, when people smoked freely in the courtroom, Darrow was sitting at counsel table during the prosecutor's closing argument. He lit a big Havana cigar and started smoking it. As the DA's argument progressed, the cigar ash grew longer and longer. Darrow had placed a straight wire down the center of the cigar, which kept the ash attached. As the prosecutor argued on, the jury paid less and less attention to him and more to whether the cigar ash would fall. The defendant was ultimately acquitted.

It is said that famed Chicago insurance defense lawyer Max Wildman once hired an attractive young woman to sit behind the plaintiff in a case concerning the wrongful death of the plaintiff's wife. The woman's job was to make friendly small talk with the plaintiff during court recesses; the idea was that the jury would observe the plaintiff's "new relationship" and lose sympathy for his loss.

Trial lawyers are always looking for an edge, an angle, with the jury. There are almost as many examples as there are lawyers who try cases. Some efforts seem more desperate, or even silly, than useful, but all are consistent with another lesson repeated by those who teach trial techniques: "Everything that happens in the courtroom counts; you never know what will have an effect on the jury." A few examples:

- One young male lawyer removed his wedding ring during trial and casually flirted from a distance with the women on the jury. According to a colleague, the technique appeared to work, at least to the extent that jurors found him "cute."
- A California lawyer saw a juror he thought was the likely foreman reading the *New York Times* each day during recesses. Thinking that bringing in his own copy of the newspaper was too obvious, the lawyer made sure that he carried needed items into court in the *Times*'s familiar blue plastic home delivery bag,

complete with distinctive logo. The juror became foreman and the lawyer won the case. But the lawyer sheepishly admits that he has no idea whether the juror even noticed the bag.

- Some lawyers wheel boxes of papers into court each day of trial to send a message to jurors that they have more evidence than can possibly be explained away. They make a display by sifting through mountains of documents to pull out the few pieces of paper that actually have relevance.

Several of Abe Dennison's tactics are similar. Dressing his clients at the Gap or JCPenney instead of the usual fashion boutiques may not descend to the same level as Wildman's hiring an attractive "friend," but in its own way it's just as fake. Planting a bus pass on a client who actually drives a Mercedes creates a deceit; is it less false if Dennison convinces his clients to actually ride the bus for the duration of the trial? Just as important, can—or should—these deceits be prevented if the impressions they leave don't directly relate to the admissible evidence in the case?

In most states lawyers must follow ethics rules, usually based on language written by the American Bar Association, designed to protect the sanctity of trials. These rules say that a lawyer may not "falsify evidence" or help a witness testify falsely, present "material evidence" the lawyer knows is false, or "make a false statement of material fact." But these rules, emphasizing the *legal* concepts of "evidence" and "materiality," or what most of us call relevance, don't directly address the collateral deceits discussed here.

What makes Honest Abe's trial tactics—and others we've described—difficult to prevent under the black-letter ethics rules is that these attempts to sway the jury are *indirect*. Dennison is not attempting actively to misrepresent relevant facts or evidence in his cases, but rather is using back-door techniques to raise subtle issues that are technically irrelevant but which might have a substantial effect on the jury. While lawyers are not allowed to talk with jurors during a trial, other than in the course of presenting evidence or arguing the case, Dennison's techniques allow him to communicate without talking.

The practical reality is that few lawyers are likely to be disci-

plined for any of these tactics, except for the kind of informal admonishment received by Roger Dodd. Sanctions for unethical behavior won't be meted out if there are no clear ethics rules. One
lawyer's "parlor trick" is another's innovative trial technique. People may question the propriety of Abe Dennison's dressing down
his clients or making it look as though they ride the bus. But few
would take issue with the criminal defense lawyer who gives an incarcerated client a nice shirt and pants to wear at trial instead of an
orange jumpsuit that says COUNTY JAIL—a strategy approved by the
Supreme Court. Yet without clear ethics standards, the actions of
both lawyers will be treated the same.

Courts are not even sure what to do when lawyers make *direct* misrepresentations in trial. A well-known case from Washington State
involved a lawyer named Thoreen, who in 1980 represented a man
named Sibbett, a commercial fisherman accused of salmon fishing
violations. Thoreen decided to test the ability of the government
agents who had arrested Sibbett to identify his client. During the
trial he had a man named Mason, who resembled Sibbett, sit next
to him at counsel table, dressed in outdoor clothing including a
plaid shirt and a vest. Thoreen acted as if Mason was his client, con-
ferring with him and even giving him a legal pad to take notes.
When Mason was referred to as "Mr. Sibbett," Thoreen said nothing. Meanwhile Sibbett sat in the audience section of the courtroom
wearing a business suit. Not surprisingly, when the government
witnesses testified, they incorrectly identified Mason as Sibbett.
Following the government's case, Thoreen called Mason as a witness and disclosed the switch.

  Though there was no question that Sibbett, and no one else, was
the man arrested by the government agents, Thoreen argued that
the failure to identify Sibbett entitled him to an acquittal. Federal
judge Jack E. Tanner was not amused. Not only did he find Sibbett
guilty, but he held Thoreen in criminal contempt for obstructing
justice by impeding the court's search for the truth. Thoreen appealed. While a federal appeals court upheld Judge Tanner's ruling,
the appellate judges gave the contempt a lukewarm endorsement.
They praised Thoreen's "admirable goal" of representing his client

zealously. But using the traditional appellate standard of "viewing the evidence in the light most favorable" to the lower court's decision, they upheld the contempt because Tanner's decision was "not clearly erroneous."

A decade later Illinois attorney David Sotomayor was held in criminal contempt by a trial judge and fined $500 for pulling a defendant/stand-in switch in a misdemeanor trial in which his client was accused of driving on a revoked license when stopped by police. Again the appellate courts sounded sympathetic to the lawyer; the state's Supreme Court upheld his contempt by a 4-to-3 vote, but the fine was reduced to $100. While the cases were superficially similar, Sotomayor's behavior was very different from Thoreen's.

The arresting officer was the only witness. Having the defendant at counsel table makes almost any in-court identification more a ritual—even a charade—than an actual identification. So over lunch before the brief trial, Sotomayor, knowing that court rules required only that the defendant be present somewhere in the courtroom, decided to seat his law clerk next to him, and the defendant in the back. He never misrepresented that the person sitting next to him was the defendant, and didn't dress up the defendant or dress down the stand-in, both of whom wore similar modest attire. Indeed, the trial judge who found Sotomayor in contempt also dismissed all charges against the defendant. Criminal trial lawyers rallied to Sotomayor's defense—the president of the National Association of Criminal Defense Lawyers said, "We ought to give the guy a medal"—but to no avail.

There is a real issue whether the conduct of David Sotomayor—done to test the proof of a witness's identification beyond a reasonable doubt—is any worse than indirect efforts to falsely impress or mislead the jury. Thoreen and Sotomayor were punished because what they did more closely fits within ethics rules prohibiting misrepresentations of "material evidence." On the other hand, if the misrepresentation is on a less central point, judges will often do nothing, or simply admonish the lawyer and instruct the jury to disregard the inadmissible evidence.

The jury admonishment might go something like this: "The testimony you have just heard is hereby stricken. You are admonished not to consider it for any purpose. I instruct you to deliberate as though you never heard it." But many lawyers believe it's impossible for jurors to "unring the bell" and forget what they see or hear, no matter what the judge says. A Brown University psychology professor conducted a study in the mid-1990s that not only supports this view, but concludes that the more emotional the lawyer's message, the harder it is for the jury to ignore. The study also found that judges actually "enhance the biasing effects of evidence" by instructing jurors to ignore it.

Given this state of affairs, and ethics standards that are narrowly worded and difficult to apply, there's an enormous temptation for lawyers to take liberties with what they say and do in trial. The bottom line is that whether their techniques are direct or indirect, overtly misleading or an attempt at subtle persuasion, related to the evidence or only to matters technically inadmissible, lawyers are likely to try to see what they can get away with.

Still, most lawyers have limits, and they even seem to have some consensus about what these limits are. In 1996, in connection with a seminar conducted by the authors through the legal on-line service Counsel Connect, attorneys debated several of the trial tactics discussed here, and were polled about their opinions on three of them. Ninety-two percent of those responding said that a lawyer who, like Max Wildman, hired an attractive young woman to approach the plaintiff in a wrongful death case acted unethically. At the other end of the spectrum, 80 percent said that a lawyer who, like David Sotomayor, put his client in the audience to test whether an eyewitness can accurately identify his client acted ethically. While Wildman's trick does not directly affect the court proceedings and Sotomayor's does, and while Wildman was not punished for his manipulation though Sotomayor was, we agree with this consensus.

Sotomayor's trick served a specific and legitimate purpose—testing the ability of an eyewitness to identify the accused, not because he's sitting in the expected place in court but because he actually committed the offense. In contrast, the deception of the attractive woman approaching the plaintiff has *no* legitimate purpose whatever. That effort was designed solely to mislead the jury. Though it did not involve "material evidence," the tactic is not, like "Honest Abe" Dennison's, confined to altering his own persona or even those of his clients. The opposing party has been directly, unwittingly, and unfairly drawn into this scheme, and in a way that directly affects an issue most relevant to the case—how much money should be awarded.

The courtroom is no place for a free-for-all. At the same time, it is foolish to expect that lawyers will not try to put their personal stamp on a trial. We don't endorse Abe Dennison's conduct or his advice to his clients about how to act, but they are tactics that affect his own clients and don't alter the evidence in the case. These are best considered as part of the "game," almost impossible—and perhaps unnecessary—to regulate. We are convinced that when these tricks become too cute or go too far, they will not only fail to persuade jurors, but alienate them.

The only other item surveyed during the Counsel Connect seminar resulted in a split decision: whether it was ethical for Abe Dennison to hire a female Chinese-American law student to assist him in a difficult case with racial overtones.

Positioning the law student next to the white male client and scripting her as a friendly, caring, and concerned presence, is an entirely self-created effort. It is not a reaction to the other side's presentation, but merely an attempt to influence a jury sitting in judgment of a white man accused of raping an Asian woman. This is similar to the likely unprovable accusation that Christopher Darden was put on the O.J. Simpson prosecution team because he is black. But using a lawyer or law clerk's race, ethnicity, or sex is hardly an unusual occurrence. For years, a career public defender of our acquaintance took many of the serious sex crimes in her office partly because she knew that, as a woman, she could be a more effective advocate in the eyes of a jury.

It's understandable—perhaps inevitable—that lawyers will try anything imaginable to win within the bounds of the rules. Dennison's technique is not prohibited by any ethics rules, if only because they don't cover this territory. But in the larger sense, is it appropriate behavior? While Dennison's reasons for hiring the Chinese law student may be offensive to some, the technique can be effective. If a lawyer's job is to present the client in the best possible light and using a *willing* law student helps achieve that goal, it is difficult to condemn it. What would cross the line is if Dennison *ordered* his firm's clerk or associate to work on a case because of her race, ethnic background, or sex. Yet many lawyers would consider this, too, a necessary part of the job.

Racial issues can mingle with issues of freedom of speech and religion, raising the question of whether a particular piece of clothing, for example, involves a trial tactic or religious expression. Throughout his drug trial, Washington, D.C., mayor Marion Barry wore an African kente cloth scarf. The cloth is largely an expression of African-American pride, said to mean "Whatever happens, it will not tear," and thus epitomizing the struggle of black Americans. But when D.C. attorney John T. Harvey III wore a similar cloth at the beginning of a jury trial for what he described as both cultural and religious reasons, the judge ordered Harvey to remove it. Most D.C. jurors are black, and the judge saw the scarf as an effort to bias the jury.

The D.C. judge pointed to a New York case that required a lawyer/priest to remove his clerical collar during trial. But four years later a different New York court allowed the same priest to wear the collar, ruling that any bias could be dealt with by admonishing the jury. Probably no court can be sure of the degree to which a kente cloth, collar, yarmulke, or turban is worn for religious reasons and not simply to influence the jury. Again, a lack of clear ethics standards and the absence of rules balancing the two fundamental constitutional rights of religious freedom and the right to a fair trial mean that courts have no consistent guidance in dealing with these issues. When a lawyer's dress is more clearly a nonreligious expression, courts are more willing to say no. There's ample precedent for Marcia Clark having to remove her angel pin, including one Kansas case in which a lawyer was instructed that he could not appear in court in a World War II German officer's uniform complete with Nazi insignia.

"Playing the race card" has become one of the most sensitive and thoroughly discussed issues about the courtroom behavior of lawyers. In the last few years many of the nation's most highly publicized trials have had a major racial component, most often involving tension between African-Americans and whites or Asians:

Bernhard Goetz's subway shootings; the beatings of Rodney King and Reginald Denny; Marion Barry's drug trial; the death of a black man in Howard Beach, New York; and the O.J. Simpson cases.

Without putting it in context, "playing the race card" is merely a catch phrase. There are several ways in which the issues of race— or sex or ethnicity—become part of a trial. Some cases necessarily involve these issues. Racially and ethnically motivated incidents can and do occur; so do sexual harassment, sex discrimination, and criminal sexual behavior. No one seriously quarrels with lawyers emphasizing the issues of race, ethnicity, or sex in these cases. Legislatures have also recognized the issue by enacting hate crime statutes that allow special prosecutions where a crime appears to be racially or ethnically motivated, and shield laws that prohibit evidence of the prior sexual conduct of alleged rape victims.

But what about playing the race card, as Abe Dennison did with his law clerk, where race itself is not directly an issue in the trial? After O.J. Simpson was acquitted in his criminal trial, many accused Simpson's chief defense counsel, Johnnie Cochran, of injecting race into the trial by playing the race card. Cochran's own co-counsel, Robert Shapiro, turned up the heat by accusing his colleague of dealing the card "from the bottom of the deck."

But the race card often finds its way into the deck of courtroom tactics, even when race itself is not directly an issue. After all, most racism in America is *indirect*. The decision to play this card is not made in a vacuum. Experienced trial lawyers know that it is rarely productive simply to raise the issue of race without being able to tie it to something in the case—what the police did, what a witness said, what opposing counsel has charged.

In *Simpson*, the facts of the case alone placed race in the courtroom long before the defense team "inserted it." A famous, highly popular black man stood accused of murdering his attractive, young white ex-wife, after having abused her in the past. To ignore that these facts alone raise racial issues is, in author Toni Morrison's words, to be in "massive denial" about the real world. Perhaps, as former chief federal appeals court judge A. Leon Higgenbotham put it, people were confused between "the rhetoric of living in a color-blind society and the reality of living in a race-conscious nation."

In defending O.J. Simpson, Johnnie Cochran used the race card in context, tying it not just to his client's race, but to what the police did and said. The race card became powerful when police officers—*white* officers—made statements that could reasonably be attacked as false, especially the sworn testimony that they did not immediately consider Simpson, the rejected former husband, a suspect. As Judge Higgenbotham pointed out, California juries are instructed by the trial judge that "a witness, who is willfully false in one material part of his or her testimony, is to be distrusted in others." The race card grew enormously in value when a key police witness, Mark Fuhrman, turned out to have used crude racial epithets on many occasions. Finally, the card was effective because it was played well and at the right time, trumping the cards played by the other side. It's not surprising that under these circumstances the race card helped lead to an acquittal.

Criticism of "playing the race card" in *People v. Simpson* is grossly misplaced. Race was a factor in the case from the outset. The prosecution's witnesses only magnified the issue. Had Johnnie Cochran emphasized race in a trial where the only racial "issue" was his client's skin color, the tactic would have been far less effective; he might not have used it at all. But when Cochran used the issue of race in *Simpson*, it was the natural outgrowth of the circumstances of the case. Cochran effectively made Simpson racism's victim, and in the process, as Henry Louis Gates Jr., chair of the African-American studies program at Harvard, put it, the trial recast "O.J. as a metaphor for [racial] division." But given the same facts and the same cops, any competent Los Angeles public defender, white or black, would have used the race card in the trial of any accused black man whom the public had never heard of.

The Simpson defense team was attacked not just for playing the race card in its jury argument, but also in its selection of the jury itself. The laws of most states allow lawyers to ask judges to remove jurors who show bias, called "challenges for cause," and to challenge a certain number of others based on the attorneys' own subjective evaluation. There is no question that many trial lawyers make assumptions about what kind of jurors—race, ethnicity, sex, and socioeconomic status—will best serve their purposes. The Simpson team and its jury consultants used both challenges for cause and their own peremptory challenges and wound up with a jury that was largely black and even more predominantly female.

At its worst, jury selection allows lawyers to try picking a jury in a way that could easily be called racist. "The goddamned Chinese won't give you a short noodle on a verdict," Melvin Belli told the Association of Trial Lawyers of America in 1982. "You've got to bounce them out of there. In the last case that I tried, I used all my challenges getting rid of those sons of the Celestial Empire." Belli was almost as famous for his ability to offend as for his work as a trial lawyer, but he is not alone. During Jack McMahon's abortive 1997 campaign for Philadelphia district attorney, his opponent made public a training videotape in which McMahon showed young deputies how to avoid having blacks on their juries.

Are these strategies appropriate? Not if a lawyer bases a challenge to a juror entirely on race, according to the United States Supreme Court. But so long as the lawyer can cite some other reasonable basis, it is almost impossible for a judge to second-guess counsel's motives for challenging that juror. This doesn't make it right to use false excuses, but it does mean that challenging jurors only because of their race, ethnicity, or sex, while improper, remains relatively easy to do.

Choosing jurors in the blatant manner Belli's comments and McMahon's video suggest is both unethical and offensive. But most good lawyers are too smart to adopt such strategies. The Simpson team removed potential African-American jurors during the selection process; the prosecution team removed whites. It's absurd to think that Johnnie Cochran and his colleagues would have kept on the jury a woman who worked in a shelter for battered women simply because she was black, or a former military police commander with a strong belief in the integrity of law enforcement officers just because he was African-American. The Simpson team was looking for jurors who were willing to question the truthfulness of police officers. That may be more true on average of blacks than whites, but there was far more to the Simpson team's selection strategy than race.

The practical reality is that even the most blatant race-based jury selection will affect only a few jury seats. The jury in the Simpson case was predominantly black because the jury pool from which it was selected was heavily black; this was why many were surprised when District Attorney Gil Garcetti moved the case from a wealthy, predominantly white West Los Angeles area to the poorer, much more heavily black downtown venue. The police officers accused of beating Rodney King were guaranteed a largely white jury in their state prosecution not because of jury selection methods but because the case had been moved from ethnically diverse Los Angeles to the white middle-class suburb of Simi Valley. McMahon's efforts to pick a jury without blacks in downtown Philadelphia would meet with no more success than Belli's attempts to pick a jury in his hometown of San Francisco with no Chinese-Americans, who form one of the largest segments of that city's jury pool.

Besides, most juries are smart enough to see through race-based selection, which, after all, doesn't take place in isolation. The other side's lawyers are also in court, with the same opportunities to challenge jurors, doing what they can to select a jury that meets *their* "profile," and, presumably, protesting vocally if they see cheating by the other side. Indeed, one of the elements of the profile is intelligence. F. Lee Bailey has been quoted as saying that "when you see a lawyer trying to pick a smart jury, you know he's got a strong case." Bailey then described an argument he once had with fellow defense lawyer Percy Foreman about who had picked the stupidest jury. But usually it's the defense team, not the prosecutor, that wants a smart jury. Philadelphia DA McMahon's infamous videotape advocated avoiding not only black jurors, but *smart* ones: "Smart people will analyze the hell out of your case. They have a higher standard. They take those words 'reasonable doubt' and they actually try to think about them."

In the aftermath of the Simpson case and the first Menendez trial, in which the jury failed to reach a verdict on the guilt of two young southern California brothers accused of killing their wealthy parents, criticisms of the jury system mushroomed. "The jury as an institution is an anachronism," Yale criminal law professor Kate Stith told the *Washington Times* during the Simpson criminal trial. That same article quoted attorneys who argued that while smart jurors might be able to deal with complex trial issues, long trials mean jury pools filled with what one lawyer described as "unemployed people who don't have any appreciation for the value of a dollar." A 1987 federal court study showed that the percentage of jurors who are college graduates is a third lower in longer trials than short ones.

Mark Twain is often quoted on juries filled with "fools and rascals," and contemporary commentators cite Twain's observation that successful people always seem to avoid jury service. Bailey is cited for his "stupid jury" contest with Foreman. Jury selection consultants do little to help their public image, emphasizing on TV talk shows and in magazine roundtables how valuable their services can be and, implicitly, how well they can manipulate the process to pick the perfect juror. It seemed at times that Simpson consultant Jo-Ellan Dimitrius had more air time during her client's case than most of the TV hosts interviewing her.

Much recent criticism has focused directly on these jury selection consultants. One 1996 law review article offered the absurd and unfounded conclusion that an ethics rule was needed to prohibit using jury consultants because they are so adept at their jobs that they "predetermine the jury's verdict." Books focused on questions such as whether overweight jurors are more sympathetic to criminal defendants because they too lack self-control, a strategy attributed to trial lawyer extraordinaire Gerry Spence, or, in the words of one book reviewer, "will Presbyterians be more or less generous . . . than Congregationalists? Do software writers count as warm and fuzzy prose writers, or are they too much like engineers, 'too analytic'?"

The conclusions of many of these commentators are twofold: first, juries are simply not smart enough, too easily manipulated by high-priced selection consultants and smooth-talking lawyers; and second, the jury system needs fundamental change. One suggested change makes sense: Get cameras out of the courtroom, so that the proceedings are not distorted by the participants' awareness of their fishbowl-like visibility. Other suggestions make less sense. Some advocate using professional jurors, trained in the law, who won't be taken in by lawyers' tricks. But that sounds an awful lot like a panel of judges instead of a jury of one's peers. Others argue for allowing jury verdicts to be less than unanimous, but they forget that the evidence doesn't back them up. The Simpson and Simi Valley verdicts were unanimous, and often a hung jury is the result of a minority protecting against the tyranny of the majority. The Menendez brothers' *second* trial resulted in quick convictions.

The attack on juries' intelligence and their susceptibility to manipulation is baseless. So are the efforts to replace the current jury system with some other form of decision making. Interviews with dozens of respected and talented trial lawyers show that—be they prosecutors or defense lawyers, civil plaintiffs' lawyers or defense counsel—they share an almost universal respect for the intelligence of juries. "Sure, you can try to 'spin' your story, but you can't bullshit a jury," says one West Coast trial lawyer and trial practice teacher. "Their collective wisdom and common sense is incredible." The world is a far more sophisticated place than in Clarence Darrow's day, or even during the heyday of *Perry Mason*. We have the Internet, cable television, and real courtroom dramas played out daily on the six o'clock news, and then analyzed by experts on CNN. And overall, far more college graduates sit on juries than fifty years ago.

Juries are so smart, in fact, that they themselves may provide the best protection against the trial tricks of lawyers. They are uncanny at seeing through false fronts. That's why those who teach others the art of trying cases always remind their students to be themselves. This is not to say that juries are infallible or can never be manipulated. But as often as not, they pick up on threads overlooked by the lawyers. In those jurisdictions where jurors are allowed to ask questions, they often ask about obvious issues the lawyers simply failed to clarify, such as "Were the victim and the defendant alone at the time?" Overall, juries are groups of honest citizens doing their best to reach a fair result. They do an excellent job.

While law practice is much more closely regulated than it was fifty years ago, trial conduct has been affected less than most other areas of law. Given vague ethics standards, the principal formal regulation comes from the way individual judges run their courtrooms. But a more effective check on the behavior of lawyers is that juries will rebel against tactics that ring false. Smart lawyers know this; they'll try their tricks but be careful not to patronize or underestimate their juries. In the sometimes free-for-all theater of the courtroom, we need the intelligence and common sense of juries more than ever.

■

There is no epilogue to the story of Abe Dennison. He will not be disciplined by the bar or even brought up on charges. A judge is likely simply to warn him, and even more likely to do nothing. His most questionable strategy—hiring the Chinese-American law student— is the one least likely to be sanctioned. So how much Abe has gotten away with will depend on how the jury reacts. And in the long run, the jury's response will determine how much Abe learns to put the brakes on his trial games.

CHAPTER 8

Lawyers as Liars

Sometimes we have to round off the sharp corners of the truth.
—Oliver Wendell Holmes the Elder,
   physician, author, and father of the famed Supreme Court justice

I've never been involved in legal negotiations where both sides didn't lie.
—Law professor Charles Craver, an expert on
   negotiation and settlement

My opinion is, no lying. Strike one blow for naïveté.
—U.S. magistrate judge Wayne Brazil

Maya Jeter is a lawyer specializing in immigration matters. One day she meets with Solomon Tovarich, an old client whose family Maya has helped over the years.

"Maya," says Solomon, "my best friend Mischa's family is visiting from the Ukraine—his brother and sister-in-law and their beautiful daughter, Elena. And they say things are no better there. Sure, it's better for some than the old days, but for Jews it's even worse. Mischa's brother says it's too late for them, but Elena is twenty and wants to emigrate. But with the quotas filled, it's impossible. I was thinking, I'm a widower, my kids are grown, I got a good job, maybe I could marry Elena. She's a beautiful young lady, intelligent. She could stay here, go to college."

"You know, Sol," Maya tells him, "marrying a foreigner to avoid immigration quotas is a serious crime."

"Of course I know. Why do you think I came to you?"

Maya, suspicious of Tovarich's motives and wanting some time to think before answering him, asks him to come back later in the day, "after I look up some recent immigration rulings."

This looks like such a sham, thinks Jeter. She can't imagine that Tovarich has done much more than meet Elena a few times before. But she can't be certain. She realizes it's possible that she's being judgmental and that's she's misread the situation. After all, Tovarich wouldn't be the first man of sixty to be happy marrying a woman just out of her teens. *Yes, it bothers me,* figures Jeter, *but does that mean it's illegal?*

When Tovarich returns that afternoon, Jeter sits him down and tells him the following:

"Okay, Sol, I'll go through it piece by piece. The key issue is whether your marriage to Elena is one of convenience. That is, are you marrying her for real, or to get her a legal 'status adjustment' that would let her stay in the States? Marrying her so she can live here would be defrauding the Immigration and Naturalization Service."

"So what will Immigration do?" asks Tovarich.

"Well," continues Jeter, "the INS can't investigate every marriage, but they do check out a sizable number. And they investigate a much higher sample of people who fit their sham marriage 'profile.' I guarantee that with your age difference and the full immigration quota, you'll fit right in that profile."

When Tovarich asks what would happen if the INS investigated, Jeter tells him that "it's a question of fact" whether any marriage is real or a sham: "The INS can only look at how the two of you act and what you say to decide if you're legitimate. So if you can prove that you spent months together before you got married, or exchanged long letters of devotion and affection, or were always together on important occasions, all that would help show that your marriage is for real.

"I'll guarantee you something else," adds Maya. "If they do investigate, they'll interview you separately and ask you both where you were on various dates you should remember—July fourth, Thanksgiving, your birthday, hers. They'll ask you where you've been every day of the week just before the interview. They'll ask what kind of toothpaste and soap she uses. If your answers don't match, they'll use it against you. But if it's clear that you've really been together, you'll have a strong case for a marriage made in heaven."

When she finishes, Solomon turns to his lawyer and smiles. "Thank you, Maya, that's very helpful. Every day I'm more in love."

.

Lawyers are perennially rated among the least beloved people in America. Perhaps the foremost reason is that almost everyone thinks they lie—from late-night talk show hosts performing monologues and reporters writing hit pieces to legal scholars, judges, and even lawyers themselves.

According to noted University of Pennsylvania ethics professor Geoffrey Hazard, lawyers, imbued with the adversary theorem, often seem like willing coconspirators in their clients' lies. "Shading the truth and telling lies occurs in almost every case, I am sure," says Professor Hazard. "But we have created this adversarial system that encourages it." Judges agree as well; the president of the National Judicial College says that perjury—and not "a little white lie here or there"—occurs "in almost every case."

The adversary theorem raises at least two distinct issues about lawyers and lying. One is whether attorneys are ever justified in lying, or helping a client to lie. But this question can't be answered without addressing the first issue: defining what "lying" is. Are direct lies any worse than shading the truth, or simply remaining silent and leaving a false impression? Deciding if a lawyer is at fault for lying shouldn't turn on whether the lie is direct or indirect or spoken or silent, but rather on whether the circumstances permit something less than the truth.

Iowa law professor Gerald B. Wetlaufer thinks lawyers should both own up to the fact that they lie and do so under his broad definition: any effort "to create in some audience a belief at variance with one's own." Citing the *Random House Dictionary*, which goes beyond direct falsehoods to define *lie* as "something intended or serving to convey a false impression," Wetlaufer argues that concealments and omissions are also lies. In a 1990 article he cataloged the ways in which lawyers lie—and fool themselves into believing either that they don't or that the lies don't "count." Many sound all too familiar. We summarize:

- *"I didn't lie,"* which includes "My statement was literally true" (though misleading), "I was speaking on a subject about which there is no absolute truth," and "I was merely putting matters in the best light."
- *"I lied, if you insist on calling it that, but it was . . .":* "ethically permissible" (and thus okay); "legal" (and thus okay); "just an omission"; or "ineffectual," because it was just a white lie or because it was simply not believed.
- *"I lied, but it was justified by the very nature of things."* This includes situations where lying is considered part of the rules of the game, such as negotiations, where most lawyers feel that candor defeats the very purpose of the exercise.
- *"I lied, but it was justified by the special ethics of lawyering,"* especially the duties owed clients: loyalty, confidentiality, and, of course, zealous representation.
- *"The lie belongs to someone else,"* usually the client, so that the lawyer is "just the messenger."
- *"I lied because my opponent acted badly."* This includes "self-defense," or "having to lie" before the opponent does, and lying to teach the opponent a lesson, or because bad behavior means the opponent has forfeited any right to candor.
- *"I lied, but it was justified by good consequences,"* that is, justice triumphed.

Each year we ask incoming San Francisco law students whether they see themselves as seekers of truth and justice. When we ask if one of the primary roles of a lawyer is to seek the truth, less than 10 percent say yes. And these are students in their second day of law school orientation. The vast majority, though, believe that lawyers *do* have the duty to seek justice. But can justice be maintained when truth is so routinely slighted?

Sissela Bok, a philosopher and an acute observer of the legal system, doesn't think so. She believes that more than justice is in jeopardy when lies are permitted. "The harmlessness of lies is notoriously disputable," she writes. "What the liar perceives as harmless or even beneficial may not be so." Bok examines lying in the context of our whole society, in which "the veneer of social trust is often thin." Lying, she argues, can damage or even destroy this trust. When trust is damaged, the whole community is damaged; when trust is destroyed, "societies falter and collapse." Justice is one of the casualties.

Even those with less apocalyptic views question whether lawyers can successfully seek justice without giving equal credence to truth. Yet in many ways our legal system seems to foster lying—at least under the broad definitions used by Wetlaufer and Bok. The history and tradition of the legal profession is replete with examples of small deceits. A fundamental tenet of the adversary theorem is that lawyers need not be completely candid with the other side or even the court. For example, even when the discovery process works—with no war to the death over disclosing every scrap of paper—the lawyer seeking the information must still push just the right lever before getting the cheese.

Are there occasions when lawyers *should* be permitted to lie? Can any of Professor Wetlaufer's colorful excuses become a justification? Most lawyers feel that when they are negotiating a case, it's impossible to be completely truthful and still engage in what Wetlaufer calls "strategic speaking." By its very nature, negotiation involves some measure of misleading the opponent, concealing one's true position, and—to use the poker parlance often adopted to describe the process—running a bluff. On one hand, the lawyer must be truthful; on the other hand, misleading the opponent, or at least allowing the opponent to be misled, seems a necessary part of the "game." Negotiation is not, and never will be, a matter of "putting all our cards on the table."

In 1975 Alvin B. Rubin, then a federal judge in Louisiana, wrote an article eloquently imploring "principled practitioners" to hold themselves to a simple ethics standard in negotiation: "The lawyer must act honestly and in good faith." He saw the adversary system as "means, not end," and argued that "client avarice and hostility neither control the lawyer's conscience nor measure his ethics." His article was widely reprinted, and it struck a chord with many lawyers. It began a debate on the ethics of negotiation that continues to this day. His complaint that there was no ethics rule requiring lawyers to be candid to opponents helped lead to a new, broader American Bar Association rule on lying. And his aphorisms—he also posited that "gamesmanship is not ethics"—received warm murmurs of support.

But Judge Rubin, possibly intentionally, set the bar too high. Most believe, as Michigan law professor James J. White said in an article aptly titled "Machiavelli and the Bar," that the "essence of negotiation" requires "even the most forthright, honest, and trust-worthy negotiators" to actively mislead their opponents.

Some years ago the magazine *Inside Litigation* interviewed fifteen law professors, trial lawyers, and judges about how much they would lie in negotiating the settlement of a case. The group was asked whether it was acceptable to leave the other side with a false impression, so long as the lawyer didn't directly lie. Nine voted yes, making a distinction between "bald-faced lies" and misleading by silence, while only four voted no. And yet most of the group was familiar with a well-known Minnesota case from the early 1960s, *Spaulding v. Zimmerman*.

In *Spaulding*, a lawyer was defending the driver in a serious auto accident that injured the plaintiff, a young man in his late teens. The lawyer insisted that the plaintiff be examined by a doctor working for the defense. That doctor discovered something that the youth's own physician had missed: a life-threatening aortic aneurysm that could burst at any time, and had likely been caused by the accident. The defense lawyer said nothing, settling the case for less money than certainly would have been paid had the other side known of the aneurysm. Fortunately, the plaintiff learned of his condition later when taking an army physical and had corrective surgery. Then he asked the court to reopen his settlement. Because the youth was still legally a minor, the judge had the power to set the settlement aside, which he did. But he refused to punish the defense lawyer, saying that the attorney had no obligation to reveal the aneurysm, even though his silence misled the youth in a way that jeopardized his life.

This case generated a great deal of comment in the legal community. Law professors wrote articles arguing that here was one case where surely a lawyer had a moral imperative to reveal the harm—and where lying by omission was just as serious as an affirmative lie. Yet one professor who had written extensively on the need to take personal responsibility in *Spaulding* voted for silence in the *Inside Litigation* poll because "it's not my job to do their job."

The magazine roundtable raised another important issue: May lawyers lie about whether they are authorized by their clients to settle a case for a particular amount? On this question, the group split straight down the middle. Several cited an exception to the ABA's ethics rule on lying—or what the rule calls making a "false statement of material fact"—that "estimates of price or value . . . and a party's intentions as to an acceptable settlement" are *not* ordinarily considered "statements of material fact." This language may reflect the practical reality that if lawyers had to tell the truth about their settlement positions, no negotiations would take place. But read literally, this comment is absurd. Nothing could be more "material" to a party than the value of the case.

Professor Wetlaufer pleads for lawyers to "stop kidding ourselves," call a lie a lie, and admit that lies can and do succeed. Wetlaufer believes that once lawyers accept this dose of realism, they could focus on lies that are not justified either "by the rules of the game or by our duties to our clients" and try to limit the circumstances in which lying is permitted. He argues that many lies are "impermissible" even if not directly forbidden by the rules.

Wetlaufer is right. Many lies—using his broad definition—are both unnecessary and wrong, even in negotiation. On the other hand, expecting lawyers to be completely candid with each other is neither realistic nor advisable. As long as any vestige of the adversary theorem remains, clients have the right to a lawyer who speaks on their behalf, advocates their position, and looks at the case from their point of view. Unless this concept is completely abandoned, lawyers will continue to advocate, and the cost will be a certain degree of candor.

It's interesting that the greatest consensus among the roundtable experts was that they reached one conclusion under a technical reading of the ethics rules—call it the "I-can-get-away-with-it" response—and another when they considered whether they personally would behave that way. The average practicing lawyer—in the field day in and day out, closing deals, negotiating settlements, and, most likely, telling opposing counsel what he or she thinks the other side should hear in order to get the desired result—has little time for this distinction. As long as this lawyer expects the opposing counsel to play the negotiating game by I-can-get-away-with-it rules, the likelihood is that these rules will govern the game. When we asked lawyer-mediators at a recent conference whether they thought lawyers tell the truth even in confidential caucuses with the mediator, they uniformly said no.

What does this say about our justice system's methods of negotiation and dispute resolution? As long as those who make the rules continue to beg the question of which lies are acceptable, negotiation will continue to be a free-for-all where almost anything goes. When bar regulators are ready to create some serious ground rules of how the game is played, with appropriate penalties for unfair play, negotiations could at least move closer to having truth become part of the exercise. For instance, disclosing a client's true "bottom line" may well end the negotiation. But instead of putting lawyers in the position of having to lie, as the rule does now, it could simply forbid lawyers from asking their opponents their ultimate positions on value.

Until changes are made across the board, lawyers are on their own, limited largely by their own sense of fairness and the practical advantages to being truthful—what Judge Rubin describes as "good conduct [that] exacts more than mere convenience." Speaking more bluntly, Professor Charles B. Craver, an expert on negotiation, agrees that there must be "a level of candor if one is going to practice law," but he admits part of his reason for saying so is that candor is often a good tactic.

The adversary system fosters deceit whether the lawyers are involved in negotiation, litigation, or the day-to-day advice they give while putting deals together, drafting wills and estate plans, or helping clients comply with government regulations. Like Maya Jeter, lawyers routinely explain to their clients the law and how it relates to the client's particular situation. In the traditional phrase, lawyers serve their clients as both "attorneys *and counselors* at law." Without a lawyer's advice, clients would be forced to decide what to do without being fully informed of the legal consequences of their decisions. Providing this information is an obvious part of the lawyer's task.

But providing the information comes with a risk: that the client may use what's learned for a dishonest or fraudulent purpose. All lawyers remain obligated to give advice, so even the most honest among them will find it necessary to draw a distinction between advising the client of the law and the available legal options, and assisting the client's commission of a fraud.

Hofstra ethics professor Monroe Freedman provides this example: A defendant, on trial for his life, has killed another man with a penknife but insists that it was in self-defense. The lawyer asks the client, "How often do you carry the penknife?" The client asks, "Why do you need to know?" It is "entirely appropriate," says Freedman, to answer the client's question truthfully—carrying the knife regularly tends to show that having it was normal, while carrying it only on that day, or infrequently, might show an intent to kill. Left on his own, the client may not understand the import of the lawyer's question; he may feel forced to guess what the "right" answer is, and could guess wrong. So "the lawyer must apprise the defendant of the significance of his answer. There is no conceivable ethical requirement that the lawyer trap the client into a hasty and ill-considered answer before telling him the significance of the question." Advising the client of that significance is not helping the client to lie, but telling him what he has a right to know.

Judge John D. Voelker, who served on the Michigan Supreme Court in the 1950s, provided one of the most famous examples of the fine line between advising a client and assisting in a fraud. It comes not from one of Voelker's opinions, but from his novel *Anatomy of a Murder*, which he wrote under a pseudonym, and which became both a best-seller and a blockbuster movie. An army lieutenant, played by Ben Gazzara in the movie, is accused of murdering a man named Barney Quill, shortly after Quill raped Gazzara's wife. Jimmy Stewart, representing Gazzara, tells his client that of all the defenses to murder, only one—that Gazzara had a "legal excuse"—might apply. Stewart tells Gazzara that he is just explaining the "letter of the law," but Gazzara thinks Stewart has something more in mind:

BEN GAZZARA: Go on.

JIMMY STEWART: Go on with what?

BEN: With whatever it is you're getting at.

JIMMY [smiling]: You're bright, Lieutenant. Now let's see how really bright you can be.

BEN: Well, I'm working at it.

JIMMY: Now because your wife was raped, the sympathy will be with you. What you need is a legal peg so the jury can hang up their sympathy on your behalf, you follow me? [Pause while Gazzara thinks hard.] What's your legal excuse, Lieutenant? What's your legal excuse for killing Barney Quill?

BEN [thinking]: Excuse. Just excuse. [Stands up and walks to window, his back to Stewart.] Well, what excuses are there?

JIMMY: How should I know? You're the one who plugged Quill.

BEN [staring out window, thinking]: I must have been mad.

JIMMY: No, bad temper's no excuse.

BEN [walking back toward Stewart]: Well, I mean I must have been crazy. [Pause.] Am I getting warmer? [Jimmy walks to door, starts to open it.]

BEN [insistently]: Am I getting warmer?

JIMMY: I'll tell you that after I talk to your wife. In the meantime, see if you can remember just how crazy you were.

Eventually Gazzara comes up with the legal "excuse" of killing under an "irresistible impulse," a kind of temporary insanity defense discovered by Stewart's law associate in the dark recesses of an old Michigan case.

Unlike advising the penknife holder, this scene involves a lie. Stewart's suggestions are an active effort on his part to create a false defense that will be presented through his client's testimony. But distinguishing between legitimate advice, on one hand, and assisting fraud and falsehood, on the other, can have a lawyer walking a thin semantic tightrope.

This isn't just the stuff of movies. In 1997 Baron & Budd, a Dallas plaintiffs' asbestos firm, danced on this same tightrope before falling off. Defense attorneys uncovered a memo in which the firm advised its clients to "STOP TALKING IMMEDIATELY" if their lawyer interrupts, because "your attorney is trying to fix something you said wrong." The memo instructs clients to listen closely to any "suggestion" made in their lawyer's questions, and offered examples: "You meant that insulating cement was used on steampipes, didn't you?" or "You didn't see the product before the 1960's, right?" Judge Voelker couldn't have scripted it better.

Here's the American Bar Association's comment on how to walk this tightrope:

> A lawyer is required to give an honest opinion about the actual consequences that appear likely to result from a client's conduct. The fact that a client uses advice in a course of action that is criminal or fraudulent does not, of itself, make a lawyer a party to the course of action. However, a lawyer may not knowingly assist a client in criminal or fraudulent conduct. There is a critical distinction between presenting an analysis of legal aspects of questionable conduct and recommending the means by which a crime or fraud might be committed. . . .

Did Maya Jeter correctly make this "critical distinction" in advising Tovarich? Clearly, she could have directly pointed the way to fraud by telling Tovarich exactly what to do: "Court Elena every minute while she's here on her visitor's visa; spend every holiday and birthday with her; look for a new apartment together, and furnish it; write her love letters, and have her do the same." But the advice she gave Tovarich, couched in terms of the law as it relates to the facts of his case, sounds like the kind of legal analysis considered acceptable by the ABA rule. True, Tovarich may still commit fraud, and he may do it based on Jeter's advice, but he was at least entitled to her objective and expert counsel.

Is this a "critical distinction" without a difference, a mere matter of semantics? We think not. Without such distinctions, even if they are semantic fine lines, clients would be deprived of the advice of their attorneys anytime they *might* use the information in an improper way. On this occasion, the American Bar Association rule makes sense.

•

It's not always easy for lawyers to know when they've crossed the line into affirmatively assisting their clients' illegitimate purpose. They are understandably reluctant to "play God" with clients by assuming that their legal skills are being used fraudulently. Often it's impossible to really "know" their clients' motives. And the only ethics guidance they have is vague, particularly the ABA rule that forbids "a false statement of material fact" but fails to address whether that extends beyond direct misstatements to omissions far less direct but ultimately no less misleading. The ABA itself has written seemingly contradictory ethics opinions on the issue.

Still, lawyers must draw a line somewhere, and that line must be well short of where it was placed by the New York firm of Singer, Hutner, Levine & Seeman in representing O.P.M. Leasing, Inc. O.P.M. was founded in 1970, the brainchild of two partners, childhood friends, and brothers-in-law, Myron Goodman and Mordecai Weissman. O.P.M.'s business involved purchasing computers from IBM and then leasing them to companies like Rockwell International, AT&T, and Polaroid. The more O.P.M. leased, the more banks were willing to lend money for more computers, using the leases with the megacompanies as collateral. By the late seventies O.P.M. was one of the country's five largest computer-leasing companies— all of it done, as the name of the company implied, with O.P.M.— other people's money.

There was just one major problem: The entire business was a fraud. Not only were most of the leases fake, most of the computers never existed. The same computer would be used again and again for different leases and different loans. O.P.M.'s biggest "client," Rockwell, was largely a name on forged leases, created by Goodman crouching under a glass-top table to shine a flashlight through signature pages that Weissman traced onto fake documents. In all, according to investigative reporter Stewart Taylor, between 1978 and 1981 alone, O.P.M. obtained almost $200 million in loans from nineteen lenders secured by forged Rockwell leases.

Not long after it opened its doors, O.P.M. became Singer, Hutner's biggest client. The lawyers had no indication of anything amiss until June 1980, when Goodman, knowing his accountant had discovered the Rockwell fraud and was threatening to tell all, first swore his attorneys to secrecy and then told them he had done something wrong—something he couldn't fix because it would take millions of dollars he didn't have.

Goodman kept his story vague, but the accountant hired his own lawyer, William J. Davis, to meet with O.P.M.'s counsel. Davis later described his meetings with senior partner Joseph L. Hutner as "a macabre dance." He says he offered Hutner the accountant's letter outlining the fraud, but Hutner "didn't want it [and] didn't want to know what was in it." Hutner behaved, said Davis, as if he were about to "clamp his hands over his ears and run out of the office." Meanwhile Goodman, while admitting to past mistakes, swore to his lawyers that his days of dishonesty were behind him.

But the lawyers knew it wasn't that simple. The accountant's message had gotten through: a Singer, Hutner memorandum drafted during this period referred to evidence of multimillion-dollar frauds. To get that money, O.P.M. had used the law firm's own "opinion letters" about the worthiness of the loans, which in turn were based on fake documents. Even worse, the firm knew that in the accountant's opinion, O.P.M., "in order to survive, would probably have to continue the same type of wrongful activity."

Given all this, Singer, Hutner considered stopping all its work for O.P.M. But no firm wants to lose its largest client; if Goodman's assurances could be taken at face value, all his "mistakes" were in the past. The lawyers decided to seek the advice of an outside expert in legal ethics. They chose Henry Putzel III, who had taught ethics at Fordham University and came recommended by the law school's dean. Putzel gave Singer, Hutner the answers the firm wanted to hear.

First, Putzel concluded that despite the accountant's opinion, Singer, Hutner knew of "no fact which in any way indicated the commission of an ongoing fraud." Therefore, said Putzel, the firm had no duty to say anything about what had happened in the past, including telling the banks that *existing* loans were based on false information. Second, relying on Goodman's new assurances, the firm could even continue to close new loans for O.P.M. Third, it was not necessary for Singer, Hutner to check to be sure each new O.P.M. deal was legitimate so long as Goodman swore in writing that it was, which of course he was only too happy to do.

So during the summer of 1980 Singer, Hutner continued to assist O.P.M. in obtaining new loans. But the lawyers couldn't stick their heads in the sand forever. In September, after Goodman had admitted more details about his past frauds and acknowledged that they totaled almost $100 million, the law firm finally decided to resign as counsel. But with Putzel's approval, Singer, Hutner did not resign at once. Rather, it set up a staged withdrawal between September and December to ensure that the client was not abandoned without a lawyer. Incredibly, the lawyers stayed on despite Goodman's admission that O.P.M. had continued to defraud lenders even after his June "confession" and promise of reform—because he swore yet again that all fraud had finally stopped.

O.P.M. found new lawyers to represent them—Peter Fishbein and his firm, Kaye, Scholer, Fierman, Hays & Handler. In October Fishbein called his old friend Hutner to ask whether there were any problems with O.P.M. that had caused Singer, Hutner to give up its largest client. But Putzel instructed Hutner he could tell Fishbein nothing without violating O.P.M.'s confidentiality. The end result was that Kaye, Scholer, knowing nothing of O.P.M.'s past history, assisted O.P.M. in obtaining another $15 million in bogus loans before the fraud was exposed.

When O.P.M.'s house of cards collapsed and the tangled web of litigation began, everyone got a lawyer, including the lawyers, Singer, Hutner, and the lawyers' lawyer, Putzel. O.P.M. went into bankruptcy and Goodman and Weissman were sent to prison. Lawsuits flew, and Singer, Hutner wound up paying $10 million. The firm collapsed, but the principals went on practicing law, none sanctioned by the bar, and all claiming they had done the right thing.

Most sanctimonious was Putzel, whose legal brief defended the advice he had given Singer, Hutner: Under the adversary system, "a lawyer's primary obligation . . . must be to his client, rich or poor, likeable or despicable, honest or crooked." There are times, Putzel's lawyers argued, when lawyers are "duty-bound to stand up for and protect liars and thieves." But here, by advising Singer, Hutner essentially to turn a blind eye toward the truth, Putzel had encouraged the lawyers to stand up and *assist* liars and thieves to become better at lying and thieving.

The O.P.M. case should have served as a lesson to all lawyers about the dangers of collaborating in a client's fraudulent conduct. But the firm that was left holding O.P.M.'s hand after Singer, Hutner fled— that most clearly should have learned this lesson indelibly from experience—apparently never caught on. Five years after representing O.P.M. during its self-destruction, Kaye, Scholer and firm leader Peter Fishbein signed on as counsel to Charles Keating's Lincoln Savings & Loan.

The savings-and-loan scandals of the late 1980s left a black mark on the country's financial world that is still visible. Hundreds of institutions failed, some because they were overextended and incompetently managed, especially through the purchase of junk bonds; many others went under because of banking improprieties and even outright fraud. No scandal inflamed the American public more than the case of Lincoln Savings & Loan. This story was not about mismanagement but about overt fraud. By the time federal bank regulators took over Lincoln in 1989, the cost to the public of bailing out those defrauded by the California-based S&L was put at $2.6 *billion*. When the dust finally settled, Keating, the man who controlled Lincoln, had been sent to prison on fraud charges, and two of Lincoln's law firms—Kaye, Scholer, and Jones, Day, Reavis & Pogue, one of the country's five largest firms—had agreed to pay fines of $92 million for their involvement.

While Lincoln went about defrauding the public through its loans and investments, Kaye, Scholer assisted in the cover-up. Lincoln employees backdated documents to make certain investments look "legal," stuffed loan and investment files that contained almost nothing with fake research and underwriting information to make it appear that the deals were proper, and "sanitized" other files by removing negative information about borrowers or risky investments. The lawyers knew all of this. And yet not only did they do everything in their power to stonewall regulators from the Federal Home Loan Bank Board during two routine examinations, they actively tried to throw them off the scent.

To *American Lawyer* investigative reporters Susan Beck and Michael Orey, Kaye, Scholer acted more like "Charles Keating, Jr.'s PR firm" than Lincoln's attorneys. Among the claims Kaye, Scholer made in a formal report to the bank board were these:

- "Lincoln unquestionably is not in unsafe and unsound condition. To the contrary . . . Lincoln's new management has created an extraordinarily successful, financially healthy institution."
- "Lincoln prudently manages and thus minimizes the risks associated with real estate lending."
- "The ultimate proof of the pudding of Lincoln's comparative advantage, its sound investment selection, and its prudent underwriting is the unqualified success of Lincoln's program."

In 1989 Congress created the Office of Thrift Supervision (OTS) to clean up the S&L mess. When the OTS filed a notice of charges against Kaye, Scholer in March 1992, and then used its administrative powers to freeze the firm's assets, it dropped a bombshell that shook the insular world of large-firm practitioners to its core. Kaye, Scholer responded with a thorough defense and a lengthy declaration from Professor Hazard, then at Yale, supporting its conduct. But within days the firm—its assets frozen, its lines of credit being called in by its banks—settled its dispute with the OTS for $41 million, and Fishbein and another partner agreed never again to represent federally insured deposit institutions.

Kaye, Scholer and Fishbein maintained their innocence throughout, and placed the blame for the settlement on the OTS's high-handed tactics, especially freezing the law firm's assets. Indeed, many observers saw the money freeze as an abuse of governmental power. Still, many of those same critics were convinced that Kaye, Scholer's focus on the OTS's tactics was intended to deflect scrutiny from the firm's own improper conduct.

Just as the Lincoln Savings & Loan scandal and the criminal trial of Charles Keating became headline stories in the mainstream press, the Kaye, Scholer case became a cause célèbre in legal circles. It spawned symposia, seminars, and endless articles from legal reporters and lawyers alike focusing on when lawyers must come forth with the truth. In his first monthly *National Law Journal* ethics column after Kaye, Scholer settled with the OTS, Professor Hazard summarized his defense of his client. This defense rested on an assumption that Kaye, Scholer was not merely advising Lincoln during a routine bank audit, but was acting as trial lawyers do, fighting the bank board as an adversary. Being "litigation counsel," argued Hazard, meant that under the adversary system, Kaye, Scholer had no obligation to be candid with the board.

Kaye, Scholer's protestations did not dissuade New York State disciplinary authorities from investigating the conduct of Fishbein and other Kaye, Scholer partners, but the investigation was eventually closed with no action taken. Then, in August 1993, the American Bar Association issued this ethics opinion: "In representing a client in a bank examination, a lawyer may not under any circumstances lie to or mislead agency officials, either by affirmative misstatement or by omitting a material fact." But, the opinion then hedged, there is "no duty to disclose weaknesses in [the] client's case or otherwise reveal confidential information." Many saw the opinion's ambivalence as a defense of Kaye, Scholer's actions.

Another ABA opinion, issued just a year earlier and based on facts similar to the O.P.M. case, had taken a much stronger stand: A lawyer could no longer represent a client if it meant assisting the client's continuing or future fraud. This opinion also said that if a client uses its law firm's work to perpetrate a fraud—as O.P.M. used Singer, Hutner's favorable opinions about pending loans—the lawyers may publicly "disavow" this work, even if it was done in good faith, in order to prevent it from being used by the client for a fraudulent purpose.

It is difficult to reconcile these two opinions. The one based on Kaye, Scholer is largely a defense of the adversary theorem in its purest form. The earlier opinion is known as the "noisy withdrawal" opinion because it permits lawyers to publicly refuse to be exploited by their clients for illegal purposes. It is hard not to believe that the difference between these two opinions has something to do with the prominence of Lincoln's two law firms. If *they* were considered unethical, then so would lawyers in scores of similar powerful firms across the country. Seen in this light, it's not surprising that the ABA passed a resolution in August 1993 opposing the tactics used by the OTS; after all, the OTS fought power with power and won.

Why did Kaye, Scholer think it could get away with helping Keating and Lincoln defraud the public? Harvard law professor

David Wilkins points out that the law firm's lead counsel, Fishbein, was "a life-long litigator who had never previously represented a federally insured institution." Wilkins blames what happened on the failure of the firm to have any means to examine, much less control, the conduct of its "most prestigious, powerful and profitable partner." In other words, there was no one to stand up to Fishbein, nor any mechanism for doing so.

As for ethics expert Geoffrey Hazard, he had been retained by Kaye, Scholer in 1981 after Singer, Hutner dropped O.P.M. on the firm without warning of O.P.M.'s frauds. Back then, Hazard had strongly criticized Singer, Hutner's ethics expert, Putzel. O.P.M.'s lawyers *should* have disclosed the situation to Kaye, Scholer, Hazard argued, in order to prevent their client from perpetuating a fraud. But by 1992, retained to defend Kaye, Scholer's failure to disclose Lincoln's frauds, Hazard had completely changed his tune.

In the mid-1990s New York became the first state to set up a system capable of disciplining entire law firms for unethical conduct. What part the O.P.M. and Kaye, Scholer matters played is not known, but the New York City bar, which led the fight for law firm discipline, focused on two points: first, law firms develop their own cultures, which have a substantial effect on the ways their attorneys practice law; and second, an entire law firm should be accountable for the behavior of all its lawyers.

Are there any circumstances other than negotiations where a lawyer is justified in lying—where a credible argument can be made that Truth must suffer in order for Justice to be protected? We've already examined criticism of this idea, from Wetlaufer's excuse that "I lied, but it was justified by good consequences," to philosopher Bok's insistence that lies always damage the fabric of society. But can lying ever be excused because a "higher" interest—justice—is being served?

In March 1997, just before jury selection began in the Timothy McVeigh trial, the *Dallas Morning News* reported that McVeigh's lawyers had a written confession from their client admitting he had driven the truck filled with explosives that killed 168 people in Oklahoma City. There was no question that the confession, if it existed, was inadmissible in court: It had been made only to the defense team, and the *Morning News* acknowledged it had obtained its documentation from a member of that team; this made the statements a confidential attorney-client communication. But the story was still damning to McVeigh both in the court of public opinion and in the minds of prospective jurors. Chief defense counsel Stephen Jones, about to select a supposedly "unbiased" jury in a case involving the worst act of terrorism in our country's history, needed instant damage control.

At first Jones said the confession was a hoax—it didn't exist. Within a day Jones changed his story, claiming that the "confession" had been concocted by the defense to persuade a reluctant witness to talk. The witness would talk only if he was not suspected; the "confession," Jones said, was created to lull the witness into speaking with the defense. The press, especially the legal trade press, immediately focused its attention on whether Jones was justified in lying. Interestingly, little attention was focused on the irresponsible reporting by the *Dallas Morning News*, which made disclosures that served only to harm McVeigh, since no jury would ever hear them in court.

The press figured Jones was a liar one way or the other: Either he had lied by creating the "concocted" confession and fooling a witness, or the confession was actually the truth, in which case Jones had lied to the press. Legal ethics experts lined up on both sides of the issue. Many cited the American Bar Association's ethics rule, which prohibits making false statements not just to the court or opposing counsel, but to any "third person." Either the witness, if the confession was a fake, or the press, if the confession was true, would qualify as a "third person." Talk circulated about whether Jones should be referred for discipline to the state bars of Oklahoma, his home state, and Colorado, where the trial was held.

No one knows whether this "confession" was true or concocted. Assuming for the moment that it was true and Jones lied to the press, those criticizing him for this—especially the press—were throwing stones from glass houses. Jones was obligated to try to get his client a fair trial. Already confronted by a horrible case with a wealth of evidence against him, he found himself faced with disclosure of his client's confession. With a real confession, Jones had three choices: admit its truth, effectively damning his client in the eyes of the public and the potential jurors; remain silent, knowing that this would have the same effect as an admission; or come up with a plausible denial.

Under these circumstances, the third choice was effectively his only alternative. The others would have had him choose truth over justice, not just his sworn duty to his client, but McVeigh's right to a fair trial as well. Jones didn't have that luxury.

Concocting a confession to persuade a witness to talk raises a more difficult issue. Many ethics experts who approved of this said it amounted to a lawyer simply doing his job. "Lawyers are not truth-seeking, unless the truth happens to help clients," said Professor Stephen Gillers. Others pointed out that the prosecution often does worse things. Even Houston's district attorney justified Jones's fake confession ploy as a matter of strategy, commenting that if he had a witness who wouldn't talk as long as his mother was alive, he would "send someone from the funeral home out and say his mother was just killed." But to argue that Jones was justified because prosecutors lie even more is to invoke the doctrine of relative filth—"I can do it because *they* are doing something worse."

There are, though, two other justifications for Jones's conduct. First, our justice system has long recognized the need to balance truth with justice. The term "legal fiction" is a euphemism for an untruth. Yet these fictions pervade our courts: allowing incarcerated defendants to appear during trial in normal attire and without handcuffs; rules that keep the jury from hearing untrustworthy "hearsay," or evidence of what one person told another; evidence that judges strike because the prejudice it causes "outweighs its probative value." These rules prevent juries from hearing about a defendant's forced confession, or the prior sexual conduct of a rape victim. Legal fictions are just as common in civil cases, where most trials are preceded by "motions *in limine*," or requests from both sides to limit the evidence to be presented. Experienced judges acknowledge that the entire truth is never heard in the courtroom, in order to serve the ends of justice.

Second, there are times when we all confront the moral dilemma of telling the truth versus doing harm. These situations range from the relatively benign—answering a spouse who asks, "How do I look?"—to the most serious—Nazi storm troopers asking whether there are any Jews on the bus. In the movie *Liar, Liar,* Jim Carrey, on his truth-telling day, answers the question "How do you like my dress?" with the honest response "Whatever takes the focus off your hair." Most of us would lie without remorse about either an unfashionable dress or an innocent fugitive. But lawyers face serious moral dilemmas when they feel they must choose between the truth as they know it and justice as they see it.

When Professor Monroe Freedman was asked about Stephen Jones's conduct, he recalled his days working on housing discrimination cases. He would employ "testers" to meet with real estate agents to see if black couples were being treated differently than whites. These testers, he acknowledged, were a lie; they weren't seeking housing, but evidence. Freedman says he's not comfortable with lying, but believes that it's hard to make categorical statements that lawyers should never do it. "I have done it myself," he admits, "and I would do it again."

Epilogue:
Solomon Tovarich Meets the INS

Three months went by before Maya Jeter heard from Solomon Tovarich again. He called to say that he and Elena had just been married and that they wanted Maya's help filling out the necessary forms for Elena to be able to stay in the country.

"So how's it going, Sol?" asked Jeter.

"Good, good," said Tovarich. "Elena is signed up for classes at State; she's great, she likes it here. She's adjusting fine."

"And what about you?"

"I'm great! Everything is working out just fine, just great."

"Listen, Sol," said Jeter, "let me call you back tomorrow about your case. I've got a brief I've got to get out this afternoon."

That evening Maya Jeter thought about whether she wanted to represent the couple. She'd been suspicious of the whole thing from the start, and her brief conversation with Sol did nothing to allay her concerns. But Maya knew Tovarich well enough that she couldn't be quite sure of his motives any more than when he first came to see her. He had always been hard to read. Maya realized that it came down to what Solomon and Elena really felt about their marriage, something she'd never know for certain. That meant that the ethics rules allowed her to go either way: She could take the case, but nothing compelled her to do it.

The next day Jeter called Tovarich back and made an appointment to meet him and Elena. She remained unconvinced about the marriage, but she reasoned that she had no way of knowing whether it was a sham. Besides, Tovarich and his family had been good clients who paid their bills on time. She tried telling herself that she could always refuse to represent the couple if it was obvious from their meeting that the marriage was a hoax. But she knew that was unlikely to happen, because Tovarich was too smart; the time for her to say no was *before* they met. Sure, she had misgivings, but after all, she thought, she was an immigration lawyer, and this was what immigration lawyers did.

CHAPTER 9

Keeping It Secret
(Or, What You Don't Know
Can Hurt You)

Secrecy and a free, democratic government don't mix.
> —Harry S Truman, as quoted in an
> oral biography by Merle Miller

To close a court to public scrutiny of the proceedings is to shut off the light of the law.
> —Texas Supreme Court justice (later congressman)
> Lloyd Doggett, architect of Texas's open court records rule

My agenda has nothing to do with truth and justice. It has to do with winning. —Louisville attorney Gary Weiss, defending
> lawyers' efforts to prevent evidence from being disclosed
> in court in a large lawsuit against Prozac

E. J. Boyette was a forty-eight-year-old computer program- mer when he died, leaving a wife and five kids. Always active, Boyette had worked out three times a week, and on the weekends he rowed with a group of guys he knew from college. Shortly after his forty-seventh birthday he noticed that he was getting tired easily and was often short of breath. He made an appointment with his doctor, who referred him to a cardiologist. After extensive tests, the cardiologist recommended surgical placement of a new kind of heart valve from the Jones/Henning/Wharton Company that had been highly praised in all the medical journals.

At first everything seemed fine. Boyette was released from the hospital, started mild workouts, and had even begun dreaming of joining his rowing mates on the water again. But after three months Boyette's physical condition began deteriorating quickly. In another month he was dead. His widow consulted attorney Andrea Hardy, a partner in a small firm that represents plaintiffs in injury cases.

Andrea began her practice working at a large firm, but after a few years she grew dissatisfied. She felt she had lost her way as a lawyer. So ten years ago, she took a pay cut to go to work for the firm of Geisel & Yanahiro. She never regretted it. Eventually she became a partner, and last year her partners renamed the firm Geisel, Yanahiro & Hardy. Best of all, Andrea developed a specialty in product liability cases. She came to see her work—prosecuting lawsuits against companies that market dangerous products—as making a real difference. Hardy took the Boyette case and filed a wrongful death suit against Jones/Henning/Wharton.

Now, eighteen months later, after extensive discovery and a review of thousands of documents, Andrea and her paralegal have just found a memo that seems to show that the company knew its first-generation heart valves had design flaws that could cause some patients to get worse and even die. She and her paralegal can barely contain their excitement. They quickly draft a new and very specific demand for the other side to produce more documents, which Andrea believes will include the smoking gun she can use to prove that the manufacturer knew the heart valves were defective. Not only would this prove the company's liability, but it could well mean a good possibility of punitive damages, awarded to punish the manufacturer for distributing a product it knew was dangerous.

Opposing counsel George Burger reacts as he has to every document request: He fights it tooth and nail. But the discovery judge finally orders Burger to produce the documents. On the appointed day for delivery, Andrea is surprised to find Burger himself at her office. He asks if they can talk.

"Look," he says, "I'll hand over these documents in a minute. I think you know what's in them. But there's something I'd like you to consider. We'll offer you five million dollars right now to settle the case. There are just two conditions: the amount we pay must be secret, and all the documents you've gotten from us must be returned. All of them, including copies." Andrea is dumbstruck. Until this moment Burger had maintained his client's innocence and never breathed a word about settlement. She knows $5 million is a lot more than she's likely to get for the case at trial, even with punitive damages. And the fee would easily be the largest her firm has ever received. She's sure the documents in George Burger's briefcase include the smoking gun she's looking for.

Andrea tells Burger that she'll have to review the documents and discuss things with her client before making a decision. "Fine," says Burger, "I'll give you a week." Later that day, with her paralegal and her law partners gathered around her, Andrea reads three memos from senior Jones/Henning/Wharton officials that conclusively prove that the manufacturer knew the heart valve's design was defective before Mr. Boyette's valve was implanted. One memo summarizes 107 incidents in which the valve was considered a contributing cause in a patient's death. The other two discuss how the company should deal with the design flaw, eventually concluding that nothing should be done to take it off the market until a new product could be developed to replace it.

Andrea knows she must talk to Mr. Boyette's widow. But she ponders what to advise her about accepting Burger's offer. She loves her practice because she gets to expose dangerous products, not conceal them. She knows that if she agrees to keep the documents secret, other people with heart valves like Mr. Boyette's could be in danger, even die. But she also knows the guiding principle that her first duty is to her client, not the public at large. And the amount her client has been offered is enormous.

•

It's one thing for plaintiffs' lawyers to play the adversarial game by matching their big-firm counterparts blow for blow at trial and during discovery. Lawyers argue, with some reason, that tough tactics in these arenas are necessary to the adversary system—and that they occur on a two-way street where both sides operate with equal vigor and skill. But the adversary theorem can work in far more insidious ways, especially when money—lots of money—is at stake.

When big money is put in front of a lawyer in the form of an offer to settle at a premium amount, it's likely that something more is involved than in the usual case. Often that something is information—the kind of information that is damning to one side and a potential gold mine to the other; information that could cause a company to pay off individual litigants handsomely if they are willing to keep a secret.

Unlike jury verdicts, lawsuit settlements almost never include findings of fault. But if the public is aware that millions have been paid to settle, most people will think that there must be fault somewhere. If damaging information is also disclosed, the perception will be even more damning. Besides, when lawyers get access to such information, it means that a single isolated lawsuit can turn into a separate case each time someone makes a similar complaint about the product.

In this light, it's understandable that companies accused of selling defective products or causing toxic spills, hospitals accused of harboring incompetent doctors, and religious or fraternal organizations whose elders are accused of child abuse all have a keen interest in keeping the settlement of any individual claim top secret. These defendants want to keep quiet not just the settlement's amount, but the evidence that led up to it, and sometimes the very existence of the settlement itself.

Some of the arguments for secrecy are good ones. First, not all claims are legitimate; some are filed for sensationalism or publicity, and others are attempts to reach into deep pockets. Still others, while filed in good faith, may not have merit. Just because a car has defective brakes doesn't mean that the brakes caused the driver's accident; maybe the driver was drunk or simply inattentive. Even if the brake defect played a part in the accident, there may also have been other contributing causes.

Most important, even if a single claim is valid, it doesn't validate all similar claims. A priest may have molested one child but not another; a doctor who makes a fatal mistake with one patient may never make another. Defective brakes may have caused Driver #1's accident, but that does not mean that Driver #2's car, the same make and model, crashed for the same reason. Not every set of brakes fails. Besides, not every settlement means that the brakes were defective. No company wants its name linked with accusations of defective products, whether true or false. It may be smarter to settle with a sympathetic plaintiff who has a reasonable—but by no means certain—chance of winning at trial if it means that the evidence of defective brakes will remain secret.

Those who favor secret settlements believe that if the facts of each individual case become public, greedy plaintiffs' lawyers and unscrupulous clients would be encouraged to file frivolous lawsuits. Harvard Law School professor Arthur Miller, perhaps the most articulate spokesperson for this view, claims that there is no proof at all that suppressing "anecdotal evidence," or what he calls "stories," has ever denied the public vital information on issues of public health and safety.

There is undoubtedly some truth to this view. Allegations in a lawsuit don't prove anything. Nor does an isolated settlement, which a company may enter to protect itself from the publicity of going to trial. Even an occasional jury verdict doesn't prove a product is defective in every case, only in that particular one. But neither Professor Miller nor the Product Liability Defense Council, whose members are companies sued for defective products and whose foundation helped finance Miller's work, is able to point to evidence that open settlements actually encourage frivolous lawsuits.

More significantly, an examination of some of the cases Miller mentions shows that many are far more than mere "anecdotes." Some involve companies that entered into hundreds of secret settlements to protect their products, despite having strong evidence of their danger. Other cases appear to be the tips of large and dangerous icebergs that might cause serious harm if the public isn't warned.

The makers of the prescription drugs Zomax, Halcion, and Prozac all experienced problems with their products, and all took great pains to keep their settlements secret. Eventually the evidence about each drug became public anyway. With Halcion, much of the exposure came from an English investigation. In the case of Zomax, disclosure came only after a scientist experienced a potentially fatal allergic reaction and decided to investigate. Zomax was eventually taken off the market, but by that time it was reportedly responsible for a dozen deaths and over four hundred severe allergic reactions, almost all of which were kept quiet through secret settlements worked out by McNeil, the drug's manufacturer.

The Dalkon Shield intrauterine device was taken off the market, but only after numerous secret settlements that left the public in the dark long after the dangers of the product were known to those involved in the litigation. Attorneys for A. H. Robins, the Dalkon Shield's manufacturer, even tried to condition settlements on the plaintiffs' lawyers' promises never to take another Dalkon case. This is a clear violation of the ethics rules of almost every state, which prohibit buying off lawyers in this way for public policy reasons.

In 1984 a woman named Maria Stern went to trial against Dow Corning and won a $1.7 million judgment for damage caused by her silicone breast implants. When Dow Corning offered to settle on appeal on the condition that neither Stern nor her lawyers could ever refer to the damaging information they had discovered, Stern felt she had no choice. She knew that any other course meant years of appeal with an array of the best legal talent aligned against her before she would see a penny. She finally accepted the deal.

The public remained in the dark about breast implants for years afterward. So did the Food and Drug Administration, whose head, Dr. David Kessler, angrily complained that it had taken the FDA seven years to find out what the lawyers litigating breast implant cases had known all along but kept secret. Once he learned of the evidence, Kessler acted quickly, insisting on a ban on the further use of silicone implants. Since the ban, tens of thousands of women have contacted the FDA complaining of serious injuries caused by their implants. Legal and scientific experts are still arguing whether silicone implants are truly dangerous, but this argument begs the more fundamental question of whether the public has a right to know what the risks are when it's buying a product.

No product with a suspicious track record has been more thoroughly defended by more lawyers and on more fronts than General Motors pickup trucks with side-mounted gas tanks. In Chapter Three we saw how GM's lawyers took the offensive when they sued Ralph Nader, the Center for Auto Safety, and others for defaming their client's product. Meanwhile, other GM lawyers were quietly settling individual cases involving exploding side-mounted gas

tanks with amazing frequency. According to its own records, GM
settled approximately two hundred such cases while continuing to
argue that the tank mountings were perfectly safe. Almost all the
settlements required that all information be kept secret from anyone not a party to the case.

It is difficult to believe that the settlement of hundreds of lawsuits
about dangerous drugs or exploding gas tanks results merely from
unsupported individual claims. There is a point beyond which
"anecdotal evidence" takes on a clear pattern. Where that pattern
points to the existence of a danger to the public health and safety—
or even the serious *possibility* of such a danger—it is time to ask
whether our legal system can afford to allow such secrecy.

Not only does suppressing evidence deny information to the
public, but it unbalances the scales between plaintiff and defendant.
Plaintiffs' lawyers have to start each case from scratch—from the
beginning of a difficult discovery process—with no evidence about
previous cases, and without being able to share either information
or ideas. Meanwhile, defense attorneys are aware of the entire history of litigation over the product. They're able to learn from experience, developing new, higher hurdles for plaintiffs' lawyers to
leap in order to get the same information others already have but
promise not to reveal.

The adversary theorem plays a major role in this suppression of
evidence about potential dangers to the public. If a lawyer's obligation is to put the needs of each individual client first, then the public welfare is likely to finish a distant second at best, if not a poor
third to the lawyer's own fees.

Many lawyers who defend product liability cases argue that
their duty to their clients *requires* them to promote secret settlements that conceal the clients' mistakes. The rules governing their
conduct allow for little sentiment, either for the opponent or for the
public. Lawyers are taught that short of lying to or misleading the
court, they owe their clients their best efforts. To defense lawyers,
this means pushing for secrecy if they can get it. Plaintiffs' lawyers
like Andrea Hardy have the same duties to their clients under the
same ethics rules. Many feel impelled by their duty of loyalty to
their client to accept a settlement that benefits that client, even when

they recognize that secrecy could harm the public as a whole. They also know that while they can advise the client what to do, the client has the ultimate right to decide whether to settle the case.

There is one other major player involved in the issue of secrecy: the judge. Many agreements about secrecy occur well before settlement. Courts have the power to issue "protective orders," orders that require one side to disclose information and documents to the other, but only on the precondition that the information will not be used outside the case. Often these orders require returning the documents when the case is over. Protective orders are ordinarily issued for one of two reasons: the protected information contains "trade secrets," such as state-of-the-art designs that could be stolen by competitors if made public; or more generally, in the words of the federal discovery rule, "to protect a party or person from annoyance, embarrassment, oppression, or undue burden or expense."

It's difficult to argue that information about a defective car part or a drug's dangerous side effects is entitled to protection as a "trade secret." Competitors are hardly likely to steal the information about another company's defects and use it themselves. So lawyers seeking to keep discovery secret often rely on their clients' rights of privacy. "Litigants do not give up their privacy rights simply because they have walked, voluntarily or involuntarily, through the courthouse door," argues Professor Miller. And, says Miller, no plaintiff, just by paying a court filing fee, should be able to force a defendant to disclose "intensely personal and confidential information." Courts exist to serve "private parties bringing a private dispute."

Still, plaintiffs also have an important right—the First Amendment right to free speech. Here that means the right to tell what they have learned about their case. Our courts have always been open to the public, ever since the English ended the secretive Star Chamber that darkened the courts in the days of Henry VIII. Free expression depends on the court being a *public* forum, not the private arena Miller describes. And free expression means that once you discover information about a case, you should be free to share it as you see fit.

Our courts, including the United States Supreme Court, have decided that when these two rights conflict—one side's right to privacy and the other's right to freedom of expression—the presumption favors openness, unless there is "good cause" for a judge to believe that protecting the information is necessary, and that it furthers a "substantial government interest." The United States Supreme Court protected a religious group's list of members on this basis, citing the constitutional right to freedom of religion. But protection from "annoyance" and "embarrassment" hardly seems to rise to that level.

Since few written court opinions have dealt with these issues directly—fewer still where the public's health and safety may be at risk—the average trial judge has enormous discretion to decide what should be protected from disclosure. Unfortunately, not all judges are up to this task. Some simply don't want to decide; they would rather have the lawyers work it out. If the parties can't agree, some judges believe that the safest thing is to protect everything. One such order, in the case of a woman who killed her own mother while in a mood-altered state caused by Halcion, prevented disclosure of any information about the drug.

Most judges feel that if the lawyers agree on what should be kept secret, why should they object? Almost every court has a policy that settlements should be encouraged; settlements not only resolve disputes but help clear the court's calendar. If secrecy encourages settlement, judges are reluctant to intrude. Some observers have estimated that as many as nine out of ten judges will agree to a protective order if both sides support it. And plaintiffs' lawyers often agree because it's the quickest, least expensive, easiest way to get the information they want.

Judge H. Lee Sarokin, a federal judge in New Jersey who heard two of the first product liability suits against the tobacco industry, tried to keep the information in those cases open to public view. "I must confess," he told a reporter some years later, "that for a considerable period of time, as a routine matter I signed consent orders [if] the parties agreed and the lawyers agreed. . . . But I slowly came to the realization that there were other interests involved." Those interests, of course, belonged to the public.

Product liability cases are not the only places secret settlements are used. And concealing documents, either by protective orders or by returning them to their original owners after settlement, is not the only way that information about lawsuits is kept secret. A few examples:

- A home for the mentally disabled secretly settles a case accusing the home's administrator of sexually abusing someone with Down's syndrome; the administrator privately admits molesting over a dozen others.
- The Catholic Church's Chicago archdiocese secretly settles a molestation case, ostensibly to protect the child, while at the same time criticizing the boy's parents from behind the veil of secrecy. An investigation by *Chicago Lawyer* estimated that four hundred lawsuits had been settled by the Catholic Church in the previous decade—almost all of them secretly.
- Baker & McKenzie, the country's largest law firm, settles an AIDS discrimination case reminiscent of the movie *Philadelphia* by getting a promise of silence.

When doctors, lawyers, health care facilities, and churches are sued, they are often not satisfied merely to keep the settlement and the evidence secret. Reporters and other interested lawyers know how to search local court dockets for lawsuits. So defense attorneys sometimes insist that plaintiffs' lawyers join them in stipulating that the names of the parties be changed from the real names to, say, the law firm of Doe & Roe, or the XYZ Nursing Home. Some states, among them California, allow the parties to stipulate to reverse the jury's decision. This way, the real winners get paid and avoid appeal—but the losers avoid having a judgment against them. Or the lawyers might stipulate to "depublish" any written court opinions that provide information future plaintiffs could use. In Maria Stern's breast implant case, these changes were actually made at Dow Corning's insistence *after* the jury trial and award, by a stipulation to vacate the verdict and seal the court record from public view.

Since the names are changed, it is difficult to tell how often this happens. Usually, though, these stipulations require the approval of a judge. It might be assumed that such approval would only rarely be given. But a case settled means another matter removed from a crowded docket, leading some judges to do little more than rubber-stamp these requests without examining the reasons for secrecy.

Defense lawyers justify their part in these procedures as simply doing their job. They justify the court's actions too by arguing, as Professor Miller put it, that a court is not designed to be an "information clearinghouse" and that judges are ill-equipped to be "informational ombudsmen" for the public.

Plaintiffs' lawyers generally exhibit more reluctance to engage in these concealments, but often they feel they have little choice. They have an obligation to accept good settlements, and in many cases they believe they won't get a settlement without agreeing to secrecy. Even if they feel that secrecy is morally unjustified, their duty to their client overrides their reservations. They also fear that turning down these settlements puts them at risk in trial, where their client can always lose, even with a good case, against a large and capable defense team before a jury of twelve strangers. And always increasing the enormous pressure they feel are the substantial fees—all contingent on the outcome of the case—that they will receive for accepting the secret settlement.

Sometimes the effort to keep evidence secret from the public simply goes too far, even in a world where the rules say that the client comes first. That was the case in the Louisville trial of *Fentress v. Eli Lilly & Co.*

In September 1989 Joseph Wesbecker, a forty-seven-year-old printing worker with a ten-year history of mental illness and at least two suicide attempts, armed himself with an AK-47, walked into the Louisville printing plant where he had worked, and started shooting. By the time the horror stopped, Wesbecker had killed eight people, wounded twelve more, and finished things off by blowing his own brains out. One month before, Wesbecker had begun taking Prozac; the lawyers for the shooting victims soon focused on Prozac as the cause of Wesbecker's extraordinary violence.

The *Fentress* case, named for one of Wesbecker's victims, was the first of 160 cases pending against Prozac to go to trial. Lilly and its lawyers were understandably determined to defend Prozac with everything they had. By the time *Fentress* went to trial in the fall of 1994, Prozac had become the aspirin of antidepressants—the wonder drug everyone was talking about and millions were using. Prozac represented almost one-third of all Lilly sales in 1994—$1.7 billion. A great deal was at stake. If Lilly lost, the other plaintiffs waiting in the wings would gain strength and resolve. But if Lilly could win an outright victory, those plaintiffs might think twice about their cases.

Fentress was considered a relatively weak Prozac case—one that Lilly was confident it could win. Most of the other lawsuits focused on people who had taken the drug themselves and claimed to experience serious adverse reactions. But in *Fentress*, the plaintiffs themselves had never used Prozac; they claimed harm by a *third party*, Wesbecker. They would have the difficult task of proving that Prozac caused Wesbecker to act as he did.

The case went to trial in Louisville before Jefferson Circuit judge John Potter, who combined a keen, Harvard-educated mind with a courtly, soft-spoken southern manner. Throughout the case the plaintiffs' lead attorneys, Paul Smith, of Dallas, and Nancy Zettler, of Illinois, pushed Judge Potter to allow evidence about another Lilly product, the anti-inflammatory drug Oraflex. Oraflex had been taken off the market in 1982 because it was too dangerous. In 1985 Lilly pled guilty to twenty-five criminal counts of failing to report adverse reactions to Oraflex, including four deaths, to the federal Food and Drug Administration. The company's chief research scientist was found guilty on fifteen counts. Smith and Zettler wanted to use Lilly's failure to report the truth about Oraflex as evidence that they had done the same thing with Prozac. But Judge Potter refused to allow it, saying it was marginally relevant at best, and would prejudice the jury more than it would prove anything.

Then, after weeks of trial, Lilly and its lawyers made a bad mistake. Lilly executives testified that the company had an excellent reputation for reporting problem incidents with their drugs—what they euphemistically called "adverse events." Lilly's top scientist, the man whose predecessor had been convicted years before, testified that the FDA "repeatedly said that we, Lilly, have the best system for collecting and analyzing and reporting adverse events."

This testimony was in direct conflict with Lilly's criminal failure to report "adverse events" about Oraflex. Since much of the plaintiffs' case rested on Lilly's accuracy in reporting problems with its drugs, plaintiffs' counsel immediately renewed their request to bring in the Oraflex evidence. This time, on December 7, 1994, noting that "Lilly has injected the issue into the trial," Judge Potter agreed.

Judge Potter's ruling set off a flurry of activity around his courtroom. Plaintiffs' and defense lawyers twice jointly asked for long recesses. Then a dozen or more junior lawyers on the case, mostly local counsel from Louisville, arrived. The press descended on the scene. Groups of lawyers huddled together in courthouse corridors. In midafternoon the lawyers asked the judge to postpone the case for a day. By now a strong scent of settlement was in the air.

But when Judge Potter reconvened the case the following afternoon, he was surprised by what he heard. Chief plaintiffs' counsel Smith announced that the plaintiffs would rest without presenting the Oraflex evidence unless the trial went to its second phase, which would address the amount of the financial award. That stage would occur *only* if the jury decided in the first phase that Lilly was liable. If the jury found Lilly not liable, the case would be over, and the Oraflex evidence would never be heard. The plaintiffs' high-risk strategy puzzled Judge Potter; they could lose their whole case without presenting their best evidence. Potter asked the lawyers whether they had reached a settlement. He was told unequivocally that they had not.

The plaintiffs rested their case, and closing arguments were presented to the jury the very next day. By December 12, only three court days after Potter's ruling allowing the Oraflex evidence, the jury rendered its verdict: By a 9-to-3 vote, the minimum three-fourths majority, Lilly was found not liable. The case was over. In January 1995 Judge Potter formally entered his order in *Fentress v. Eli Lilly* dismissing the case after verdict by jury.

As soon as the verdict was in, Lilly and its lawyers trumpeted their victory across the country. "We were able, finally," said John McGoldrick, of Newark, New Jersey, one of Lilly's lead attorneys, "to get people head to head in a courtroom and say 'Put up or shut up.' . . . [T]his is a complete vindication of the medicine." Company spokesman Ed West candidly told Louisville *Courier-Journal* reporter Leslie Scanlon that Lilly hoped the verdict would send a message to the other Prozac plaintiffs across the country, and that many of the 160 pending Prozac cases "would be dismissed or just dropped."

Had John Potter not been the judge, the *Fentress* case might have ended there. But Potter was troubled by the events of early December. He asked himself why any lawyer would fight so hard over the key Oraflex evidence and then not present it in the most important part of the case. Despite what the lawyers had told him, Potter suspected that some kind of deal had been made. But he decided to be patient. He waited to see whether the plaintiffs would file a notice of their intent to appeal, a routine matter after losing a case. They did not.

When the time for appeal had run out, Potter called the lawyers from both sides to his chambers. The lawyers continued to deny that a settlement had been reached, but the meeting left Potter even more convinced that they had secretly settled the case—that Lilly had traded money for keeping the potentially damning Oraflex evidence out of the trial. But the case was over; Potter had no jurisdiction, except as to his own order of dismissal. In April 1995, stating "it is more likely than not that the case was settled," Potter filed an unusual document: his own motion to change his post-trial order from a dismissal after verdict to "dismissed as settled." He set a hearing for May.

Judge Potter's motion shook and divided the Louisville legal community. Richard Hay, then president of the Kentucky Academy of Trial Attorneys, told reporters that if money had been traded for evidence, the trial was a "sham," like "taking a dive in a boxing match." But Louisville trial lawyer Gary Weiss told the *Courier-Journal*'s Leslie Scanlon that he saw nothing wrong. A lawyer's work "has nothing to do with truth and justice," Weiss proclaimed. "It has to do with winning. . . . Paul Smith wasn't hired to be a private FDA. . . . He was hired to win money."

Meanwhile, counsel for both sides remained silent. In late April Lilly spokesman Ed West acknowledged that both sides had agreed not to appeal, but he refused further comment other than to tell the *Courier-Journal* that "the case was not settled." Admitting settlement, after all, would weaken Lilly's public proclamation that it had won the case outright at trial. By mid-May the lawyers on both sides joined forces to file an objection with Kentucky's appeals court to Judge Potter's hearing anything about what they considered a closed case.

Lead plaintiffs' lawyer Paul Smith finally spoke in mid-May: "There was no secret settlement. . . . This was a hard fought case." Lilly's lawyers continued their press silence. Only West and Lilly vice president Stephen Stitle spoke on the record for the company. "There was no agreement or even any discussion about settling the case without allowing the jury to decide," wrote Stitle in a letter to the *Courier-Journal*. But Stitle's letter, couched in the best legalese, failed to reveal whether the jury was being allowed to decide real issues or whether it was unknowingly taking part in a sham trial.

The *Fentress* lawyers' objections to Judge Potter's motion sent the case to the appeals court and forced Potter to hire an attorney himself. He found his lawyer in the newspaper. Potter had read Richard Hay's comments about a sham trial, called him up, and asked how outraged Hay was about the case. "Enough to represent you," Hay replied. Together Hay and Potter filed a brief in the appeals court that was both blunt and direct: "It is unbelievable that the plaintiffs would reach a settlement, and then want to keep it secret, particularly where the essence of their claims was that Lilly covered up information. Their public silence has been bought and paid for. [¶] Secrecy is certainly not important to the millions of people taking Prozac and the thousands of doctors prescribing Prozac. They want the truth." Potter didn't contend that Prozac was dangerous, only that the public had the right to know all the relevant information, pro and con.

The public portion of the *Fentress* settlement story had just begun. On June 12, 1995, the appeals court heard arguments, and three days later sided with Lilly and the *Fentress* plaintiffs, ruling that Judge Potter no longer had jurisdiction over the case. Potter appealed to the Kentucky Supreme Court.

During the spring and summer of 1995, bits and pieces of the settlement gradually came out. Before the June appeals court hearing, Lilly spokesperson West admitted that Lilly had agreed with plaintiffs not to present the Oraflex evidence. And before the fall Supreme Court hearing, lawyers for both sides acknowledged that they had indeed settled all money issues and had agreed to go through only the first, liability phase of the trial no matter what the result. Still, no one would disclose any details.

In their appeal to the Supreme Court, Potter and Hay took a new tack. They deemphasized the importance of public disclosure and focused instead on the fact that the lawyers had not been candid with the judge. As their first brief made clear, both Potter and Hay believed that the *Fentress* parties had denied the public vital information when Lilly "bought and paid for" the plaintiffs' silence. But that argument had gotten them nowhere in the court of appeal. By emphasizing the lawyers' lack of candor and honesty in their second brief, they had a much better chance of getting the attention of the Supreme Court. After all, lying to or misleading a court is a clear, unambiguous ethics violation and, just as important, doesn't sit well with judges.

In the new brief Potter and Hay cited transcripts of hearings in chambers. The most charitable assessment of these transcripts was that both sides' lawyers had been less than candid with the court. It was also reasonable to interpret these transcripts more strongly— that the lawyers had simply lied to the judge.

In one meeting in chambers, while the jury was deliberating, a juror came forward and told Judge Potter that she had overheard settlement negotiations going on in the hallway. She repeated this with the lawyers present and was then excused. Potter turned to the lawyers and said, "Does anybody have anything they want to say?" A moment later he asked again, "Does anybody have the slightest clue?" "No," said chief plaintiffs' counsel Smith. "I can't imagine," said defense lawyer Edward Stopher. Stopher may possibly not have known of the settlement, but no one else in the room full of lawyers said a word.

The lawyers all knew that their agreement meant that phase two of the trial, determining the financial damages, would never occur under any circumstances. But they repeatedly misled Judge Potter about the trial going on to this second phase. Smith asked the judge for "ground rules" about what he could say about the second phase in his closing argument in phase one. The defense lawyers played their roles, objecting to Smith's saying anything at all about phase two. When the judge discussed how much of a break should be taken between the two phases, the lawyers continued to play their parts, with Smith kiddingly asking whether his Christmas presents could be sent care of the court. When Potter suggested that the two sides meet for settlement if the plaintiffs won phase one, chief defense counsel Joe Freeman Jr.—the same Joe Freeman we met in Chapter Three, when he was sanctioned for discovery abuses in the Isuzu rollover cases in Atlanta—assured Potter that a Lilly executive with authority to settle would be available, even though he knew that Lilly had already agreed to the terms of the settlement.

Meanwhile in Indianapolis, Lilly's hometown, a series of Prozac cases was consolidated for trial before federal district court judge S. Hugh Dillin. Paul Smith had been lead counsel in those cases, too. Smith's presence was important because he was in charge of taking depositions and gathering documents for all cases before Judge Dillin, not just his own. During the summer of 1995, while the Louisville case was going through appeals, Smith suddenly withdrew as lead counsel in Indianapolis. Several of the other plaintiffs' lawyers asked the judge to find out whether Smith had settled his Indianapolis cases as part of the *Fentress* settlement. Smith refused to say and the judge refused to investigate.

On May 23, 1996, the Kentucky Supreme Court decided the case of *Hon. John W. Potter v. Eli Lilly* unanimously in Judge Potter's favor. Commenting bluntly on the conduct of the lawyers for both sides in *Fentress*, the court said that "there was a serious lack of candor with the trial court, and there may have been deception, bad faith conduct, abuse of the judicial process or perhaps even fraud." Hay and Potter's strategy—focusing on the affront to the court rather than the public's right to know—had worked. The court opinion concentrated not on the secrecy of the agreement but the deceitful conduct of the lawyers. Although the court said that the "only result" of exposing the secret *Fentress* agreement "is that the truth will be revealed," the decision was less a victory for open settlements and more a demand that the judge be included in the secret.

Judge Potter, though, still saw the larger issue. Armed with

Supreme Court authority to conduct an investigation and hold a hearing, Potter asked deputy state attorney general Ann Sheadel to conduct the investigation, giving her the power to subpoena documents and question witnesses under oath. Sheadel's March 1997 report uncovered new twists to the story. A complex agreement did exist between Lilly and the plaintiffs, one so secret that it was never fully reduced to writing. Sheadel uncovered a written summary of the verbal agreement, though no lawyer would admit preparing it and no plaintiff was allowed to have it.

The plaintiffs and their lawyers had agreed not to present the Oraflex evidence. In exchange, the plaintiffs would be paid whether they won or lost phase one. Only if the jury deadlocked would the deal be off. And if the plaintiffs won, they'd get a bonus if the jury found Lilly to be more than 30 percent at fault, and another if the fault was over 50 percent. But Lilly, after all, had not pulled the trigger; Wesbecker had. That made such high percentages of fault extremely unlikely, meaning that the plaintiffs were paid for their silence more than anything else. Even Sheadel failed to uncover the settlement amounts.

As for chief plaintiffs' counsel Paul Smith, part of the agreement was that *all* of Smith's Prozac cases, including those in Indianapolis, would be settled, and half his overall expenses paid by Lilly. Thus Smith may have been the single person with the most to gain by settling the *Fentress* case.

Judge Potter set a hearing to take sworn testimony on March 27, 1997. The hearing never happened. On March 24, in a surprise move, attorneys John Tate for Lilly and William Nold for the plaintiffs presented Judge Potter with a proposed new order in *Fentress*, showing that the case was dismissed "as settled," exactly what Potter's original motion had demanded two years earlier. The judge signed the order.

On March 25 Leslie Scanlon's lead in the *Courier-Journal* read: "Eli Lilly & Co. acknowledged yesterday what Jefferson Circuit Judge John Potter has tried for two years to get the drug-maker to admit: That it 'settled' the Prozac case by striking a secret agreement with plaintiffs." Plaintiffs' lawyer Nold admitted the case had been settled. But on March 26 the paper printed a "correction": Lilly denied admitting that the case had "settled" before the jury verdict, despite the order Tate presented to the judge.

On March 27 Tate, now armed with that order, appeared before the Kentucky appeals court in another effort to avoid a hearing in front of Potter. Tate argued that Potter had violated judicial ethics and was on a "vendetta" against Lilly. He called it a "lie" to brand the *Fentress* trial a sham. The next day Judge Potter, realizing his involvement had become a distraction from the main issue, wrote a brief order removing himself from *Fentress*. "Put simply," his order said, "the spotlight should be on what . . . is under the log, not the person trying to roll it over."

By this time the judge had accomplished what he had set out to do: set the record straight. The collusive settlement was no longer secret. But of the approximately 160 active Prozac cases in December 1994, less than half remained. The Kentucky court of appeal determined that any further hearings on the *Fentress* matter would be closed to the public. While the local press and a few legal trade papers had picked up the story of the Lilly settlement, the *Fentress* case had inexplicably received almost no attention in the national media. Plaintiffs' attorney Paul Smith was still practicing law in Dallas. And the only thing that anyone ever learned about the amount of the settlement was the comment of a Louisville lawyer who represented one of the *Fentress* plaintiffs in a divorce. The amount, he said, was "tremendous."

Cases such as *Fentress* take secret settlements to a new level. Instead of merely hiding information about a potential danger to the public, *Fentress* offered *disinformation* about those dangers, by bargaining away the use of important evidence. This kind of behavior is by no means unique; what is unusual is that the lawyers were caught by an exceptionally courageous judge.

Shocking as it may be, the behavior of the lawyers in the *Fentress* case is easy enough to explain. The defense lawyers would argue that they were "just doing their job." They sought not to win an individual case, but to protect their client's most important asset, Prozac. Their strategy was to minimize damage on a national scope. Indeed, what happened in *Fentress* did not prove that Prozac was unsafe. It only proved the lengths to which the defense team was willing to go both to deny people the right to judge Prozac for themselves and to cloud that judgment by suppressing the available information.

For the plaintiffs' attorneys, the issues were different. Many lawyers commenting on *Fentress* were critical of the plaintiffs' counsel. But aside from deceiving the court, several admitted that they too might have done the same thing if their clients were offered "tremendous" sums. These lawyers understood the dilemma: The ethical lawyer's duty is to represent the client's interests within the bounds of the law; the consequences to the public are secondary. But this black-letter rule of ethics is at odds with ordinary, everyday morality. Hiding information about a potential danger to the public is wrong, and fooling the public with a false state of the evidence is even worse. Nevertheless, as one West Coast attorney put it, if Lilly offered him $1 million for each client so long as he left out certain evidence, his first duty would be to do what his client wanted, including taking the money. "On the other hand," he continued, "you have to ask, 'What about the other victims in the other cases?'"

Not all lawyers would be so concerned. Greed is a powerful force. *Fentress* showed how money can be used by the defense to change the plaintiffs' counsel from sworn enemies one day to allies in a cover-up the next. Did Paul Smith allow greed to govern his actions? Only he can say, but most lawyers would at least be tempted. For years at a time, these lawyers spend thousands of hours and hundreds of thousands of dollars fighting cases against bigger and better-financed opponents. They recover their fees and expenses only if they win. If the day ever comes when the opponent offers "tremendous" sums to settle, almost any lawyer would give it serious consideration, no matter what conditions are placed on settlement.

In September 1995 *American Lawyer* published a feature piece about the Louisville Prozac case. The magazine asked six "ethics experts" about the conduct of the *Fentress* lawyers. All agreed that misleading the judge was wrong, but five of the six defended the agreement itself as within the bounds of ethics, even though it came down to paying money to suppress evidence. This strong consensus raises the issue of whether the ethical conduct of lawyers is sufficiently tied to the ordinary moral conduct of human affairs.

We cannot expect morality to come only from the bench. There are not nearly enough judges like H. Lee Sarokin, who believe that part of their job is protecting the public interest. Fewer still are willing to take the risks John Potter did to test a secret deal. So unless the rules of the game are changed to prevent settlements that conceal information important to the public, these settlements—and trials like *Fentress*—are certain to continue.

Lawsuit secrecy need not be a foregone conclusion. In some situations plaintiffs' lawyers have been able to stand up to defense counsel and refuse to settle unless the information they obtained remains public. Plaintiffs' lawyers settled two hundred Minnesota Dalkon Shield cases in 1984 while insisting that all documents and depositions they had obtained remain available to other plaintiffs. But they had the help of federal judge Miles Lord, who took a strong stand against defendant A. H. Robins's efforts to maintain secrecy. In many more cases, without the force of a law behind them, lawyers feel powerless to insist on such conditions.

Such laws have begun to develop. In 1990 Texas approved Rule of Civil Procedure 76a, which broadly prohibits secret agreements. It starts with the proposition that all court records must be open. No judge may seal something from public view, even if the lawyers for both sides agree, unless the judge finds that a "specific, serious and substantial interest" needs protection and that secrecy is the only way to accomplish it. Those who really need secrecy—abused children, for instance, or vulnerable elderly victims of fraud—can get it, but those hoping only to hide their own mistakes cannot.

Texas's rule has three other important components. First, it covers not just the usual court records and proceedings, but *all* documents, whether filed with the court or merely given to the other side during discovery. Second, court orders and opinions can *never* be sealed, so the names can never be changed, or the decision "depublished," to protect the guilty. Third, secrecy orders can be challenged not just by the parties but by anyone, including the press or consumer groups.

Rules like Texas's don't become law without a fight and without personal commitment. Congressman Lloyd Doggett was the driving force behind this rule, first as a member of the Texas legislature, where he helped draft it, and then as the Texas Supreme Court justice who spearheaded the rule's approval by a 5-to-4 vote. In his impassioned arguments to protect the public welfare, Doggett quoted Supreme Court justices, philosophers, and presidents from Jefferson to Nixon who had taken a stand against secrecy.

Before the rule was passed, opponents bombarded the court with warnings: openness would create dire economic consequences; no one would settle without keeping matters secret; challenges to secrecy orders would clog the courts. None of these things happened. In the rule's first three and a half years, there was only one successful challenge to a secrecy order.

Since 1990 about a dozen states have adopted some prohibition on keeping secrets from the public. Some states' laws are limited and weak, but a few make a real difference. Florida's 1990 Sunshine in Litigation Act directly prevents secret settlements and secrecy orders that conceal information about "public hazards," a phrase the legislature defined broadly. In 1993 Washington State passed a similar law, the Public Right to Know Bill.

But no rule or law works perfectly. Both the Texas rule and the Florida law have great strengths, but also significant weaknesses. Like most standards, they have a certain amount of wiggle room, which means they still depend on individual judges who are willing to take strong stands. Many judges, perhaps less resolute than John Potter, focus on encouraging settlement, and see secrecy as often being the easiest path to that goal.

More important, neither Texas nor Florida directly addressed the behavior of lawyers. Nothing prevents Texas plaintiffs' lawyers and defense counsel from working together to convince a judge that *their* case is that rare one where secrecy is needed. Florida prohibits secrecy agreements between attorneys but has no specific penalties. Parties who enter secrecy agreements in Washington are liable for violating consumer protection laws, but that still doesn't directly punish the *lawyers*. Lawyers from both sides are right where they have always been—in the position of vigorously representing their clients while putting aside the needs of the public. The current ethics rules don't forbid lawyers from acting this way; if anything, the client-first principle fosters it.

The few far-reaching "sunshine" laws remain under continued attack. A 1993 Texas court case limited outsiders' challenges to secrecy orders, while a 1992 lawsuit attacked Florida's law on the grounds that corporations have constitutional rights to privacy. In other states, the effort was over before it began. In 1991 the California legislature considered Senate Bill 711, a far-reaching proposal that would have made secrecy orders and agreements illegal in cases concerning defective products, environmental hazards, and financial frauds. The bill passed both houses of the legislature but was vetoed by Governor Pete Wilson.

California Senate Bill 711 included a provision that would actually have disciplined lawyers who engaged in secret settlements. This statute had the right idea. If lawyers' ethics rules required that attorneys could no longer put their clients' interests ahead of the public health and safety *and* that they would be disciplined for doing so, lawyers would be unlikely to continue to find loopholes around "sunshine" laws. Until then, many will insist that it is their affirmative ethical duty to do this, even where the public is at risk. And innocent people will be injured or die as a result.

Epilogue:
The Boyette Settlement

After receiving the documents and the $5 million offer, Andrea Hardy spent most of that night and the following day closeted in the conference room with her two partners trying to decide how to advise the Boyettes. There were two things on which all three partners quickly agreed: that hiding evidence of a dangerous product like the heart valve was wrong; and that $5 million and the lawyers' one-third contingency fee were very large sums of money.

The partners all knew that advising the Boyettes was part of Andrea's job. Some lawyers give advice objectively, laying out the pluses and minuses as if on a balance scale. Others argue forcefully for what they think is best. At first Andrea took the position that she should tell Mrs. Boyette to turn the offer down: "How can we tell the family to accept this offer when we know people will die if they're not warned?" "But how can we tell them *not* to accept it?" argued Norman Yanahiro. "Our duty is to our client, right? Are we supposed to tell Jeanie Boyette to turn this down? She's got five kids, two still in high school, three in college. Are you telling me you're allowed to impose your moral judgment on her?"

Joe Geisel believed in "going by the book," so he spent most of the day looking for guidance in the state's Rules of Conduct Governing Lawyers. He found several references to a lawyer's duty of "competent," "diligent," or "zealous" representation, but nothing preventing a lawyer from accepting a secret settlement, even when the public could be harmed. When Geisel pulled out the written court opinions, he found several cases that allowed secret settlements as long as all parties agreed. No cases directly discussed harm to the public. "It's clear, Andrea," he finally concluded. "*Nothing* prohibits this settlement. If anything, the rules support Norman— our duty is to do what's best for the Boyettes." "But what *is* best for them?" Andrea replied heatedly. "They've got to live with this, too. How will they feel about letting other people die? Isn't that part of what they need to be thinking about?"

Eventually Andrea softened her position. She agreed she would present both sides to Jeanie Boyette without making her own recommendation, and let the family decide. She met with Mrs. Boyette and her oldest child, John, told them the amount of the settlement offer, and explained George Burger's two secrecy conditions. She told them they would probably never get as much money, even at trial. She also reminded them how other people with similar heart valves could be hurt or even die unless the truth became known. But she stopped there, without giving them her own personal recommendation—to turn the settlement down because of the enormous moral costs.

That night, thinking back on what she had said, she regretted she hadn't made the big speech—about other patients like Mr. Boyette whose valves had not yet failed; about other families who'd suffered a loss like the Boyettes', and what they would have to go through to fight their case from scratch; and about the fact that while they should not expect $5 million, the Boyettes were still likely to do very well at trial. She knew how persuasive she could be in advising her clients, and she knew she had pulled her punches.

Andrea and her partners had talked excitedly about how much they might earn—one-third of $5 million was an awful lot of money—but she was pleased that no one seemed to lose sight of the fact that their advice shouldn't be colored by the size of their own paycheck. Still, Andrea wondered to what extent her fees were in the back of her mind as she spoke to the Boyettes. After all, those fees meant college tuition not just for the Boyettes but for her own two children. She was not surprised when John Boyette called the next day to say that the family had met, discussed the offer, and decided to accept it.

In the weeks that followed, Andrea Hardy second-guessed herself a hundred times. Her clients were good people. She wondered how they would feel about the blanket of secrecy six months or a year from now. She knew that her opponent still would have settled for a reasonable sum just to avoid the exposure of a trial. She was losing sleep, and when she slept she dreamed about heart valve victims lying in a row in the hospital, or the press conference she never held at which she announced to the world the smoking-gun evidence she'd found.

Andrea finally went to her partners and told them that she never wanted to be in the same position again, forced to choose between the public safety and the duty to her clients. She proposed adding a provision to the firm's fee contract: "Client is aware that Geisel, Yanahiro & Hardy will not agree to accept settlement of Client's case if the settlement would keep from public disclosure evidence of a danger of substantial physical harm to members of the public. By agreeing to have GY&H represent Client, Client also agrees not to accept a settlement under such conditions."

Andrea's partners agreed to include this language in their contracts. So far no client has turned the firm down because of the provision, and a few have even complimented her for including it. But Andrea knows that it's one thing for clients to accept these ground rules at the beginning of the case, when they see themselves in the same light as other victims, and another thing entirely at the end of a case, when real money is on the table.

Andrea and her partners also know that when an offer to settle is made, they have an ethical duty to present it to their clients. The client always controls the ultimate outcome of the case, and Andrea wouldn't want it any other way. Because a client has the ultimate decision over whether to settle or not, and has the right to fire the lawyer at any time, Andrea knows it may be impossible to hold her clients to this agreement. And because their state's ethics rules require them to put their clients' interests first, they also know that concern for the public safety is a luxury the partners can't always afford.

CHAPTER 10

Class Actions:
Public Protection or
Windfalls for Lawyers?

A powerful force for public good.
> —Attorney Arthur Bryant, whose public interest law firm
> has a "Class Action Abuse Prevention Project,"
> giving his opinion of class actions generally

Legal jargon that the average citizen cannot understand.
> —Former Maine senator William Cohen, describing
> a typical class action notice

First Thing We Do, Let's Pay All the Lawyers
> —Headline in the *New York Times*, 1997,
> after settlement of secondhand smoke tobacco class action
> included $49 million in attorneys' fees

Joseph and Joella Winston both teach at the local high school in the midsized midwestern city where they grew up. Joseph teaches math and coaches football; Joella teaches English. About eight months ago the Winstons received a document in the mail. The return address on the envelope said "In re Tri-County Computer Litigation." Inside were two documents, both printed, single-spaced, 8½-by-11-inch booklets. The first page of each booklet had the words "In re Tri-County Computer Litigation," a case number, the names of two law firms, and the address of the local United States District Court. The first booklet, twelve pages long, carried the title **"Class Action,"** and underneath that, **"Notice of Pendency and Settlement."** The second document, five pages long, said **"Proof of Claim and Release Form,"** and under that, **"General Instructions."**

The Winstons had never heard of any of the lawyers, and couldn't figure out why they had received the documents. They knew Tri-County, because it was the largest computer retailer in the area. They had bought their own home computer there a few years ago. The first document began, in capital letters: "PLEASE READ THIS NOTICE CAREFULLY. IT RELATES TO THE PENDENCY AND PROPOSED SETTLEMENT OF THIS CLASS LITIGATION AND IF YOU ARE A CLASS MEMBER CONTAINS IMPORTANT INFORMATION AS TO YOUR RIGHTS TO OBTAIN A SHARE OF THE SETTLEMENT FUND DESCRIBED BELOW."

The Winstons weren't sure what the settlement was about. They hadn't heard about it or read anything in the newspapers. But they sat down and read both documents. The section of the document entitled "The Proposed Settlement" was four single-spaced pages long and had eleven subsections. By the time they finished reading, they were almost as confused as when they had started.

The next day Joella called the local bar association's lawyer referral service to see whether she could get a legal opinion on the document. She paid a $25 fee to speak to a lawyer for a half hour. He explained that a class action case had been filed against Tri-County over a misleading promotion. The case had just settled. If the Winstons had bought a computer from Tri-County during the period in question, they might be part of the class and eligible to receive part of the settlement. "But," he said, "these cases are complicated. Your best bet is to call the law firms listed on the forms."

The next day the Winstons called the 800 number listed in the document under the heading "To Get Further Information." They called three times, but each time they got a recording that repeated the same general information they already had. At this point they understood neither what the case was all about nor how it could affect them. They were irritated that some lawyers had made them part of a lawsuit without their permission, and frustrated that the forms were so complicated and that they had no one to call for advice.

The first listed firm on the class action notice sent to the Winstons was Stockhauser & Plevin. For the last thirty years Gabriel Plevin has practiced law just a few miles from the Winstons' home. While his partners focused on "transactional" work—writing contracts, doing wills and living trusts—Plevin became the firm's litigator. Increasingly he has turned to handling class action cases. In recent years, with two young associates to help him, he has made class actions virtually his entire practice.

Plevin doesn't have the large staff or enormous war chest it takes to do mass torts or discrimination class actions with millions of class members, but he finds many smaller, regional problems that are well within his grasp. He enjoys the work, reasoning that he performs a service for consumers while at the same time making more money than ever before. Almost every settlement he reaches—he learned early on that class actions rarely go to trial—includes an agreement by the defendant to pay his fees. In the beginning, finding good class actions was hard, but in the past few years Plevin has developed a nose for them. He rarely goes out looking for class actions anymore; usually they come to him.

He got his last big case on the golf course. He was playing in a foursome with Sam Kim, who owns a large hardware store in town. Between holes Sam told Gabriel how annoyed he was with Tri-County Computer. "I thought the deal in the paper was clear: Buy a computer with monitor and get a free printer. I knew it was a bottom-of-the-line model, but it had to be better than the junk I'd been using. I ended up buying three computers, one for the office, one for home, and one for my granddaughter, but I never got a single printer."

"What happened?" asked Plevin. "Well," said Kim, "when I bought the computers, they said the printers were out of stock. I had my manager call every few weeks after that, but they never had the printers. Finally, last month they told her that the free offer had expired. Expired! Look, I know about inventory, and I can tell you they *never* had enough printers. And the model in the offer was discontinued, so they had no way to get any more."

Plevin was suddenly more interested: "Wait a minute, Sam. Are you telling me that by the time you bought your computers,

Tri-County had no way of giving you the printers?" "Not a chance," said Kim. "I'll bet they were discontinued before the deal was ever in the papers. Otherwise why do you think they'd give them away?"

Plevin knew that if Tri-County promised goods it couldn't deliver, it was guilty of deceptive advertising. More important, if Tri-County had sold enough computers during the offer period, that could make for a great class action case. So far Tri-County had made out like a bandit; people weren't going to sue over a $150 printer. If Gabriel filed a case on behalf of a "class" that included everyone who bought a computer but didn't get a free printer, he could get the customers something and make himself some money. And the case would be easy: All he'd have to find out in discovery was how many computers Tri-County sold and how many printers they failed to deliver. "Sam," said Gabriel, "tomorrow I'm going to go look up that Tri-County ad on microfiche. If they made the offer the way you told it to me, how'd you like to be a plaintiff in a class action?"

.

Class actions are the best way for people to fight back together against the small injustices that they would otherwise have to suffer in silence alone. But class actions also present unprecedented opportunities for unscrupulous plaintiffs' attorneys to abuse the ordinary people they're supposed to represent, while collecting large fees for themselves. Arthur Bryant, executive director of Trial Lawyers for Public Justice (TLPJ), whose Class Action Abuse Prevention Project is an "industry" watchdog, calls class actions "a powerful force for public good." He knows that the alternative may be "no litigation at all," since the damage done any one individual is so small. But Phoenix lawyer John P. Frank, who has served on several committees that advise the courts about class action rules, has called them a "racket" and a modern "Lawyers' Relief Act." Indeed, consumer groups such as Bryant's TLPJ have been constant thorns in the side of class action counsel, objecting to settlements because the fees are too high and the rewards to class members too low.

Class action lawsuits have been around for a long time. But not until the rise of the consumer movement in the late 1960s did they become popular. Just as the public was becoming aware of the defects and dangers of ordinary commercial products, a change in the federal class action rules made it possible for each individual member of a particular "class" of people to collect money damages. No longer were class actions limited to injunctive relief, which could force changes in a company's behavior but not award money.

With money at stake, the number of class actions rose swiftly. At first the lawsuits focused mostly on the kinds of complaints that didn't make economic sense for individuals to pursue: defective toasters, blenders, and other small appliances; credit card and loan companies overcharging interest and underpaying refunds; car rental companies that insisted on selling unnecessary insurance; and many, many more.

As time went on, lawyers began using class actions more frequently for bigger-ticket items: defective car parts, fraudulent stock offerings, discrimination in hiring or promotion, toxic spills, and even "mass torts" involving hundreds of thousands, sometimes millions, of people, such as cases charging that breast implants and asbestos exposure cause widespread illness.

On one hand, class action lawsuits provide broad, unprecedented opportunities to redress abuses that affect the ordinary person. Here are some examples:

- Bausch & Lomb marketed the *exact same* contact lenses in three separate packages, the Optima at $70 per pair usable for a year, the Medalist at $90 for a dozen pairs marketed as usable for one to three months, and the Sequence 2 at $80 per dozen but supposedly usable for only one to two weeks. A class action suit forced the company to stop the fraudulent pricing practice and awarded $34 million in cash and $34 million more in merchandise to victims of the scheme—up to $5.00 in cash and $5.00 more in products for each pair purchased.

- Over two thousand victims of a fraudulent investment scheme were left with nothing but a bankrupt defendant on his way to prison. San Francisco attorney William Bernstein filed a class action that forced Fireman's Fund, the defrauder's insurance company, to pay 100 cents on the dollar to the victims. Fireman's Fund paid $55 million in all, several times the policy limits, because the investments had come with certificates of "guaranteed insurance."

- Mobil's AV1 aircraft oil was found to be defective; a class action settlement required Mobil to pay for a complete tear-down inspection and reassembly of over six hundred small aircraft that used the product.

- After lawyers filed a class action suit charging that State Farm Insurance discriminated against women in hiring its agents, a group of about a thousand women received a total award of over $150 million. Individual women who could prove that they were better-qualified than the men who were hired received between $135,000 and $800,000 each.

On the other hand, despite these and countless other successes, class action lawsuits also give unprecedented power to lawyers and precious little control to class members. Class action lawyers have the power to create their own class, define its scope, recruit the individuals who will act as the class's authorized "representatives," settle claims in ways that offer little benefit to the individual class members but reward the lawyers with fees as large as eight figures, and even join forces with the defense to settle cases before they are filed. The agreement of class members is often more of an afterthought than a necessity.

Class actions are very different from typical plaintiff/defendant cases, even those with many individual plaintiffs. In multiple-plaintiff cases, each individual remains a separate client, entitled to the lawyer's loyalty to his or her particular case. Class actions don't—indeed, *can't*—work that way. The sheer number of potential class members means that if each were considered an individual client, with the full right to settle only upon individual approval, it would be impossible to ever pursue, much less resolve, a class action case.

Any lawyer might be tempted to make a quick buck on a quick settlement or pocket a big paycheck by accepting a little less than a case's real value. That temptation is greater in class actions, where there is no close relationship between the lawyers and the class members they serve. In ordinary plaintiffs' cases, the lawyers come to know their clients personally—their history, family, needs, desires, and personalities. In class actions, even the named class representatives are usually little more than pawns taking the lawyers' direction. Unlike lawyers who get premium fees while agreeing to secret settlements, class action attorneys can hardly claim that their fees result from going the extra mile in the zealous representation of their individual clients.

The ethics rules lawyers are sworn to follow make no mention of class actions; the rules simply don't take these special kinds of cases into account. The result is that they provide almost no useful guidance to lawyers about their responsibilities to class members. This leaves each jurisdiction—the individual states and various federal courts—free to interpret these responsibilities as it sees fit. It also reinforces the wide latitude that lawyers have to decide issues affecting the class.

Courts ultimately have to pass on the fairness of all class action settlements. But most courts give far less weight to the class members' views than to the lawyers' recommendations. Even the individual class representatives, whose names actually appear in the case title and who are supposed to speak for the whole class, have little control. They usually speak through their lawyers, and when they don't, they often have little credibility with the judge.

Toward the beginning of the case, a judge must approve the "certification" of the class by finding sufficient common characteristics among its members to group them together. The judge also approves the selection of the plaintiffs' class counsel. This judicial approval is often a much bigger hurdle than approving the settlement. Once the class is "certified," many lawyers feel it is just a matter of time until the case can be settled successfully, at least from the lawyer's point of view.

Despite their clear oversight responsibility under both federal and state law, many judges are no more likely to closely scrutinize a class action settlement than the settlement of any other case. Judges view settlement as good, and presume settlements to be fair. If most cases didn't settle, court dockets would become overwhelmed. Besides, the trial of a class action, far more complicated than most cases, would take much more court time than the average case.

Some of the best consumer attorneys in the country serve as

plaintiffs' class action counsel. But even the best lawyers admit that some of the strongest temptations any attorney can face are those that confront class counsel. They often work on their cases for years, only to face a trial that is even more daunting, in both time and expense, than the most complex individual case. With stakes so high and the potential payday so great, lawyers can easily fool themselves into believing that a settlement that falls a little bit short is still worth taking.

Temptation comes in the form of an offer from defense lawyers, who would often rather pay substantial attorneys' fees to their opposing counsel than much greater sums to the individual class members. Even where the class members are to receive money, it is often difficult to tell how much it will be, despite the estimates given to the court by the lawyers. The money paid is often both indirect and uncertain—indirect because it may be in the form of coupons or future discounts, and uncertain because payment may be conditioned on class members jumping through a series of hoops that make it difficult to qualify for payment.

Sometimes money is not the main issue. Many class actions seek "equitable relief," or changes in a defendant's behavior that would ensure that the abusive practice—overcharging, manufacturing defective products, employment discrimination, and so on—will never happen again. Often defendants would rather pay money than agree to changes that could profoundly affect the way they do business. When it comes to equitable relief, it's relatively easy for even honorable class action counsel to fool themselves into thinking they are getting the class members what they want—money—even if there are insufficient guarantees that the defendant's behavior will change.

In 1994 an Alabama state court judge approved a settlement in a class action against the Bank of Boston. The case charged the bank with holding escrow account interest that belonged to the class members, rather than paying it to them as it was earned. The 715,000 class members each had had mortgages issued through the bank at one time or another. Both the plaintiffs' lawyers and defense counsel told the judge that their settlement was worth over $40 million. But many familiar with the case disputed this claim as grossly inflated. According to the *New York Times*, the maximum individual recovery was only $8.76. Besides, no one disputed that the money belonged to the class members; the only question was *when* it would be paid. Nevertheless, the judge approved the settlement and $8.5 million in class counsel's fees.

According to Illinois federal judge Milton I. Shadur, the bank had offered the class the same deal two years before the final settlement, *except* that the plaintiffs' lawyers would get only $500,000 in fees. To make matters worse, under the first offer, the bank would pay the fees, but under the final settlement, the fees were to be paid out of the class recovery. Since class members who no longer had mortgages had no funds left in the bank, the entire attorneys' fees bill had to be paid by those who still had their mortgages.

This gave the case the unique feature of charging some class members far more in fees than they "won" in back interest. One Maine couple recovered $2.19 from the class action, but had to pay $91.33 in fees for the attorneys. They were not alone; many people claimed they never even knew they were members of a class until they had "miscellaneous deductions" used to pay the lawyers charged to their escrow accounts. They fought back, filing their own class action against the plaintiffs' attorneys and the bank for fraud. But the second case was never heard on its merits; it was eventually dismissed because it was filed too late, after the time for objections had run out.

The Bank of Boston settlement aroused the ire of many, including the attorney general of Florida, where the bank's principal mortgage company was located; the consumer group Public Citizen, whose Brian Wolfman called it the "most notorious" class settlement; and other plaintiffs' class lawyers, who took pains to distance their own practices from the case. Judge Shadur was most direct, calling the case the "Willie Horton of the class action." But lawyers for both the plaintiffs and the bank pointed out that a judge had approved the settlement knowing its terms and after hearing all the objections. Besides, the bank did change its accounting practices as part of the agreement. "Nothing fraudulent or improper took place," one of the chief plaintiffs' counsel, Chicago's Daniel Edelman, told the *New York Times*.

The Bank of Boston case is not the only one in which consumer attorneys questioned Daniel Edelman's conduct. His critics, including lawyers for Public Citizen and the Center for Auto Safety, contend that in a series of class actions in consumer credit cases, Edelman's settlements did more to line his own pockets than to benefit the class members he represented. These lawyers acknowledge that Edelman knows his way around class action cases, but say that too often he settles them quickly and cheaply, turning a quick profit for himself.

Anyone who has ever read a car lease knows how difficult it is to understand. Several class action lawyers came to believe that these contracts were more than just tough reading; credit companies were overcharging on car leases. Edelman has been among the most active lawyers filing class actions against car leasing companies—Toyota Leasing, Wells Fargo Leasing, and Ford Motor Credit, among others. While other lawyers have also filed class actions against these companies, Edelman seemed to outstrip everyone in the speed with which he has filed—and settled—his cases.

In one case against Ford Motor Credit, Edelman presented a settlement to the court that called for $425,000 in penalties, $675,000 in cash rebates, and up to $1,200,000 in future credits on car leasing payments. Edelman's proposed fees were a mere $250,000. But a closer look at the proposed settlement appalled consumer lawyers, who filed formal objections to the settlement with the court.

First, the settlement covered several years of Ford Motor Credit leases, and a class of about two million people. This meant that the average recovery would be about $1 per consumer for potentially fraudulent charges that could total hundreds or even thousands of dollars in a single lease. To make matters worse, the settlement called for the $425,000 penalty to be paid at the rate of $4.25 to 100,000 class members chosen at random. The rest would get nothing. This settlement seemed almost like buying a "scratcher" card from the state lottery; in fact, the objectors argued that the settlement was exactly that—an illegal lottery.

In a case against Wells Fargo Leasing, Edelman filed a class action and reached a settlement almost immediately. Each class member would receive a nontransferable $75 coupon that could be used toward the payment of any Wells Fargo lease—*except* the class member's current lease. Once again, other class action attorneys and consumer groups strongly objected, arguing that this deal had no practical value whatever to the average consumer. The class members won absolutely no relief on the current lease. To get any benefit at all, they would have to lease another vehicle, finance it again through Wells Fargo Leasing—the very company that had been sued—and requalify under Wells's standards. Edelman's fee petition showed only twenty hours of attorney time, but his fee claim was for $75,000.

In some ways, these cases are like the quick-settling fender benders we discussed in Chapter Six, but the damage done to the public interest is far greater. A bad class action settlement has a Typhoid Mary effect, infecting everyone in its path. Once a class action settlement is approved, it cuts off not only the named representatives' claims, but the claims of all those in the class. Class actions on the same subject can be filed by different lawyers in different parts of the country. But the case that becomes the first to settle generally preempts all the others and becomes *the* case in which the rights and remedies of all class members are decided. Public Citizen's Wolfman calls this preemption the single biggest problem in class actions.

What takes place is a kind of reverse auction. Instead of the bids going up during the auction, there is a "race to the bottom." The defendant shops a settlement to each separate group of plaintiffs' lawyers, settling with those who are willing to take the least for their clients. The lawyers who settle are rewarded with attorneys' fees. Those who insist on more benefits for the class can be ignored and often shut out entirely. At their worst, these settlements are as collusive as the worst secret agreements, with plaintiffs' lawyers not merely succumbing to temptation but abandoning their responsibilities to the class for their own personal gain.

There are three possible ways out of such settlements. Some lawyers carve out more limited classes, such as statewide groups. That's what happened in another series of cases involving Ford Motor Credit. Lawyers in four statewide class actions accused FMC of "force placing" insurance, or forcing customers to buy collision and comprehensive insurance from its own wholly owned subsidiary. The subsidiary then charged outrageously high rates, as much as

$6,000 for collision and comprehensive insurance alone, with no liability coverage. When car owners couldn't pay, their cars were repossessed.

Attorney Barry Baskin settled a class action covering California customers for $58 million and a permanent injunction against the practice. Similar cases were settled in Florida, Arizona, and Missouri. These states' residents were fortunate: Their claims were resolved before a nationwide class action filed by Daniel Edelman preempted the claims of FMC customers in the other forty-six states. The national class action settled for about the same amount as the California case alone, but with many more class members, individual recoveries averaged much less.

The second way to avoid an inadequate settlement is simply to object. A judge must hold a "fairness hearing" before approving any class action settlement, and any class member may object to the settlement because it doesn't provide sufficient money or other relief. But objections are given little weight by judges who are more interested in clearing their dockets than in carefully scrutinizing the merits of a settlement. A better chance of success exists when the named class representatives themselves object, or where consumer groups such as Public Citizen or Trial Lawyers for Public Justice organize and represent objectors at the fairness hearing. When the Washington, D.C.–based Center for Auto Safety made known its objections to the Ford Motor Credit leasing settlement, the judge canceled the fairness hearing and ordered the parties to explore further options. Even so, only rarely does a judge find a settlement unfair.

Many jurisdictions allow a judge to approve a settlement even if every single named class representative objects, despite the fact that the representatives are supposed to speak on behalf of the entire class. And while organized legal opposition to settlement helps, it only modestly reduces the long odds. In order to succeed, the objectors must overcome the collective will of both parties to the case. The defense, through its lawyers, and the class, through its counsel, will appear before the court as a united front arguing strongly why the settlement is fair.

The easiest path to settlement, of course, is when there are no objections at all. After reaffirming in published settlement notices that "any member of the Settlement Class may object," one group of San Francisco class counsel took to adding this startling language: "If your objection is found to be frivolous, you may be subject to monetary sanctions." Since the class was also warned that only by objecting would participants "receive any further notice of subsequent hearings, including any further fee hearings," the lawyers created an obvious catch-22: Class members had to object to stay informed, but were threatened financially by the class's own lawyers if they exercised that right. Class counsel who make such threats are clearly out of line. But the damage has already been done to class members who were thinking about objecting.

The third way out of a class action settlement is the only one within the control of the individual class member. Class action members have the right to opt out of settlements and preserve their own claims against the defendant either in an individual lawsuit or, on some occasions, by participation in another class action that might provide better results. Originally, class action suits seeking monetary damages included only those who chose to "opt in" to the class, but this limited the ability of class actions to provide the widest benefit to consumers. When the class action rules were modified in 1966, one controversial change created a presumption that all class members would be included in the class. Opting in was no longer necessary. Rather, a class member would have to choose to opt out. One judge likened this to belonging to a book club, where the member automatically gets the club's selection unless it's specifically declined.

The change in the law may have broadened the application of class action suits, but it came at the cost of class members' independence. Often, as in the Bank of Boston case, people don't even know they are class members, much less that they can opt out. The rule change was made with the understanding that any court that hears a class action must "direct notice to the members of the class of the right of each member to be excluded." But saying this and accomplishing it are two different things entirely.

Giving notice to hundreds of thousands of people, whether by mail or through newspapers and advertisements, is never easy even if the court and the lawyers make the best possible effort. Besides, the notices are dense and complicated. Often individual class members don't understand their rights to opt out until the period for doing so has already expired. For those individuals who do opt out, the small size of their claim makes it a practical impossibility to pursue their own cases unless they can band together with others in another group lawsuit.

In 1993 a federal court in Atlanta approved the settlement of a reported $368 million class action settlement over airline price-fixing. The case involved a class of over four million people and resulted in attorneys' fees of $14 million. While these fees totaled less than 4 percent of the claimed recovery, the settlement was "paid" not in cash but in coupons good for $10 or $25 off future fares. Restrictions on these coupons limited their use; most significantly, the coupons couldn't be "stacked" at one time, but were usable only in small increments: $10 maximum on any fare under $250, and $25 on any fare under $500. This created a traveler's nightmare that makes using frequent-flier miles easy in comparison. The airlines say it's impossible to determine how many coupons have been used, but most observers estimate it to be a minute fraction of their face value.

Perhaps the most controversial coupon case involved a product that has merited considerable attention elsewhere in these pages: General Motors pickup trucks with side-mounted gas tanks. At the same time that lawyers across the country were filing hundreds of individual injury and wrongful death cases against GM, plaintiffs' class action lawyers filed several cases on behalf of all truck owners who had *not* been injured, charging that the defective gas tank mounting increased the chances of future injury and lowered the value of the trucks. In July 1993, in federal court in Philadelphia, GM and the plaintiffs' lawyers proposed a class settlement covering roughly 5.7 million owners of these trucks. The owners would get coupons good for $1,000 off their next light-duty truck; the plaintiffs' lawyers would get $9.5 million.

Consumer groups, including two organizations founded by Ralph Nader, the Center for Auto Safety and Public Citizen, strenuously objected to the settlement. They argued that the coupons were virtually worthless, for several reasons. First, they were transferable only to family members or upon sale of the truck; second, they were not usable with any other discount, promotion, or rebate; and third, they were valid for only fifteen months after settlement. Judge William H. Yohn Jr. disagreed, and in December 1993 approved both the settlement and the $9.5 million in attorneys' fees. Yohn chose to accept an economic analysis provided by the settling lawyers that claimed over one-third of the coupons would be used, giving the settlement a total value of between $1.8 and $2.0 billion.

Although 5,000 truck owners chose to "opt out" of the settlement and another 6,400 filed formal objections, Judge Yohn considered this number "infinitesimal" and construed the silence of most class members as approval: "[T]he approval or silence of more than 99% of the class members demonstrates that the vast majority of the class members favor the settlement." Yohn also shunted aside the Center for Auto Safety's charges that hundreds had been killed and thousands injured in fires caused by the defective gas tanks, and its insistence that the settlement should address the safety issues. "The only thing more defective than these trucks was Judge Yohn's decision," the center's executive director, Clarence Ditlow, said later.

The objectors took their case to the federal Third Circuit Court of Appeals. A year and a half later they got a surprising and pleasing result. In a 103-page ruling, a unanimous court excoriated the settlement, calling it "unfair and inadequate" and comparing it to "a GM sales promotion device." The original settlement "provided absolutely nothing to those unwilling or unable to purchase another GM truck and . . . did nothing about the allegedly dangerous vehicles left on the road," wrote Judge Edward R. Becker. Becker also sharply criticized the large attorneys' fees awarded, calling GM's failure to raise any objection to the $9.5 million in fees a "smoking gun" that signaled a "questionable settlement." The case was sent back to Judge Yohn for further review. A few months later the Texas Supreme Court threw out a similar settlement in another case involving a GM truck with a side-mounted gas tank because of its concerns about another $9.5 million attorneys' fee award.

The federal appeals court decision was hardly the last word on

GM truck coupons, however. Back before Judge Yohn, plaintiffs' lawyers filed a new complaint and conducted additional discovery in order to meet the tough standards set by the appeals court. Meanwhile, other groups of plaintiffs' lawyers focused on similar class actions that had lain dormant in several other states. In 1993 a Louisiana state court judge had certified a class of GM truck owners just two months before the proposed Philadelphia settlement. In July 1996, with the Philadelphia case foundering, the Louisiana judge allowed most of the Philadelphia class members to join that action, and then approved a settlement that again involved $1,000 coupons.

And again objectors complained. While the settlement was eventually approved, the complaints may finally have made a difference. Instead of the restrictive coupons offered in Philadelphia, the Louisiana coupons could be transferred to anyone, creating a "secondary market" that gave the coupons an actual street value. The street value was enhanced because the coupons could be used together with other promotions, and were valid for most GM cars as well as trucks. Perhaps more important, GM agreed to spend $4 million on researching vehicle fires, and—a point insisted on by the Center for Auto Safety—the plaintiffs' lawyers agreed to designate $1 million of their fees for research on a retrofit project that would explore, for the very first time since the trucks were produced in 1973, the possibility of remounting the gas tanks in a safer way.

Plaintiffs' counsel petitioned for fees in an amount approximating the $19 million total of the Philadelphia and Texas cases combined. Even though the Louisiana settlement was a clear improvement, Philadelphia class counsel still maintains that their accord was reasonable. "I come from folks who drive trucks," said one of the Philadelphia case's lead lawyers, San Francisco's Elizabeth Cabraser, implying that she knew what truck owners really want. Cabraser claimed that a quick settlement was important because the trucks were all at least ten years old. She argued that $1,000 could mean a down payment toward a new vehicle for many truck owners, and claimed that Ford and Chrysler would likely have honored the $1,000 GM coupons to keep their prices competitive.

Cabraser said that the Philadelphia settlement was "the best we could get at the time," though the Louisiana settlement was indisputably better for the class. As for Public Citizen and the Center for Auto Safety, both eventually withdrew their objections in Louisiana. For the center's Clarence Ditlow, the new settlement was "still a bad deal," and the economic value "a pittance." He continues to believe that the coupons won't be enough of a discount for most owners to buy a new truck, and that as a result, they will continue to "ride at risk." But Ditlow accepted the practical reality that the settlement had at least *some* value—enough that it would be upheld on appeal.

Neither the Center for Auto Safety nor Public Citizen took part in the request for legal fees, but interestingly, General Motors, which hadn't objected to either the Philadelphia or Texas payments, filed an objection in Louisiana. The center suspected it was because of the $1 million earmarked for retrofit research. "GM not only won't pay its own money for safety, it doesn't want to spend anyone else's either," said Ditlow.

In recent years there has been a dramatic expansion in the use of class actions in mass injury cases. Although class actions were not originally intended to resolve individual injury claims, in 1980 New York federal judge Jack B. Weinstein ordered that all cases of those claiming to be injured from exposure to Agent Orange during the Vietnam War be consolidated in one mass action in his court. Later a federal appeals court upheld the judge's certification of this class, even though it recognized that each individual's claim was different. This opened the door to mass tort class actions in a variety of cases: toxic spills, the Dalkon Shield intrauterine device, silicone breast implants, and asbestos exposure. No longer were the stakes small and each class member's claim similar; these claims could be both substantial and materially different from each other.

There were advantages to these mass tort class actions: the efficient use of the courts, consistency in court rulings, the attempt to ensure that all those injured got some measure of relief. But these giant cases, some with classes numbering in the millions, presented a host of new problems. Defendants feared that unscrupulous plaintiffs' attorneys could file questionable class actions and then force what federal appeals court judge Richard Posner has described as "blackmail settlements" fueled by "a small probability of an immense judgment" that could "hurl [an] industry into bankruptcy."

On the other hand, there are many valid mass tort claims. Turning them into class actions presented an unprecedented opportunity for defendants and their lawyers to "buy peace" by settling all claims, past, present, even future. By structuring classes to include not only those who had actually been injured by a defendant's product but also those who *might* become injured in the future, a defendant could buy not only peace but peace everlasting. In order to do this, though, defense counsel would need the cooperation of plaintiffs' lawyers. In a series of asbestos exposure cases in the early 1990s, they got it.

In 1991 these asbestos cases were consolidated in federal court in Philadelphia. They pitted plaintiffs' groups against twenty companies whose workers had been exposed to asbestos and who banded together to form the Center for Claims Resolution, or CCR. On a single day in January 1993, two plaintiffs' law firms filed a class action complaint, CCR's attorneys filed an answer to that complaint, and the two sides submitted an agreed-upon settlement. The deal was done even before it was filed. The settlement purported to resolve the claims of "all persons" who had been "exposed occupationally" to asbestos by one of the CCR companies, as well as the families of those exposed. But only those who had already become ill from asbestos-related diseases would receive any compensation. Others who faced the danger of future illness, and their families, might receive money according to various formulas, but little was guaranteed.

The class filing was as diabolical as it was ingenious. The settlement made it possible to opt out, but in order to do that, people would have to know that they were part of the class in the first place. Many people who had been exposed to asbestos never knew, and would never find out unless they became ill. Given the passage of time since exposure, the only practical way to tell people about the class's existence was through general publicity—television and print ads and an 800 number. But for those who didn't know they had been exposed, or others such as construction workers who had worked many jobs for innumerable employers whose names were long forgotten, this notice would be of little help.

Even worse, the class included both present and *future* spouses and family members of those exposed to asbestos—spouses not yet married, and children not yet conceived or even contemplated.

Because the case was settled before it was filed, the class was presented for certification as a prepackaged deal. The lawyers wanted only to settle and never intended to litigate—a task many considered impossible because of the case's complexity and the inclusion of future victims. Nevertheless, the federal trial court in Philadelphia approved the settlement and enjoined everyone covered under the class from pursuing their own individual claims. Consumer groups, including the Class Action Abuse Prevention Project of Trial Lawyers for Public Justice (TLPJ), appealed to the Third Circuit Court of Appeals, where Judge Becker again wrote for the court, as he had in the GM truck case. Becker rejected this settlement as well, saying that it was wrong to certify a class just for settlement unless it would qualify as a class for trial. In June 1997, by a 6-to-2 vote, the United States Supreme Court agreed.

The dangers of approving class actions filed only for the purposes of settlement seem clear. Counsel for both sides would have what Leslie Bruekner of TLPJ described in testimony before a judicial committee studying the issue as "an extraordinarily strong incentive to collude against the class." The defendants would be looking for an opportunity to buy peace, while plaintiffs' counsel would be tempted by attorneys' fees "earned" primarily by being in the right place at the right time.

We need class actions, just as we need contingency fees. Both help level the playing field by giving ordinary people access to the courts. But in order for class actions to serve their intended purpose, they must be used wisely. This means that more control must be wrested from the hands of the lawyers on both sides.

Suggestions for reforming class action abuses range from the ridiculous—one law professor has suggested doing away entirely with individual class representatives—to the sublime, such as former Maine senator William Cohen's proposed legislation requiring that class notices provide clear summaries in plainly written language instead of "legal jargon that the average citizen cannot understand." Academics debate in scholarly journals about technical changes to the federal rules. Some of these changes make sense, such as requiring a series of fairness hearings rather than just one. But they don't directly address how to control the behavior of the lawyers involved.

Advocates of tort reform argue that class actions should be severely limited in scope, and succeeded in passing federal legislation (over a presidential veto) that limits securities fraud class actions. But tort reform advocates tend to speak for corporate interests rather than the public's benefit. Meanwhile, the reforms emphasized by public interest groups often seem like rearguard actions designed to prevent further erosion of consumers' rights.

Almost all reform advocates support educating judges about class actions, and raising the level of objective judicial scrutiny. But increased judicial involvement alone will not make the difference in the average class action, where public interest lawyers have not been mobilized and the judge is faced with both sides forcefully explaining how fair their settlement is. Making class action notices more understandable to the public is laudable but is easier said than done, particularly in cases that require proof from records or recollection from the distant past.

The law professor who argued that class representatives were mere "decorative figureheads" has support in some quarters. Samuel Dash, former chief counsel in the Senate's Watergate investigation and now a law professor at Georgetown, believes—and has testified—that as a practical matter, the plaintiffs' class action lawyer must also act as the de facto client.

The best reform may be the exact opposite of this approach: giving real power to the named representatives of the class. Almost every reform that lawyers discuss focuses solely on lawyers, judges, or technical changes to the law itself. But if the named representatives were truly independent of the lawyer and truly representative of the class, if there were enough representatives so that no one individual could dominate, and if these class representatives were empowered to settle the case on *advice* instead of *orders* of counsel, at least some measure of control of the class would revert to those who are actually affected by the outcome.

This could limit the ability of unscrupulous plaintiffs' lawyers— and those usually honest ones who might succumb to temptation— to settle class actions because of the fees they receive. It would also limit the ability of defense attorneys to buy peace for their clients by paying some class members at the expense of others. If named representatives are truly representative of *each segment* of the class, the entire class is more likely to be protected.

Mass tort class actions should also be curtailed. They were developed primarily as a matter of judicial economy, to centralize all claims in one single case. In and of itself, that's not a good enough reason to force people to give up their individual claims. Individual cases have been and still are used successfully to challenge the behavior of large companies.

Though mass tort class actions bring everyone under the same tent, so that fewer people are left completely out of the process, the efforts to consolidate are often too ambitious and too broad. They have ignored what federal judge William Schwarzer points out were the two overriding principles of class action cases: that one individual claim would be too small to prosecute individually, and that "common questions predominate over any individual issues" facing the class members.

Even if only the second of these principles was applied, mass tort cases would be narrowed sufficiently so that the named representatives and the class members were all in the same boat, not just the same fleet. In some cases, this could mean that issues of fault are determined in the class action, while money issues would be left up to each individual plaintiff. Where necessary, cases should be split into two or more classes, as many as are needed to be sure of a close common interest between the representatives of each class and the members. The pendulum has swung too far, from individual cases with individual redress to massive class actions that cover everyone. Two, three, or even seven classes are far more efficient than hundreds of thousands of individual claims, but much fairer than one single case.

Epilogue:
The Tri-County Computer Litigation

Gabriel Plevin had little trouble settling his class action case. It turned out that Tri-County had sold over twenty-two thousand computers during its free-printer offer but had given away only fourteen hundred printers. Not only that, but even though the printers had a street price of no more than $135, Tri-County had advertised them as "a $259 value." With these facts in his favor, it wasn't hard for Gabriel to settle with Tri-County's attorneys. Only thirteen people filed objections to the settlement, and only three attended the fairness hearing, where the judge quickly approved the settlement. True, the twenty thousand class members would get only $2.50 in cash, but they would also get a $90 Tri-County store credit good for a whole year, *if* they provided proof of purchase and filled out their claim forms correctly. That meant that Gabriel could legitimately claim that the total settlement value of the case was $1,850,000, or 20,000 times the $2.50 in cash and the $90 credit. This made Plevin's $425,000 fee seem modest by comparison.

Joseph and Joella Winston never reached a live person at the 800 number, so they finally decided to fill in the forms as best as they could themselves. They searched for the computer receipt, finally finding it tucked into an envelope with the machine's warranty. They sent in the form and the receipt, and three months later received a $2.50 check and a $90.00 store credit. Since they didn't use computers much, they gave the store credit to their son Stan, who used computers every day at college. But when Stan tried to use the credit, he was told it was nontransferable. Joseph finally went down to Tri-County with his son to pick out a piece of software Stan wanted. The family wondered whether the whole experience had been worth the effort.

Gabriel Plevin had no doubt about the value of his effort, though neither he nor Tri-County would disclose how many customers had actually filed their forms or how many actually used the credit. Local consumer advocates estimated that the total of the cash and store credit used was less than Plevin's fee.

Can It Be Fixed?
What Can We Do?

If I were asked where I place the American aristocracy, I should reply without hesitation that it is not composed of the rich, who are united together by no common tie, but that it occupies the judicial bench and the bar.   —Alexis de Tocqueville, *Democracy in America*, 1840

Ninety percent of our lawyers serve ten percent of our people. We are over-lawyered and under-represented.
                    —President Jimmy Carter, 1978

Before we become lawyers, we are human beings.
                    —Incoming University of San Francisco law student
                    Damien Cox, on his second day of orientation, 1997

Many if not most Americans think that our legal system is breaking down. The system's engine, the adversary theorem, no longer runs smoothly, but seems to sputter along on just a couple of cylinders. There are many problems:

The profession has always been a monopoly—only members of the bar can practice in our courts. But today the law is more remote and technical than ever. The general practitioner has become almost obsolete, making it harder for the average person to find the right lawyer in a highly specialized marketplace. And while today's lawyers come from more diverse backgrounds than fifty or even twenty years ago, the monopoly itself is even more entrenched than in Tocqueville's time, when people apprenticed by "reading law." Today almost every state requires lawyers to take a three-year postgraduate course at an institution officially approved by the law's largest trade organization, the American Bar Association, making the ABA itself a tremendously powerful monopoly.

Large firms have gotten larger still, and more than ever act like businesses rather than groups of professionals. Most of the largest are now LLPs, limited-liability partnerships, or PCs, professional corporations. The legal press encourages them, trumpeting those firms that grow the most and regretfully reporting on those that have fallen from grace by dropping off the list of the nation's largest. In 1997 the *National Law Journal* proclaimed that for the first time its list of the largest firms would have "bullets" after the names, "patterned after Billboard magazine's music charts," to show which are making the biggest moves up the legal hit parade.

The press also reports the starting salaries at each of the largest law conglomerates. First-year associates, typically twenty-four or twenty-five years old, start at $75,000 to $101,000 a year at large big-city firms. At those rates, chances are they are representing the corporate giants of America, not those who have difficulty getting access to the system—the 90 percent that Jimmy Carter was worried about.

Law schools also continue to grow in both number and size, even as applications decrease. The ever-expanding population of law graduates has created a glut of lawyers who can't find jobs in the profession. But law schools are profitable enterprises for universities; there's no indication that any are ready to shrink or close their doors. And despite efforts by some to diversify their student bodies and change teaching methods, most schools still look much like the *Paper Chase* institutions of a generation ago, the sole exception being a dramatic increase in the number of women.

Despite all their money and power, lawyers themselves have never been more dissatisfied with their profession than they are today. In survey after survey they say they don't enjoy what they're doing. Third-year law students prepare themselves for the big "OCIs," or on-campus interviews, knowing a job offer is their ticket to riches and, not incidentally, to repaying their student loans. Some

look forward to a rosy future, but many think of their pending employment not with warmth, affection, or even anticipation, but with
trepidation at the workload that awaits them and the compromises
they know they'll have to make for the sake of their clients—and
their jobs. Ethics rules are confusing and seemingly contradictory,
which hardly helps ease the dissatisfaction felt by both students
and lawyers. Too often these rules seem to emphasize what lawyers
can get away with, rather than showing them how to do the right
thing.

Those who write ethics rules are often far removed from understanding firsthand the needs of the average person seeking legal
services. Sometimes rule makers are subject to pressures that make
the rules political rather than ethical issues, and only rarely do
moral imperatives come into play. Complaints pour in, but those
enforcing the rules, underfunded and overwhelmed by caseloads,
focus mostly on the egregious cases. This means lawyers are disciplined for violating certain rules, while other violations—more subtle but no less important—are largely ignored.

Judges can discipline lawyers by punishing their behavior in
matters before them. But too often they take the easy way out: to
admonish but not punish, to criticize but not censure. Despite the
so-called independence of the judiciary, when judges take strong
stands, particularly against powerful lawyers or parties, as likely as
not *they* will be attacked, accused of bias, and even forced to remove
themselves from the cases on which they spoke out.

Many other judges simply suffer from a lack of training and experience in dealing with ethics issues. The zealous advocacy standard, discredited and abandoned in the 1980s in most states' ethics
rules, retains its vitality through its continued use in decisions written by judges wedded to this obsolete definition of the adversary
theorem. Many of the worst abuses lawyers have inflicted on society have come under the banner of zealous advocacy, often with
the judiciary as its herald.

This is the picture of a system that badly needs fixing. Still, we remain convinced that it needs not wholesale replacement but a major
overhaul. For all its faults, our system is based on access for all those

who need our laws and courts, and the protection from those Madison described as having "the highest prerogative of power." This is far too valuable to jeopardize.

Our system is designed so that each side can have a lawyer who is a spokesperson, a standard-bearer, whose highest duty is to the client, not to the state or the lawyer's own notion of what is right. Our Constitution protects the rights of those accused of a crime, guaranteeing them effective assistance of counsel. We have a jury system for civil as well as criminal disputes so that no judge makes the final decision on an individual's case. And unlike England, on whose system ours is based, we allow contingency fees, refuse to make people pay the other side's costs if they lose a legitimate case, and allow class action lawsuits. This means that even poor people, if their case is good enough to convince a lawyer to take a chance, can gain redress against the rich and powerful.

Winston Churchill's observation about democracy still applies to our legal system: It's the worst known, except for all the others. But the patchwork changes made to this system over the course of generations have so corrupted the adversary theorem that in some respects it's barely recognizable.

What can be done to fix it? Some areas don't need massive change. The criminal justice system can be improved, especially to distribute justice more evenhandedly among rich and poor, and among whites, blacks, and other people of color. But overall, when someone is accused of a crime, the adversary theorem operates rather well.

Other changes we might favor may simply not be realistic. For instance, the Supreme Court has held that corporations have a broad attorney-client privilege; it is unlikely that our opinion to the contrary will sway theirs. It is just as unlikely that a rule or law will soon forbid minimum billable hour requirements, limit law firms to no more than fifty lawyers, or mandate any number of changes on our wish list that have no real chance of taking place.

In many other respects, though, significant changes can occur: to the system, its institutions, the rules under which it operates, the role of the public, and the behavior of lawyers themselves. We've made specific suggestions during the course of each chapter. We now focus on more general prescriptions that might make our legal system more responsive to the needs of the clients who use it and to the society in which it operates.

Law Schools

Nowhere can changes happen more quickly, or have as dramatic an impact on the legal system, than at America's law schools. In fact, each of the ideas we suggest has already been adopted by at least a few schools.

Until the Watergate scandal a quarter century ago, few law schools focused on the behavior of lawyers. Most commonly, schools offered a single upper-class elective in legal ethics for interested students. Watergate was about not just corrupt politicians, but unethical lawyers, from President Nixon and his attorney general, John Mitchell, right down to "dirty tricks" expert Donald Segretti. Its aftermath brought a new emphasis on legal ethics. Many schools added to their ethics offerings. By the late 1970s many states had adopted a short-answer exam designed to test students on the ABA's Model Code of Professional Responsibility. Law schools followed suit by making professional responsibility part of the required course curriculum.

But in many ways not much has changed. Thirty years ago almost every law school had a core curriculum of required subjects that each student had to study for an entire year: contracts, property, criminal law, civil procedure, torts, and constitutional law. These and other required courses took up most of the first two years of law school. They were taught by the "case law" method, in which students learn the subject by studying cases in which judges decided important conceptual issues. Today most of these courses are still required and still taught in the same way. But legal ethics, or more often its close cousin, professional responsibility, is taught quite differently.

First, unlike other core courses, taught for three to four units per semester by specialists in the field, ethics classes are often two-unit, one-semester courses, taught by whichever professor can be trapped into another course preparation outside his or her main field. Students naturally conclude that ethics must be far less important than torts or contracts.

Second, unlike those other courses, most ethics classes are static reviews of the rules. Students are taught what the rules say, but far less attention is paid to what they *mean*—the concepts and theory behind the rules that give students a context for learning ethical behavior. Students leave these courses with the dubious achievement of being well prepared to pass a multiple-choice exam that tests "black-letter" ethics requirements. But "rules-based" courses give students little, if any, opportunity to think through difficult ethical dilemmas and conflicts, to determine how to balance their duty to a client with the duties to our legal system and to society, or to evaluate questions of basic moral behavior. At most schools these courses are not even called Legal Ethics, but Professional Responsibility, meaning the study of the rules. The result is that for too many students, the study of ethics becomes learning what behavior they can get away with, without ever confronting the core issue: how to behave responsibly as lawyers.

At some schools things are changing. An increasingly large number of professors now consider ethics to be their principal field. More schools have added extra course hours and other ethics-related programs. Some state bar exams have begun to give ethics essay questions. And there has been a significant increase in courses that both examine ethics issues as they occur in actual practice and grapple with the relationship between ethics and morality, instead of being limited to the four corners of the rules.

Learning concepts is better than memorizing rules. But combining those concepts with an understanding of how they apply in actual practice is better still. Few lawyers claim that they learned how to practice law in law school. Shouldn't that be a school's primary function? Surprisingly, many academics say no. They fear their schools will turn into "trade schools" that ignore essential legal theory and the process of "learning to think like a lawyer." That view is sadly misguided. It's like criticizing our medical schools for having students spend a year on the wards in a hospital. There's nothing wrong with teaching students how to do their jobs properly.

Law, unlike medicine, suffers from a wide gulf between its academic faculties and everyday practitioners, a circumstance that can get in the way of effective teaching. Academics serve useful functions—they, like medical researchers, are the profession's theoreticians; they also are, or at least should be, the experts on how best to teach. But their influence at most law schools should be balanced, as it is in medicine, with professionals who have experienced the law in the trenches, as practitioners.

The law school curriculum must also become more practical. Criminal law and torts are required of all students, though some will never handle a personal injury matter, and most will never do a criminal case. But every attorney must interview clients and negotiate cases. Courses that teach interviewing and negotiation skills should be part of the required curriculum. This not only would better prepare students for practice, but would give them an appreciation for how to deal with clients and opponents alike.

And students should spend their "year on the wards," in clinical programs where they get a chance to put their practical training to work. Schools object, arguing that running clinical programs is too expensive. Clearly, the training and oversight required for each student is far more labor-intensive than herding them into large lecture halls. But if schools cooperated with the profession to place students in practice situations, much of the training and oversight could be done by those engaged in practice.

Students should be placed where they are needed the most: in legal services programs, law offices and clinics that take low-fee clients, public defender's offices, and other settings serving the needs of the underrepresented. Schools have the power to dictate to their students; they should exercise that power by requiring every student to give time to such programs. And they can do more than that, by following the lead of a few enlightened law schools that forgive student loans for those who take lower-paying public service jobs when they become lawyers.

What do these practice issues have to do with the behavior of lawyers in the profession? Everything. Increasingly, law schools, like firms, see law as a business. Many even offer combined law and business degrees. Like law firms, schools pay close attention to their rankings: the higher their rank, the more the big-money "white shoe" firms will recruit their students; the more big firms recruit there, the more good students the school attracts.

But if the business of law stands any chance of returning to a profession, law schools will have to lead the way. First they will have to reassert the primacy of education over business in their own firmament. Then they must provide an environment where students can learn about both ethical *and* moral behavior, as well as the skills needed to actually practice their profession and the goal of serving all those in need. In short, while law schools are training young men and women to "think like lawyers," they should also be reminding them to think like human beings. If these lessons aren't taught in law school, the nation's law firms are unlikely candidates to teach them instead.

Law Firms

Once young lawyers leave their schools, their principal teachers become the members of their law firm. Like many institutions, law firms insulate their employees—including their lawyers—from the rest of the world. The larger the firm, the more insulated are its lawyers, and the more prone they are to adopt whatever values they are taught within the firm. Whether by word or deed, some firms teach their lawyers to give no quarter in legal battles, to worry only about the client without regard for society, and to stretch and shade the truth so long as it doesn't involve direct lies. When faced with difficult dilemmas, most young lawyers—like most other people—will tend to move in the direction they're being pushed. The consequences, as we have seen throughout these pages, can be damaging to society, the profession, and even the firm's own clients. Yet reaching into these insular firms to create different modes of behavior is a daunting task.

But holding law firms more accountable for unethical behavior is an attainable goal. One solution: discipline them, an approach first approved in New York in the mid-1990s. Under New York's scheme, discipline wouldn't include suspending an entire firm, but could include fines and probation, which would allow disciplinary personnel in the door to monitor the firm's activities.

States need not wait for discipline to be able to audit a firm's activities. Bar audits are already common, usually to check bank accounts. But there is nothing to prevent an enforcement agency from insisting on random audits of a firm's ethical behavior—by examining its client intake procedures, fee agreements, billing methods, and so on—so long as client confidences are adequately protected. There is no groundswell of support for these audits, but they would be a valuable preventive tool. The more monolithic and insular the firm, the more effective these measures.

Over 75 percent of our states now require lawyers to take mandatory continuing legal education courses, known in the profession as MCLE. MCLE is a good idea: It forces lawyers to continue their education, both in subject matter areas and in legal ethics, by attending courses and workshops given by skilled educational providers. In some states, though, law firms are allowed to provide their own in-house MCLE. This should be changed. When law firms give their own classes, they retain their dangerous insularity, and often reinforce and repeat mistakes. Requiring lawyers to participate with others in open programs would break down that insularity, at least for a few hours.

We would place one more requirement on law firms: mandatory *pro bono publico*, or public service work. President Carter was close to the truth when he said that 90 percent of our lawyers represent 10 percent of our people. If each law firm was required to spend fifty hours a year per lawyer to serve the needs of people who otherwise would not be represented, our society might still be overlawyered, but we would no longer be underrepresented. This idea is hardly new. The ABA even has a rule strongly suggesting it: "Every lawyer, regardless of professional prominence or professional work load, has a responsibility to provide legal services to those unable to pay," begins its commentary. But the ABA stopped short of making the work mandatory, a point with which most lawyers, not surprisingly, agree. They argue, typically, that pro bono work is an admirable goal and one they personally intend to meet, but being forced to do it amounts to indentured servitude, and provides those in need with unwilling and thus substandard counsel.

This argument is disingenuous and self-serving. Practicing law is not a right, but the privilege of a regulated profession. If bars can require continuing education, they can also insist that lawyers spend 3 percent of their time doing free work. Despite widespread support for the pro bono concept, in actuality nowhere near the necessary number of lawyers participate.

Making pro bono service mandatory would accomplish much. First, there would be enough lawyer hours to serve all those in need. Second, once lawyers are used to the idea, their pride and ego, if nothing else, will cause them to do the job well. And historically, lawyers have come to treasure this work, on behalf of real people with real problems, as among their most rewarding experiences. The enlightening effect on the profession itself would be enormous, just as it has proven to be at those law schools that now require public service work from each student.

Legal Institutions

Among America's most important legal institutions are its trade associations, the American Bar Association, the American Law Institute (ALI), countless special-interest bars, and state and local bar associations. Both the ABA and the ALI are extremely powerful; the ABA is the country's second most important legal institution after the Supreme Court. While the ABA's ethics rules are models only, every state except California has used them as a basis for its own regulations. Most states will also pay close attention to the ALI's "Restatement of the Law Governing Lawyers" when it is finally published.

But both these organizations are subject to political pressures from special interests: big firms, insurance companies, in-house counsel, malpractice insurers, plaintiffs' trial counsel, and even, in the ABA's case, legal services groups. These pressures have been most visible in the case of highly politicized battles over ALI policies, but the pressure is felt by the ABA as well. Political pressures are particularly detrimental when they affect the way ethics rules and opinions are decided.

Politics can be even more of a problem for state and local bars. Some of these associations are simply business trade groups, but many others emphasize public service, trying to meet the needs of the poor by running volunteer legal services programs, a few even staffing their programs with mentor attorneys. Large local firms are often the principal contributors to these efforts. This allows them to feel they're doing something worthwhile with a small part of their profits, and it is also a good public relations tool. But it's naturally more difficult for local bars to assert strong ethics positions when these firms oppose them.

One of the biggest problems with these associations is their persistent resistance to public participation. The public has almost no presence in the ABA and none at all at the ALI, a select group to which attorneys have to be nominated and elected. Though lawyers for poor people form a significant ABA lobbying force and the ABA has a large legal services unit, lawyers—not representative clients or members of the public—are the ones who serve on the committees and boards. Even the most enlightened local bars fail to include nonlawyers on their boards.

In recent years there has been an enormous increase in paralegals and other nonlawyers performing routine legal tasks. Most bars have protected their lawyers' turf by resisting the efforts of these paraprofessionals to work directly for clients without law firm supervision. That is unfortunate. There is an important place for trained legal workers, who, properly regulated, increase access to the legal system and provide far less expensive alternatives to hiring an attorney.

The Rules of the Profession

It would be impossible to create a set of ethics rules that is completely clear and unambiguous, so that lawyers are never in doubt about what to do. Lawyers face difficult dilemmas all the time. The hardest are those that require balancing the obligations to the client and to society. These dilemmas are not going to disappear no matter what the ethics rules say. But in some respects, those who draft the rules can do better. Too many rules have too much wiggle room. Lawyers, who after all are professionally trained wigglers, will use every inch of this room to come up with a result that will give them an advantage.

Here are some rules that should be changed:

- Rules that prohibit "material misrepresentations" or "false statements of material fact" do more to create debate about what is "material" than to give guidance. These rules should be broadened to make it clear that *no* deception by lawyers is permitted, unless specifically excepted. One California rule states it clearly: Lawyers must always use "means only as are consistent with truth," and never behave falsely, whether by statement or "artifice." Exceptions should be specific—it is not untruthful to test the prosecution's proof in a criminal case, and lack of candor is permissible in the inherently deceptive arena of negotiation.

- The limits of confidentiality should also be more explicit. A lawyer should be released from the bonds of silence whenever a client's actions have a reasonable probability of resulting in substantial physical harm to any individual *or the public*, regardless of whether the client's act is a crime or how imminent the danger. Time bombs are not imminent, but left alone, their harm is inevitable. The same is true of toxic dumping. Lawyers also should be forbidden from entering secret settlements whenever the public health or safety is likely to be adversely affected.

- The term "zealous representation" has stretched the adversary theorem beyond its reasonable limits. It should be laid to rest, and courts should be encouraged to remove the phrase from their opinions. Lawyers must still maintain all "fiduciary duties" they owe their clients, including those now required by the rules: diligence, competence, candid communication, and, perhaps most important, loyalty. But they can do this without being zealots for the causes of their clients.

- Finally, the rules on lawyers' fees now require a subjective evaluation of as many as a dozen factors to determine whether a fee is "reasonable." These should be simplified and made more explicit. Billing two clients hourly for the same time, or billing more than the time actually spent, should be prohibited unless the client gets a full explanation and specifically agrees to an arrangement that is reasonable under the circumstances.

More than ethics rules must change. Courts control the cases before them, and each has its own rules. Most of these rules could more clearly define unacceptable behavior, such as withholding information from the other side on frivolous or obtuse grounds. These rules have teeth when courts are willing to exercise their power to punish ethics violations as they occur, not just with fines that many firms treat as the cost of doing business, but with real deterrence: "issues sanctions" that can directly affect the outcome of the case, a cost few clients would want to pay.

Courts should also lead the effort to constrict the adversary system by requiring meaningful early settlement discussions and encouraging mediation whenever possible. Mediation moves disputes out of the adversarial arena into a neutral forum where all sides benefit. Some argue that when large mediation firms depend on large law firms and corporations for repeat business, mediation can magnify the imbalance of power between the parties. But mediated cases can be resolved only by consent, and when that occurs early, it puts money in the hands of people who might otherwise have to wait for years, and often saves both sides enormous legal fees.

Like courts, state disciplinary counsel must also be willing to mete out strong punishment, and for a wider range of offenses. Lawyers are rarely disciplined for gross billing atrocities despite their frequency. And they are rarely disciplined for gross conflicts of interest, even though law firms too often divide their loyalty among more than one client without clearly explaining the situation or getting everyone's consent. This inevitably results in all but one of the clients being sold short.

It is not enough for bar counsel to handle the easy cases. Rules become meaningless unless violations are punished. In making their decisions about whom to prosecute, disciplinary counsel must be assured of complete independence from other bar institutions if they are to be free of all political pressures. And they must look at the situation from the client's point of view. The ethics rules exist for the *client's* protection, not the lawyer's or the bar's.

There is far too great a disparity between the discipline meted out to lawyers in small firms and those in large firms. Despite institutional practices that may involve scores of lawyers in a single firm acting unethically in a single case, bar counsel have found it difficult to punish these lawyers. There are good reasons for this. In a large firm, it is harder to determine exactly who is responsible—for withholding documents, failing to communicate with clients, overbilling, or engaging in conflicts of interest. The firm's insularity protects its lawyers from prying eyes. Prosecutors face a daunting task of breaking down this protective shield, just as lawyers can be intimidated when litigating against these firms. But this degree of difficulty makes it all the more important that bar counsel devote the time and resources necessary to ferret out these offenders. Only by prosecuting them will it be clear both that discipline is evenhanded and that no unethical lawyer is immune from prosecution.

When lawyers have harmed their own clients, the most effective use of the rules is the legal malpractice suit. Almost all ethics rules say that a lawyer's violation of a rule doesn't equal malpractice. But in many states, the ethics rules are available for clients to use as *evidence* of malpractice. Lawyers have continuously lobbied against this, but it protects a vital client right. Other protections should include rules that prevent lawyers from negotiating away liability for their own future malpractice, or requiring their clients to agree to mandatory arbitrations that deny clients their day in court before a *jury*, not another lawyer.

Public Participation

If our legal system is to be saved, members of the society it serves must play a major role in its salvation. This requires that lawyers and legal organizations open their doors to the public, and that the public have the necessary interest and fortitude to walk in. Lawyers have a monopoly on the practice of law, but not on intelligence, savvy, or—despite the claims of some—an understanding of sophisticated ethics issues. Public input provides two vital points of view often missing when lawyers evaluate their own conduct: the client's perspective and society's.

Public involvement should be widespread and pervasive. Members of the public should serve on all important professional groups that deal with the behavior of lawyers: ethics committees, which draft rules and opinions; disciplinary boards; judicial selection commissions; and the ABA, ALI, and other trade association committees that set behavior guidelines. A public body similar to a civil grand jury could be set up in each state to monitor a broad spectrum of these activities, as well as the state's disciplinary system. This body could ensure that when rules, opinions, or other changes are circulated within the profession for "public comment," the comment truly includes the public, not just those in the profession.

Choosing these public members, of course, can become as politicized as any other process. But if members of the public are sincere *and* persistent, they will eventually get attention. The payoffs are access to the system and the opportunity to play an important role.

The Personal Responsibility of Lawyers

All the possible reforms in law schools, law firms, and legal associations, stronger and clearer rule making and enforcement, and increased public access to the profession's decision making will not be nearly enough to reform our legal system if lawyers themselves don't take individual responsibility for their behavior. The ABA's rule drafters recognized this thirty years ago when they wrote in the preamble to the now-outmoded Model Code of Professional Responsibility that "[e]ach lawyer must find within his own conscience the touchstone against which to test" one's own personal ethical standards.

Lawyers must return to being professionals, not mere businesspeople. Being professional means holding dear the lawyers' fiduciary duties to their clients. But it also means recognizing that their profession exists in significant measure to serve the needs of their society. Lawyers should continue to represent their clients loyally and diligently, always looking at matters from the client's point of view rather than their own. But they must also become officers of *society*, not merely "officers of the court."

What does this mean? So many people look at lawyers with contempt, says Michael Josephson of the Josephson Ethics Institute, because they see the way they behave and say to themselves, "You know better but you are still doing it." There are always moral dilemmas and hard choices, but lawyers make difficult decisions every day. Yet they can fool themselves into a state of ignorance. "Lawyers are among the most self-confident decision makers I've ever known," says Josephson. "But whenever it's to our advantage, we pretend not to know things. We may not always know what the truth is, but we know what a lie is. We don't always know what's fair, but we know what's unfair." Lawyers must not only accept this knowledge, but act on it by accepting moral responsibility.

This would be much easier if lawyers avoided the professional detachment that so many use to do whatever they want without considering the larger moral costs. If detachment were replaced with empathy, some lawyers would still help a client in an eviction if the law allows it. "But if I do it," says Josephson, "I must be aware that I am evicting a real human being, and that my actions can have a permanent and significant impact on that person's life." Lawyers, in short, much like anyone else on the planet, must consider whether their actions will be to their credit as human beings.

SUMMARY OF
PRINCIPAL SOURCES

The following are the significant sources used for the information contained in this volume. This summary is not exhaustive, as it does not include every specific source we used for this book, nor the vast majority of documentary and anecdotal information we have gathered over our years of teaching and working in our profession. We have attempted to include here the most significant sources and representative bases for the information in this book.

Introduction
Generally: Richard A. Zitrin and Carol M. Langford, *Legal Ethics in the Practice of Law,* The Michie Co., 1995, pp. 4–5, 238; recent polls include *National Law Journal,* August 25, 1997, and *San Francisco Chronicle,* October 1, 1997.

Chapter 1: Buried Bodies: Robert Garrow and His Lawyers
Generally: Tom Alibrandi with Frank H. Armani, *Privileged Information,* Dodd Mead, 1984; *Ethics on Trial,* televised documentary, WETA-TV, Washington, D.C., 1986; *People v. Belge,* 83 Misc. 2d 186, 372 N.Y.S. 2d 798 (1975) and 376 N.Y. 2d 771, 50 A.D. 2d 1038 (1975); "Slayer's Lawyers Kept Secret of 2 More Killings," *New York Times,* June 20, 1974; Tom Goldstein, "Bar Upholds Lawyer Who Withheld Knowledge of Client's Prior Crimes," *New York Times,* March 2, 1978.

Chapter 2: Another Day Spent Representing the Guilty

Generally: Zitrin and Langford, *Legal Ethics in the Practice of Law,* pp. 48–52, 237–49, 252–53, and Teacher's Manual, 89–93.

Charles Phillips and representing the reprehensible: David Mellinkoff, *The Conscience of a Lawyer,* West Publishing, 1973; Gerald Postema, "Moral Responsibility in Professional Ethics," 55 *New York University Law Review* 63 (1980); California Business and Professions Code §6068(h); David Margolick, "At the Bar: The Demjanjuk Episode," *New York Times,* October 15, 1993; Sam Howe Verhovek, "A Klansman's Black Lawyer, and a Principle," *New York Times,* September 10, 1993; Boswell, *The Life of Johnson,* Hill ed., 1887, pp. 47–48.

The guilty defendant, the Michigan ethics opinion, and other justifications: Michigan Ethics Opinion CI-1164 (1987); Barbara Babcock, "Defending the Guilty," 32 *Cleveland State Law Review 175* (1983); U.S. Sentencing Commission news release, August 10, 1995, citing Federal Judicial Center, Mandatory Minimum Prison Term Studies, 1992 and 1994, reported in Toni Morrison, ed., *Birth of a Nation 'hood,* Pantheon, 1997.

Cross-examining truthful witnesses and arguing less than the truth: United States v. Wade, 388 U.S. 218, 250 (1967); *Johnson v. United States,* 360 F. 2d 844 (D.C. Cir. 1966); E. R. Shipp, "Fear and Confusion in Court Plague Elderly Crime Victims," *New York Times,* March 13, 1983; Daniel J. Kornstein, "A Tragic Fire—A Great Cross-Examination," *New York Law Journal,* March 28, 1986; series of articles in 1 *Georgetown Journal of Legal Ethics* (1987): Harry I. Subin, "The Criminal Defense Lawyer's 'Different Mission,'" pp. 125 ff.; John B. Mitchell, "Reasonable Doubts Are Where You Find Them," pp. 343 ff.; and Subin, "Is This Lie Necessary? Further Reflections on the Right to Present a False Defense," pp. 689 ff.; Monroe Freedman, *Lawyers' Ethics in an Adversary System,* Bobbs Merrill, 1975, chapter 4, pp. 43–49.

PART II: POWER AND ITS ABUSE

Generally: The Mind of the Founder: Sources of the Political Thought of James Madison, edited by Marvin Meyers, Brandeis University Press, 1973; Jarett B. Decker, "Defense Lawyers on Trial," *New York Times,* June 30, 1995.

Chapter 3: Power, Arrogance, and the Survival of the Fittest

Mark Dombroff: Mark A. Dombroff, "Winning is Everything!" *National Law*

Journal, September 25, 1989; John Monk, "US Airways Fights Puni-
tives in Crash," *National Law Journal,* March 10, 1997.

Suzuki, Unocal, and Du Pont discovery abuses: David Marmins and John E.
Morris, "Judge Rolls Over Crosby Partners in Suzuki Case," *The* [San
Francisco] *Recorder,* January 29, 1992; Ralph Nader and Wesley J.
Smith, *No Contest,* Random House, 1996, pp. 115 ff.; *Mealey's Litigation
Reports: Emerging Toxic Torts,* vol. V, no. 4, May 31, 1996, and October
25, 1996; *Toxic Chemicals Litigation Reporter,* August 6, 1995; *Richardson
v. Union Oil Company of California,* 167 F.R.D. 1 (D.D.C., 1996); *Bush
Ranch, Inc. v. E.I. du Pont de Nemours & Co.,* 918 F. Supp. 1524 (M.D. Ga.
1995) and 99 F. 3d 363 (11th Cir. 1996); Don J. DeBenedictis and
Emily Heller, "Sanction 'Victory' Could Prove to Be Curse in Disguise
for Du Pont, A&B," Fulton County [Georgia] *Daily Report,* October 21,
1996; Mary Hladky, "Du Pont Suits in Georgia, Hawaii Could Be Start
of New Round," Fulton County [Georgia] *Daily Report,* November 20,
1996; W. Bradley Wendell, "Rediscovering Discovery Ethics," 79 *Mar-
quette Law Review* 895 (Summer 1996).

Increasing size and insularity of American law firms: annual *National Law Journal* law firm survey issues, including September 30, 1985, September 30,
1995, March 30, 1996, and November 10, 1997, special supplement;
Lawrence J. Fox, *Legal Tender,* American Bar Association Section of
Litigation, 1995, pp. 26 ff. and passim.

Loss of professionalism: Report of the Professionalism Committee, *Teaching
and Learning Professionalism,* ABA Section of Legal Education and Admissions to the Bar, August 1996; Fox, *Legal Tender,* pp. 29–30.

Bogle & Gates discovery abuses: Stuart Taylor, "Sleazy in Seattle," *Ameri-
can Lawyer,* April 1994; *Washington State Physicians Ins. Exch. & Ass'n v.
Fisons Corp.,* 858 P. 2d 1054 (Wash. 1993); Sharon Walsh, "State
Court Sanctions Firm for Failure to Disclose," *Washington Post,* No-
vember 29, 1993; Wendell, "Rediscovering Discovery Ethics"; Nader
and Smith, pp. 121 ff.; Alex P. Fryer, "Dismaying Discovery," *Puget
Sound Business Journal,* November 17, 1995, citing *Staggs v. Subaru of
America, Inc.*

Ethics rules and acting "zealously": American Bar Association Model Rules of
Professional Conduct and Model Code of Professional Responsibility,
as reprinted in Richard A. Zitrin and Carol M. Langford, *Legal Ethics in
the Practice of Law: Rules, Statutes and Comparisons,* Michie (1995);
American Bar Association and Bureau of National Affairs, *Lawyers'
Manual on Professional Conduct* (1998).

Dalkon Shield litigation: Morton Mintz, *At Any Cost,* Pantheon, 1985, especially pp. 194–95, 218–22, and 265–66.

SLAPP suits: Penelope Canan and George Pring, "Strategic Lawsuits Against Political Participation," 35 *Journal on Social Problems* 506 (1988); Canan and Pring, *SLAPPs: Getting Sued for Speaking Out,* Temple University Press, 1996; Comment, 39 *UCLA Law Review* 979 (1992); Paul Elias, "A Shield Becomes a Sword," *The* [San Francisco] *Recorder,* December 16, 1996; Steve Lowery, "Zip It Up," *New Times Los Angeles,* January 16, 1997; Alexandria Dylan Lowe, "The Price of Speaking Out," *ABA Journal,* September 1996; Doug Grow, "Showing Signs of Not Quitting," [Minneapolis] *Star Tribune,* February 9, 1997; Craig Whitlock, "Court Throws Out Effort to Stifle Activist Grandma," [Raleigh, North Carolina] *News and Observer,* April 8, 1997; author interviews with Clarence Ditlow, 1997 and 1998, especially April 29, 1997, and May 1997; Nader and Smith, p. 213; California Code of Civil Procedure §425.16; *Church of Scientology of Calif. v. Wollersheim,* 96 C.D.O.S. 773, February 5, 1996.

Chapter 4: A Gun to the Head of the Junior Attorney

Zealously representing Credit Suisse and others: Simon H. Rifkind, "The Lawyer's Role and Responsibility in Modern Society," speech to the Association of the Bar of the City of New York, published in 30 *The* [Association's] *Record* 534 (1975); Mark Green, *The Other Government,* Grossman, 1975; Zitrin and Langford, *Legal Ethics in the Practice of Law,* pp. 237–39, 241; Associated Press, "Despite Dissent, Law Firm Will Advise Swiss Bank in Holocaust Cases," March 4, 1997; Carrie Johnson, "Arent Fox Rejects a Client," *Legal Times,* April 14, 1997.

Big firm size, earnings: "The AmLaw 100," *American Lawyer,* July/August 1995; *National Law Journal,* "What Lawyers Earn," supplements of July 10, 1995, and June 2, 1997, and "The NLJ 250," supplements of September 30, 1996, and November 10, 1997; author conversation with William Reece Smith, October 1996; Counsel Connect on-line discussion of January and February 1997, including Stephen Gillers's comments of January 26, 1997.

The billable hour generally: William Ross, "The Ethics of Hourly Billing," 44 *Rutgers Law Review* 1 (1991); Zitrin and Langford, *Legal Ethics in the Practice of Law,* pp. 585–86; *Goldfarb v. Virginia State Bar,* 421 U.S. 773, 95 S. Ct. 2004 (1975); Kim Barnes on billing, *ABA Journal,* September 1995; author interviews with William Ross, including June 2, 1997; Aaron Epstein, "Lawyers Accused of Double-billing," *The* [Lakeland, Florida] *Ledger,* April 4, 1995.

Examples of billing excess: Carl T. Bogus, "The Death of an Honorable Profession," 71 *Indiana Law Journal* 911 (Fall 1996); Lisa G. Lerman, "How Many More Hubbells Out There?" *Los Angeles Times,* June 28, 1995; Epstein, "Lawyers Accused of Double-billing," *The* [Lakeland, Florida] *Ledger,* April 4, 1995; Karen Dillon, "6,022 Hours," *American Lawyer,* July/August 1994; Douglas R. Richmond, "Professional Responsibility and the Bottom Line," 20 *University of Southern Illinois Law Journal* 261 (Winter 1996); David Margolick, "At the Bar: Keeping Tabs on Legal Fees," *New York Times,* March 20, 1992; Kathy Payton, "The First Thing We Do, Let's Bill All the Lawyers," *The* [Raleigh, North Carolina] *News and Observer,* June 1995 Business Dateline; author interviews with William Gwire, spring 1997, including May 28, 1997.

Creative billing techniques: Zitrin and Langford, *Legal Ethics in the Practice of Law,* pp. 588–92 and Teacher's Manual, 187–89; ABA Formal Opinion 1993-379; Victoria Slind-Flor, "Some Just Say 'No' to Clients," *National Law Journal,* November 2, 1992, cited in Nader and Smith.

Law firm pressures and law firm "culture": Author interviews with William Gwire, spring 1997, especially May 28, 1997; Susan Hightower and Brenda Sapino, "Cultural Evolution: It Takes More than Money to Succeed over the Long Haul in the Law Business," *Texas Lawyer,* January 22, 1996; Lawrence J. Fox, *Legal Tender,* passim; Lawrence J. Fox, "A Nation Under Lost Lawyers," 100 *Dickinson Law Review* 531 (Spring 1996); Richard Gordon, quoted in [Denver] *Rocky Mountain News,* January 29, 1995; David Segal, "Law Firms Court Own Attorneys," *Washington Post,* December 30, 1996; Mark F. Bernstein, "J.D.," *The* [San Francisco] *Recorder,* June 9, 1997; Carol A. Leonard and Kelly A. Fox, "Sometimes, the Enemy Comes from Within," *New York Law Journal,* July 9, 1996.

Stress, dissatisfaction: Barbara Mahan, "Disbarred," *California Lawyer,* July 1992; Michael A. Bloom and Carol Lynn Wallinger, "Lawyers and Alcoholism: Is It Time for a New Approach?" 61 *Temple Law Review* 1409 (1988); Bogus, "The Death of an Honorable Profession."

Solutions: Author interviews with William Gwire and William Ross; ABA Committee on Professionalism Report, August 1996, and materials from ABA conference on professionalism, Chicago, October 1996; American Bar Association Task Force on Lawyer Business Ethics, "Statements of Principles," 51 *The Business Lawyer* 745, May 1996; Zitrin and Langford, *Legal Ethics in the Practice of Law,* pp. 588–92 and Teacher's Manual, 187–89; Dick Dahl, "Share the Pain, Share the Gain," *ABA Journal,* June 1996.

Chapter 5: Blowing the Whistle in Corporate America

Generally: Sally R. Weaver, "Client Confidences in Disputes Between In-House Attorneys and Their Employer-Clients: Much Ado About Nothing—or Something?" 30 *University of California Davis Law Review* 483 (Winter 1997); David Luban, *Lawyers and Justice: An Ethical Study*, Princeton University Press, 1989, chapter 10; Ted Schneyer, "Professionalism and Public Policy: The Case of House Counsel," 2 *Georgetown Journal of Legal Ethics* 449 (1988); author interviews with Craig Simmons, 1997, especially March 15, 1997.

A. H. Robins: Mintz, *At Any Cost*, chapter 12, especially pp. 210–18, 232–41.

Corporate attorney-client privilege: Christine Hatfield, "The Privilege Doctrines—Are They Just Another Discovery Tool Utilized by the Tobacco Industry to Conceal Damaging Information?" 16 *Pace Law Review* 525 (1996); Marshall Williams, "The Scope of the Corporate Attorney-Client Privilege in View of Reason and Experience," 25 *Howard Law Journal* 425 (1982); Elizabeth G. Thornburg, "Sanctifying Secrecy: The Mythology of the Corporate Attorney-Client Privilege," 69 *Notre Dame Law Review* 157 (1993); *Trustees of Dartmouth College v. Woodward*, 17 U.S. (4 Wheat.) 518 (1819); *Davenport Co. v. Pennsylvania R.R.*, 166 Pa. 480; 31 A. 245 (1895); *U.S. v. Louisville & Nashville RR*, 236 U.S. 318 (1915); *Hale v. Henkel*, 201 U.S. 43 (1906); *Radiant Burners, Inc. v. American Gas Association, et al.*, 207 F. Supp. 771 (N.D. Ill., 1962) and 320 F. 2d 314 (7th Cir. 1963); *Bredice v. Doctor's Hospital, Inc.*, 50 F.R.D. 249 (D.D.C. 1970), aff'd 479 F. 2d 920 (D.C. Cir. 1973); *Upjohn Co. v. United States*, 449 U.S. 383, 101 S. Ct. 677 (1981); Carole Basri and Benjamin Nahoum, "Update on How In-House Counsel Can Use and Expand the Privileges," *The Metropolitan Corporate Counsel*, June 1996.

Tobacco lawyers: *Haines v. Liggett Group, Inc.*, 140 F.R.D. 681 (D.N.J. 1992), 975 F. 2d 81 (3rd Cir. 1992), and 814 F. Supp. 414 (D.N.J. 1993); Hatfield, "The Privilege Doctrines"; Mike France, "Inside Big Tobacco's Secret War Room," *Business Week*, June 15, 1998; Peter S. Canellos, "Tobacco Lawyers' Role: Counsel or Coverup?" *Boston Globe*, December 28, 1997; "Low-Smoke Butt May Signal New Tobacco Gambit," *National Law Journal*, May 6, 1996; series of April 23, 1998, articles, including: Raja Mishra, "More Fuel for the Fire," *Houston Chronicle*; Barry Meier, "House Committee Releases 39,000 Tobacco Documents," *New York Times*; Henry Weinstein and Myron Levin, "RJR Lawyers Quashed Research, Memo Says," *Los Angeles Times*; and George Rodrigue, "Tobacco Papers Put on Internet," *Dallas Morning News*; Nader and Smith, *No Contest*, pp. 18–27; *People v. The Council for Tobacco Re-*

search, Supreme Court, County of New York, petition and memorandum of law dated April 29, 1998; Barry Meier, "Release of Tobacco Memos Brings Lawmakers' Demand for More," *New York Times*, December 19, 1997.

The ABA's rules: ABA Model Rules 1.6(b) and 1.13; Monroe Freedman, "Cases and Controversies: The Corporate Bar Writes Its Own Rules," *American Lawyer Group*, June 22, 1992; Ted Schneyer, "Professionalism as Bar Politics: The Making of the Model Rules of Professional Conduct," 14 *Law and Social Inquiry* 677 (1989); Zitrin and Langford, *Legal Ethics in the Practice of Law*, pp. 5–7; ABA Model Rules first draft, 28 *United States Law Week* no. 32, February 19, 1980; ABA Commission on Evaluation of Professional Standards, Proposed Final Draft, Model Rules of Professional Conduct, May 30, 1981.

European corporate rules: AM&S Europe Ltd. v. Commission, 1982 Euro. Comm. Rep. 1575 (1982) before the European Court of Justice; Allison M. Hill, "Note: A Problem of Privilege: In-House Counsel and the Attorney-Client Privilege in the United States and the European Community," 27 *Case Western Reserve Journal of International Law* 145 (Winter 1995).

The Pinto saga: Luban, *Lawyers and Justice: An Ethical Study; Grimshaw v. Ford Motor Corp.*, 119 Cal. App. 3d 757(1981); Gary T. Schwartz, "The Myth of the Ford Pinto Case," 43 *Rutgers Law Review* 1013 (1991); Lee Strobel articles in the *Chicago Tribune*, October 13, 14, and 15, 1979.

Corporate responsibility: Michael Josephson, speech to ABA Conference on Professionalism, October 4, 1996, Chicago; author interview with Michael Josephson, August 12, 1997; Joseph J. Fleischman, William J. Heller, and Mitchell A. Schley, "The Organizational Sentencing Guideline and the Employment At-Will Rule As Applied to In-House Counsel," *Business Lawyer*, February 1993; Rorie Sherman, "Gurus of the '90s," *National Law Journal*, January 24, 1994; John H. Cushman Jr., "E.P.A. Is Pressing Plan to Publicize Pollution Data," *New York Times*, August 12, 1997; James E. Lukaszewski, speech to Dallas Press Club, October 31, 1994, published by Executive Speaker, 1995.

Whistle-blowing lawyers and retaliatory discharge: Weaver, "Client Confidences . . ."; *Willy v. Coastal Corp.*, 647 F. Supp. 116 (S.D. Tex. 1986) and 855 F. 2d 1160 (5th Cir. 1988) aff'd 504 U.S. 935 (1992); "Texas Endorses In-House Counsel's Discharge Claim," *The Legal Intelligencer*, October 31, 1997; *GTE Products Corp. v. Stewart*, 653 N.E. 2d 161 (Mass. 1995); Jennifer Thelen, "Do In-Housers Have the Right to Sue For Wrongful Termination?" *The* [San Francisco] *Recorder*, February 27, 1995; *General Dynamics Corp. v. Superior Court*, 7 Cal. 4th 1164 (1994); *Parker v.*

M&T Chems., Inc., 566 A. 2d 215 (N.J. Super. Ct. App. Div. 1989); Zitrin and Langford, *Legal Ethics in the Practice of Law*, pp. 479–80; Leslie Levin, "Testing the Radical Experiment: A Study of Lawyer Response to Clients Who Intend Harm to Others," 47 *Rutgers Law Review* 81 (Fall 1994).

Taking responsibility: Mintz, *At Any Cost*, Appendix, pp. 259–62; Josephson, October 4, 1996, Chicago speech and author interview, August 12, 1997; Arthur Miller, *All My Sons*, Viking Penguin, 1947.

Chapter 6: Insurance Lawyers: Chasing Ambulances and Chasing Money

Generally: Katherine A. LaRoe, "Much Ado About Barratry: State Regulation of Attorneys' Targeted Direct-Mail Solicitation," 25 *St. Mary's Law Journal* 1514 (1994); Jerold S. Auerbach, *Unequal Justice: Lawyers and Social Change in Modern America*, Oxford University Press, 1976; Ken Dornstein, *Accidentally on Purpose*, Macmillan, 1997.

Number of lawsuits: National Center for State Courts, annual surveys; Andre Henderson, "Damming the Lawsuit Flood," *Governing Magazine*, September 1995.

Brooklyn ambulance chasers: Dan Morrison, "Ambulance Chasing Charges," *New York Newsday*, February 13, 1997; Bill Farrell and Stephen McFarland, "DA Kills Ambulance-Chase Scam," New York *Daily News*, February 13, 1997.

History from Drinker to changes in the advertising ban: Auerbach, *Unequal Justice*; Zitrin and Langford, *Legal Ethics in the Practice of Law*, pp. 5 ff., 558–64, and 567–71; John M. McGuire, "The Mound City Bar," St. Louis *Post-Dispatch*, March 3, 1996; *Belli v. State Bar*, 10 Cal. 3d 824 (1974); *Jacoby v. State Bar of Calif.*, 19 Cal. 3d 359 (1977); *Bates v. State Bar of Arizona*, 433 U.S. 350 (1977); *Ohralik v. Ohio State Bar Ass'n*, 436 U.S. 447 (1978).

ValuJet and TWA 1996 air crashes: All Things Considered broadcast, National Public Radio, July 23, 1996; *ABC Nightline* telecast, June 5, 1996; Laura Brown, "Lawyers Prey on ValuJet Mourners," *Boston Herald*, May 23, 1996.

Profiles of plaintiffs' lawyers: Andrea Stone, "Fighting for 'the Brave,' " *USA Today*, December 11, 1995; Tony Mauro, "Legal Eagles Plummet from the Heights," *USA Today*, March 14, 1996; Richard Connelly and Robert Elder Jr., "O'Quinn: The Long Knives Come Out Again," *Texas Lawyer*, February 19, 1996; Pamela Coles, "Implant Lawyer Is Accused of Hustling Clients," New Orleans *Times-Picayune*, April 18, 1997;

Christopher Palmeri, "A Texas Gunslinger," *Forbes*, July 3, 1995; "4 Lawyers Accused of Accident-Chasing," [Charleston, South Carolina] *Post and Courier*, April 18, 1997.

Florida 30-day solicitation ban: Florida Bar v. Went-For-It, Inc., 115 S. Ct. 2371 (1995).

San Francisco and Pennsylvania experiences and Texas "truth squad": transcripts from case of *Settle v. Civil Service Employees' Ins. Co.*, Alameda [California] County Superior Court #754597-3; Monroe Freedman, *Understanding Legal Ethics*, Matthew Bender, 1990, pp. 237 ff.; *Gunn v. Washek*, 405 Pa. 521 (1961); correspondence between authors and Kevin M. French, September and November 1997; correspondence between authors and Professor David Cummins, April, September, and November 1997.

Allstate and Liberty Mutual "no lawyer" campaigns: Richard C. Ruben, "Insurer Out to Eliminate Middleman," *ABA Journal*, September 1996; Paul Frisman, "Good Hands, Bad Deal?" *Connecticut Law Tribune*, November 18, 1996; Evelyn Apgar, "Bars in Other States Decry Insurers' No-lawyer Letters," *New Jersey Lawyer*, March 3, 1997.

Bob Manning's case and other insurance woes: David Cay Johnston, "Paralyzed Since Fall in 1962, Man Is Still Seeking Benefits," *New York Times*, May 5, 1997, and "Hearing Set on Denial of Paralyzed Utility Worker's Benefits," *New York Times*, May 6, 1997; Haig Neville, "Your Premiums Are Paid, But Are You Covered?" *Michigan Lawyers Weekly*, December 9, 1996; Lisa J. Huriash, "Parents Angry over Definition of 'Cosmetic,'" [Fort Lauderdale] *Sun-Sentinel*, December 1, 1996; Nancy West, "Proposed Bill Would Allow for HMO Appeals," [Manchester, New Hampshire] *Union Leader*, January 2, 1996; James Denn, "Denial of Claims Spurs Bill for Tougher Controls," [Albany, New York] *Times-Union*, May 26, 1996.

Conflicting roles of insurance lawyers, and lobbying the ALI: Zitrin and Langford, *Legal Ethics in the Practice of Law*, pp. 168–75, and Teacher's Manual, pp. 62–65; Jonathan Groner, "Insurance Companies Lobby the ALI," *Legal Times*, July 15, 1996; Groner, "Insurance Lobby Aims at Influential Legal Group," *American Lawyer Newspapers Group*, June 12, 1996; Michael Prince, "Insurer Lobbying of Ethics Panel Criticized," *Business Insurance*, September 9, 1996; William T. Barker, letter to editor of *Legal Times*, June 24, 1996; Counsel Connect on-line Hofstra University seminar discussion, March-May 1996.

Tort reform and "relative filth": National Center for State Courts 1994 and

1995 reports; Nader and Smith, *No Contest*, p. 265; Michael Josephson, speech to American Bar Association Professionalism Conference, Chicago, October 4, 1996.

Chapter 7: All the Court's a Stage, and All the Lawyers Players: Leading and Misleading the Jury

Generally: Zitrin and Langford, *Legal Ethics in the Practice of Law*, pp. 372–87 and Teacher's Manual, pp. 123–29.

William K. Smith "Oscars": Michael Blumfield, "Drumroll Please for the Smith Trial Oscars," *Orlando Sentinel Tribune*, December 15, 1991.

Examples of trial lawyers and trial techniques: Roger Dodd, "Innovative Techniques: Parlor Tricks for the Courtroom," *Trial*, April 1990; Christopher Palmeri, "A Texas Gunslinger," *Forbes*, July 3, 1995; Andrea Higbie, "There Will Be a Brief Recess While We Check Our Wardrobes," *New York Times*, November 25, 1994; Harriet Chiang, "Why Marcia Clark's Clothing Matters," *San Francisco Chronicle*, February 9, 1995.

Ethical rules: American Bar Association Model Rules 3.3, 3.4, 4.1; *Estelle v. Williams*, 425 U.S. 501 (1976).

Concealing clients' identities: United States v. Thoreen, 653 F. 2d 1332 (9th Cir. 1981), cert. denied, 455 U.S. 938 (1982); *People v. Simac*, 161 Ill. 2d 297, 641 N.E. 2d 416 (1994); Jan Hoffman, "At the Bar," *New York Times*, July 29, 1994.

Effect on juries: Superior Court of California, County of Los Angeles, *California Jury Instructions* §1.02; Richard P. Morin, "Evidence Ruled Inadmissible May Still Leave Its Mark on Jurors, Research Indicates," *Brown University Journal*, January 29, 1997.

Race and jury tactics, and People v. Simpson: Patrice Gaines-Carter, "D.C. Lawyer Told to Remove African Kente Cloth for Jury Trial," *Washington Post*, May 23, 1992; *LaRocca v. Lane*, 376 N.Y.S. 2d 93, 338 N.E. 2d 606 (1975) and *People v. Rodriguez*, 424 N.Y.S. 2d 600 (1979); Robert Shapiro, interview with Barbara Walters, ABC Broadcasting, October 3, 1995, as reported by *New York Times*, October 4, 1995, and *Los Angeles Times*, Sunday Opinion section, October 8, 1995; Toni Morrison, editor, *Birth of a Nation 'hood*, Pantheon, 1997, including A. Leon Higgenbotham, "The O.J. Simpson Trial: Who Was Improperly 'Playing the Race Card?'"; Maureen Dowd, "O.J. as Metaphor," *New York Times*, October 5, 1995; Michael Janofsky, "Under Siege, Philadelphia's Criminal Justice System Suffers Another Blow," *New York Times*, April 10, 1997; Laura Mansnerus, in "Week in Review," *New York Times*, April 13, 1997; *Batson v. Kentucky*, 476 U.S. 79, 106 S. Ct. 1712 (1986).

The value of juries: Barbara Bradley, "Juries and Justice: Is the System Obsolete?" *Washington Times,* April 24, 1995; "Tipping the Scales in Favor of One Side?" roundtable discussion, *Illinois Legal Times,* February 1996; Debra Sahler, "Comment: Scientifically Selecting Jurors While Maintaining Professional Responsibility: A Proposed Model Rule," 6 *Albany Law Journal of Science and Technology* 383 (1996); Walter Olson, *We the Jury* book review, *Reason,* February 1995; Thomas Sowell, "Unclogging America's Courts," [Denver] *Rocky Mountain News,* October 11, 1997.

Chapter 8: Lawyers as Liars

Generally: Gerald B. Wetlaufer, "The Ethics of Lying in Negotiations," 75 *Iowa Law Review* 1219 (July 1990); Manuel Ramos, "Legal and Law School Malpractice: Confessions of a Lawyer's Lawyer and Law Professor," 57 *Ohio St. Law Journal* 863 (1996); Sissela Bok, *Lying: Moral Choices in Public and Private Life,* Pantheon, 1978.

Lying in negotiation: Alvin Rubin, "A Causerie on Lawyers' Ethics in Negotiation," 35 *Louisiana Law Review* 577 (1975); James J. White, "Machiavelli and the Bar: Ethical Limitations on Lying in Negotiation," 1980 *American Bar Foundation Research Journal* 921 (1980); Larry Lempert, "In Settlement Talks, Does Telling the Truth Have Its Limits?" *Inside Litigation,* March 1988; *Spaulding v. Zimmerman,* 262 Minn. 346, 116 N.W. 2d 704 (1962).

Giving advice versus assisting in fraud: Monroe Freedman, *Lawyers' Ethics in an Adversary System,* Bobbs Merrill, 1975, pp. 59–75; *Anatomy of a Murder,* Otto Preminger Films, Ltd., Columbia Pictures, 1959, based on the 1958 novel by Hon. John D. Voelker ("Robert Traver"); Bob Van Voris, "Client Memo Embarrasses Dallas Firm," *National Law Journal,* October 13, 1997; American Bar Association Model Rule 1.2, comment paragraph 6.

O.P.M. Leasing and its lawyers: Stuart Taylor Jr., "Ethics and the Law: A Case History," *New York Times Magazine,* January 9, 1983; Zitrin and Langford, *Legal Ethics in the Practice of Law,* pp. 456–57; Heidi Li Feldman, "Can Good Lawyers Be Good Ethical Deliberators?" *Michigan Law Quadrangle Notes,* vol. 39, no. 2, Summer 1996, adapted from *Southern California Law Review,* March 1996.

Lincoln Savings and its lawyers, Kaye, Scholer: Susan Beck and Michael Orey, "They Got What They Deserved," *American Lawyer,* May 1992; David Wilkins, "Making Context Count: Regulating Lawyers After Kaye, Scholer," 66 *Southern California Law Review* 1147 (1993); Stephen Gillers and Roy D. Simon, *Regulation of Lawyers: Statutes and Standards,*

Little, Brown, 1993 edition; Anthony Davis, "The Long-Term Implications of the Kaye Scholer Case for Law Firm Management—Risk Management Comes of Age," 35 *South Texas Law Review* (October 1994); Geoffrey Hazard, "Ethics," *National Law Journal,* April 27, 1992.

ABA's response to Kaye, Scholer affair: ABA Formal Opinions 92-366 (August 8, 1992) and 93-375 (August 6, 1993); David Margolick, "At the Bar," *New York Times,* November 26, 1993; Amy Stevens, "Convention Notes: Lawyers Decide They Also Don't Like Getting Sued," *Wall Street Journal,* August 12, 1993; Zitrin and Langford, *Legal Ethics in the Practice of Law,* pp. 497, 502.

McVeigh's lawyer Stephen Jones, and justifications for lying: Deirdre Shesgreen, "McVeigh Attorney's Actions Spur Sharp Debate on Ethics of Fabrication," *Legal Times,* March 10, 1997; Gayle Reaves and Steve McGonigle, *Dallas Morning News* series of articles, including March 1, 1997, and March 5, 1997; Ann Woolner, "It's True: Some Lawyers Lie," *American Lawyer Group,* March 12, 1997.

Chapter 9: Keeping It Secret

Generally: Lloyd Doggett and Michael Mucchetti, "Public Access to Public Courts," 69 *Texas Law Review* 643 (February 1991); Arthur Miller, "Confidentiality, Protective Orders, and Public Access to the Courts," 105 *Harvard Law Review* 427 (1991); Stephanie Dolan, "Ethical Concerns and Obligations for Attorneys Involved in Secret Settlements and Agreements," unpublished paper, November 1995; Laura Goldsmith, "Confidential Settlements," unpublished paper, November 1995.

Arguments favoring secrecy and Professor Miller's views: Joseph Calve, "Restricting Settlement Secrecy," *Connecticut Law Tribune,* March 16, 1992.

Dangerous products litigation concealed: Bob Gibbins, "Secrecy Versus Safety: Restoring the Balance," 77 *ABA Journal* 74 (December 1991); Steven D. Lydenberg et al., *Rating America's Corporate Conscience,* Addison-Wesley, 1986, pp. 234 ff.; *Davis v. McNeilab, Inc.,* U.S. Dist. Ct., D.C., no. 85-CV-3972; Morton Mintz, *At Any Cost,* pp. 197–98; [Massachusetts] *Lawyer's Weekly,* February 20, 1995.

Stern breast implant case: Stern v. Dow Corning Corp., U.S. Dist. Ct., N.D. Cal. no. C83-2348; Zitrin and Langford, *Legal Ethics in the Practice of Law,* p. 114; Nader and Smith, *No Contest,* pp. 76 ff.

General Motors truck cases: Transcript of American Judicature Society, "Confidential Settlements and Sealed Court Records: Necessary Safeguards or Unwarranted Secrecy?" reported in 78 *Judicature* 304 (1995); author correspondence and interviews with Clarence Ditlow, 1997 and

1998, especially interview of June 23, 1997, including correspondence providing documentation; Catherine Yang, "A Disturbing Trend Toward Secrecy," *Business Week*, October 2, 1995.

Open court documents, limits on protective orders: Seattle Times v. Rhinehart, 467 U.S. 20 (1984); Larry Coben, "The Use of Portative Orders," *The Legal Intelligencer*, July 20, 1993; author interviews with Hon. H. Lee Sarokin (Ret.), 1997 and 1998, and Judge Sarokin as quoted in Jaffe, "Public Good vs. Sealed Evidence," [Newark, New Jersey] *Star-Ledger*, September 2, 1990, cited in Doggett; *Cipollone v. Liggett Group, Inc.*, 106 F.R.D. 573 (D.N.J. 1985) and 785 F. 2d 1108 (3d Cir. 1986).

Hiding molestation and discrimination: Legal Intelligencer, June 10, 1994; *Chicago Lawyer,* January 1994; *National Law Journal,* March 6, 1995.

Fentress (Prozac) litigation: Leslie Scanlon, series of articles in [Louisville] *Courier-Journal,* especially April 20, 1995, May 7, 1995, May 28, 1995, June 1, 1995, September 13, 1996, December 13, 1996, March 12, 1997, March 25, 1997, and March 28, 1997; Maureen Castellano, series of articles in *New Jersey Law Journal,* including May 3, 1995, May 15, 1995, and June 12, 1995; Nicholas Varchaver, "Lilly's Phantom Verdict," *The American Lawyer,* September 1995; *Pharmaceutical Litigation Reporter,* Andrews Publications, October 1995; David J. Shaffer, series of articles in the *Indianapolis Star.*

Efforts opposing secrecy: Texas Rules of Civil Procedure Annotated, rule 76a; Florida Statutes Annotated, §69.081; Washington State House Bill 1866 "Public Right to Know Bill" (1993); California Senate Bill 711 (Sen. Lockyer, passed August 26, 1992, vetoed); Robert Nissen, "Open Court Records in Products Liability Litigation Under Texas Rule 76a," 72 *Texas Law Review* 931 (1994); Mintz, *At Any Cost*, p. 241.

Chapter 10: Class Actions

Generally: Hon. William W. Schwarzer, "Structuring Multiclaim Litigation: Should Rule 23 Be Revised?" 94 *Michigan Law Review* 1250 (1996); Carrie Menkel-Meadow, "Ethics and the Settlements of Mass Torts: When the Rules Meet the Road," 80 *Cornell Law Review* 1159 (1995); Federal Rule of Civil Procedure 23; notes of the Advisory Committee on Civil Rules of the Judicial Conference of the United States regarding amendments to F.R. Civ. Proc. 23, 1996; Trial Lawyers for Public Justice, series of articles on class actions, *Public Justice,* quarterly TLPJ newsletter, Fall 1996 ff.; Note, "Back to the Drawing Board: The Settlement Class Action and Limits of Rule 23," 109 *Harvard Law Review* 828 (February 1996).

Initial quotes: Brian Cummings, "Both Defense and Plaintiff Lawyers Say Class Action Lawsuits Can Be Misused," *Chicago Daily Law Bulletin,* April 27, 1996.

Specific examples of "small ticket" class actions: Author interviews with William Bernstein, 1997, especially May 27, 1997, and Barry Baskin, June 1997.

The Bank of Boston case: Barry Meier, "Math of a Class-Action Suit: 'Winning' $2.19 Costs $91.33," *New York Times,* November 21, 1995; Hon. Milton Shadur, "The Unclassy Class Action," *Litigation,* vol. 23, no. 2 (Winter 1997); Kimberly Blanton, "Class-action Suit Winners Sue Lawyers," *Boston Globe,* November 22, 1995; author interviews in May and June 1997 with William Bernstein, Rob Branson, and Mark Chavez, and with Brian Wolfman, April 30, 1997.

Other Edelman cases: Author interviews with Barry Baskin, William Bernstein, Mark Chavez, Clarence Ditlow, Rob Graham, Bryan Kemnitzer, and Brian Wolfman, April, May, and June 1997.

Ford Motor Credit, San Francisco class notice, and ways to avoid unfair treatment: Author interviews during April, May, and June 1997 with Barry Baskin, Rob Graham, and Leslie Brueckner; Rinat Fried, "Class Counsel Issues Warning to Objectors," *The* [San Francisco] *Recorder,* August 31, 1998; published notice in *Food Additives Cases II (Re: Archer-Daniels-Midland Co., et al.),* Superior Court, City and County of San Francisco, 1998; Trial Lawyers for Public Justice amicus curiae brief in *Amchem Products, Inc. v. Windsor,* U.S. Supreme Court no. 96-270, pp. 12–15.

Airline coupons: Bill Rankin, "Who Benefits from Class Action—Besides the Lawyers," Cox News Service, as printed in [Springfield, Illinois] *State Journal-Register,* April 7, 1996; descriptions of coupon rules; author interviews with travel agents, Spring 1996.

General Motors pickup class actions: In re: General Motors Corp. Pick-Up Truck Fuel Tank Products Liability Litigation, 846 F. Supp. 330 (E.D. Penna. 1993) and subsequent district court opinions of February 2, 1994, at 1994 U.S. Dist. LEXIS 1094, and November 25, 1996, at 1996 U.S. Dist. LEXIS 17510, and *In re: General Motors Corp. Pick-Up Truck Fuel Tank Products Liability Litigation,* 55 F. 3d 768 (3d Cir. 1995); series of articles of April 18, 1995, including from [Cleveland] *Plain Dealer, New York Times, Washington Post, Houston Chronicle, Los Angeles Times, Dallas Morning News;* author interviews with Clarence Ditlow, 1997, especially June 2, 1997, and May 6, 1997, with Ditlow and Rob Graham; with Brian Wolfman, April and May 1997; and with Elizabeth Cabraser, May 14, 1997; "Judge Approves Settlement over Side-Mounted Gas Tanks in GM Trucks," *The Legal Intelligencer,* January 2, 1997; Charles

B. Camp, "GM Truck Settlement Rejected," *Dallas Morning News,* February 10, 1996; "TX Supreme Court Affirms Rejection of GM Class Action Settlement," *Automotive Litigation Reporter,* March 5, 1996.

Asbestos and other mass injury class actions: In re: "Agent Orange" Product Liability Litigation, 506 F. Supp 762 (E.D.N.Y. 1980) and 818 F. 2d 145 (2d Cir. 1987); Michael Hoenig, "Class Action Imbroglios," *New York Law Journal,* May 8, 1995; author interviews and correspondence with Leslie Brueckner, 1997; *In re: Rhone-Poulenc Rorer, Inc.,* 1995 WestLaw 116310 (7th Cir. 1996); *Georgine v. Amchem Products, Inc.,* 83 F. 3d 610 (3d Cir. 1996) and *Amchem Products, Inc. v. Windsor,* 117 S. Ct. 2231 (1997).

Conclusions: Jean Wegman Burns, "Decorative Figureheads: Eliminating Class Representatives in Class Actions," 42 *Hastings Law Journal* 165 (November 1990); Bill Cohen, "Cohen Introduces Bill to Protect Consumers in Class Action Suits," *Congressional Press Releases,* December 22, 1995; author conversations with Samuel Dash, including April 28, 1997.

Conclusion: Can It Be Fixed? What Can We Do?

Generally: "The NLG 250," *National Law Journal,* November 10, 1997, and November 16, 1998, special supplements; Chris Klein, "Big-Firm Partners: Profession Sinking," *National Law Journal,* May 26, 1997; American Bar Association Model Rule 6.1, Comment, paragraph 1; California Business and Professions Code §6068(d); author interview with Michael Josephson, August 12, 1997.

INDEX

ABOUT THE AUTHORS

RICHARD ZITRIN, a partner in the San Francisco firm of Zitrin & Mastromonaco, LLP., is an adjunct professor of law at the University of San Francisco, where he teaches legal ethics and coordinates the school's ethics curriculum. He also teaches trial practice at USF and legal ethics at the University of California's Hastings campus. He has extensive experience as a trial lawyer, from defending murder cases to representing plaintiffs in products liability and sexual harassment lawsuits. He was a member of the State Bar of California's Committee on Professional Responsibility and Conduct from 1990 to 1996 and served as its chair in 1994–95.

CAROL M. LANGFORD practices law in Walnut Creek, California, and teaches legal ethics at both the University of San Francisco School of Law and UC Hastings. She has also taught at UC Berkeley. She spent five years as a litigation associate at two of the nation's largest firms, Pillsbury, Madison & Sutro, and O'Melveny & Myers, before becoming a partner at a 70-lawyer San Francisco law firm. She was a member of the State Bar of California's Committee on Professional Responsibility and Conduct from 1991 to 1997 and served as its chair in 1995–96.